Ghostwriting Modernism

Ghostwriting
Modernism

HELEN SWORD

CORNELL UNIVERSITY PRESS

Ithaca & London

First published 2002 by Cornell University Press
First printing, Cornell Paperbacks, 2002

Printed in the United States of America

Excerpts from the following works by H.D. are reprinted by permission of the New Directions Publishing Corp. and Carcanet Press Ltd.: *Collected Poems, 1912–1944*, copyright 1982 by The Estate of Hilda Doolittle; *Helen in Egypt*, copyright 1961 by Norman Holmes Pearson; *Tribute to Freud*, copyright 1956, 1974 by Norman Holmes Pearson; *Trilogy*, copyright 1944, 1945, 1946 by Oxford University Press, renewed 1973 by Norman Holmes Pearson.

Library of Congress Cataloging-in-Publication Data

Sword, Helen.
    Ghostwriting modernism / Helen Sword.
      p. cm.
    Includes bibliographical references and index.
    ISBN 0-8014-3699-0 (cloth : alk. paper) — ISBN 0-8014-8775-7 (pbk. : alk. paper)
      1. English literature—20th century—History and criticism.   2. Spiritualism in literature.   3. American literature—20th century—History and criticism.   4. Spiritualism—Great Britain—History—20th century.   5. Spiritualism—United States—History—20th century.   6. Modernism (Literature)—United States.   7. Modernism (Literature)—Great Britain.   8. Occultism in literature.   9. Ghosts in literature.   10. Death in literature.   I. Title.
    PR478.S64 S96 2002
    802.9'37—dc21

                                        2001004620

Cloth printing   10 9 8 7 6 5 4 3 2 1
Paperback printing   10 9 8 7 6 5 4 3 2 1

Mediums

They shall arise in the States,
They shall report Nature, laws, physiology, and happiness,
They shall illustrate Democracy and the kosmos,
They shall be alimentive, amative, perceptive,
They shall be complete women and men, their pose brawny and
  supple, their drink water, their blood clean and clear,
They shall fully enjoy materialism and the sight of products,
  they shall enjoy the sight of the beef, lumber, bread-stuffs,
  of Chicago the great city,
They shall train themselves to go public to become orators and
  oratresses,
Strong and sweet shall their tongues be, poems and materials
  of poems shall come from their lives, they shall be
  makers and finders,
Of them and of their works shall emerge divine conveyers,
  to convey gospels,
Characters, events, retrospections, shall be convey'd in
  gospels, trees, animals, waters, shall be convey'd,
Death, the future, the invisible faith, shall all be convey'd.

        Walt Whitman, *Leaves of Grass*

Contents

Preface

Did you ever see fairies dancing on the lawn? Of course not, but that's no proof that they are not there. Nobody can conceive or imagine all the wonders there are unseen and unseeable in the world. You may tear apart the baby's rattle and see what makes the noise inside, but there is a veil covering the unseen world which not the strongest man, nor even the united strength of all the strongest men that ever lived, could tear apart. Only faith, fancy, poetry, love, romance, can push aside that curtain and view and picture the supernatural beauty and glory beyond.

> Francis P. Church, "Yes, Virginia, There Is a Santa Claus"
> (*New York Sun* editorial, 1897)

The door to the inner chamber had a double or triple bead curtain which obscured the opening. . . . My eyes have seen the veil, the double or triple moving depths of bead curtain, that in my work may still be my fascination with the movement of meaning beyond or behind meaning, of shifting vowels and consonants— beads of sound, of separate strands that convey the feeling of one weave. . . . There is something about looking behind things. There is the fact that I am not an occultist or a mystic but a poet, a maker-up of things.

> Robert Duncan, *The H. D. Book* (1969)

In 1922—the *annus mirabilis* of modernist literature, when James Joyce's *Ulysses* and T. S. Eliot's *Waste Land* both saw first publication—Sir Arthur Conan Doyle, creator of one of the most famously rational characters in literary history, published an earnest work of psychical research titled *The Coming of the Fairies*. The coincidence is jarring, but it is hardly atypical. That same year, Thomas Mann attended a materializing seance in Munich, where a decade earlier Rainer Maria Rilke had consulted a spirit medium and sought to buy a planchette to aid in automatic writing. William Butler Yeats was hard at work on *A Vision*, the 1925 spiritualist tour de force in which he sets down and systematizes the otherworldly messages received via the trance mediumship of his wife during a thirty-month period beginning in 1917. Radclyffe Hall had recently emerged from two libel cases involving spirit messages from her dead lover. And H.D. had just experienced another of the mysterious bouts of visionary consciousness that would eventually culminate, during the air raids of the Second World War, in her seance communications with a group of dead R.A.F. pilots.

Nor were these eminent modernist writers alone in their continuing preoccupation with seances, trance mediumship, automatic writing, and other forms of attempted communication with the dead. Sigmund Freud, Carl Jung, and Henri Bergson, three of the modernist era's most influential intellectual avatars, were corresponding members of the London Society for Psychical Research who wrote or lectured on the origins and effects of mankind's persistent belief in spirit survival.[1] Eliot, Ezra Pound, and Mina Loy, seemingly unlikely acolytes of the other world, all attended seances during or just after the war years.[2] And even confirmed skeptics such as Joyce, D.H. Lawrence, and Virginia Woolf, while shunning spiritualist practice, routinely filled their fiction, poetry, and essays with mediums, ghosts, seances, disembodied voices, and other invocations of the living dead.

How can we account for the striking persistence of popular spiritualism, that credulous Victorian fad, in the cynical age of literary modernism? In this book, I argue that spiritualism continued to flourish well into the twentieth century, both as method and as metaphor, not in spite of the modernist Zeitgeist but because of it. Like modernist literature, popular spiritualism sought to embrace both authority and iconoclasm, both tradition and innovation, both continuity and fragmentation, both the elitist mystique of high culture and the messy vitality of popular culture. In particular, the figure of the spirit medium—with her multiple perspectives, fragmented discourse, and simultaneous claims to authority and passivity—offered a fertile model for the kinds of cultural and linguistic subversions that many authors were seeking to accomplish through their own poetics. To borrow the famous words of Yeats's "unknown instructors," spiritualism and mediumship provided modernist writers with compelling new "metaphors for poetry."[3]

This book seeks to provide a systematic account of literary modernism's vexed and often embarrassed fascination with popular spiritualism, a wide-ranging yet distinct cultural phenomenon with roots in nineteenth-century social and religious reform.[4] Spiritualism is not the same as occultism, with which it is often confused; whereas the latter promises ancient, esoteric knowledge to a select group of initiates, the former is accessible to anyone who can construct a homemade Ouija board or hire a storefront medium. Its very popularity, in fact, has led many intellectual elitists to view popular spiritualism as an inherently suspect phenomenon. The modernist writers discussed in this book, however, were well aware, sometimes in spite of their own misgivings, that great art can draw its vigor from precisely such unlikely and even unsavory sources. Yeats, for one, justified his forays into what he called the "low haunts" of popular spiritualism by depicting literary inspiration as an illicit affair, a back-alley insemination: "Muses resemble women who creep out at night to give themselves to unknown sailors and return to talk of Chinese porcelain . . . or Beethoven's Fifth Symphony."[5]

Taking its cue from Yeats's metaphor of the slumming muse, *Ghostwriting Modernism* seeks to illuminate the relationship between mediumistic discourse—a destabilizing, low cultural, often implicitly feminized mode of speech and writing—and modernist literary aesthetics. This is not a book about ghost stories, although stories about ghosts do, inevitably, appear in its pages. Nor do I concern myself much with what Tzvetan Todorov calls "fantastic" literature, which forces the reader to hesitate between rational and supernatural explanations for mysterious phenomena. (Most spirit mediums, as we shall see, considered their spiritualist experiences to be entirely rational and scientifically explicable.) Likewise, Freud's "uncanny"—"that class of the frightening which leads back to what is known of old and long familiar"—is mentioned only in passing.[6] (Popular spiritualism tends to induce blissful seriousness among its practitioners and scornful hilarity among its detractors; for neither group is fright much of an issue.) Instead, I focus on some of the more subtle ways in which mediums and communicating spirits unsettle seemingly stable ontological—or, as Jacques Derrida would have it, "hauntological"—boundaries between self and other, absence and presence, materiality and spirituality, life and death.[7] Literary modernists and spiritualists alike, I argue, are concerned less with penetrating the "unseen world" of the supernatural than with exploring what Robert Duncan calls the "double or triple moving depths of bead curtain" separating that world from ours: the materialized "movement of meaning" that at once marks and effaces the borderline between seemingly discrete states of being. Like the mediums extolled by Walt Whitman in the poem I have chosen as this book's epigraph, modernist-era spiritualists revel, paradoxically, in earthbound materiality: "materialism and the sight of products . . . poems and materials of poems."

So many people have contributed to this book in small but material ways—providing references, lending books, offering anecdotes about seances and Ouija boards—that I cannot possibly acknowledge them all here. A number of institutions and individuals, however, deserve individual thanks.

For generous research fellowships in support of this project: the National Endowment for the Humanities, and the Office of Research and the University Graduate School at Indiana University, Bloomington.

For permission to publish portions of this book that have appeared elsewhere: *American Literature* 66, 3 (1994) ("James Merrill, Sylvia Plath, and the Poetics of Ouija"); *Modern Language Quarterly* 60, 1 (1999) ("Necrobibliography: Books in the Spirit World"); and *Texas Studies in Literature and Language* 41, 2 (1999) ("Modernist Hauntology: James Joyce, Hester Dowden, and Shakespeare's Ghost").

For access to invaluable resources: the British Library; the Beinecke Library (Yale University); the Lilly Library (Indiana University); and especially the Interlibrary Loan department of the Indiana University Library, which procured obscure spiritualist publications for me from dozens of libraries in at least fifteen different states.

For guidance, criticism, assistance, suggestions, and support at various stages of this book's development: Jane Augustine; Diana Collecott; Eibhlín Evans; Ralph Freedman; Sandra Gilbert; Susan Gubar; Kenneth R. Johnston; Bette London; Timothy Materer; Andrew H. Miller; Adalaide Morris; Perdita Schaffner; Janet Sorensen; Hugh Stevens; Leon Surette; Harriet Tarlo; Stephen P. Watt; Perry Willett.

For their astute and always scholarly devotion to hauntology: Simeon Berry; Katie Harse; Craig Owens; Julie Wise.

For expert research assistance regarding some very arcane subject matter: Lauren Proll-Orem.

For meticulous professionalism and saintly patience: Bernhard Kendler.

For friendship and intellectual succor: Marjorie Howes.

And finally, for a life worth living: my mother, Lois Sword, and my ghost-father, Charles Sword; my blithe and spirited children, Claire Allegra, Peter Rangi, and David Asher; and my beloved husband, Richard Sorrenson, who enriches my words, my work, and my heart.

Ghostwriting

The distance that the dead have gone
Does not at first appear—
Their coming back seems possible
For many an ardent year.

And then, that we have followed them,
We more than half suspect,
So intimate have we become
With their dear retrospect.

Emily Dickinson

There is no other life, only the one.
The world of the spirits that comes afterward
is the same as our own, just like you sitting
there they come and talk to me, just the same.

William Carlos Williams, "The Horse Show"

Spiritualism is "the belief that the dead communicate with the living, as through a medium."[1] Although such beliefs have existed in one form or another in virtually every human culture since the dawn of civilization, the birth of spiritualism in its modern form—what I call "popular spiritualism"—is generally dated to 1848, the year in which two young girls in upstate New York first reported hearing the mysterious rappings that they identified as code messages from otherworldly spirits. Although the famous Fox sisters were later discredited (one of them confessed, many years after the fact, that they had simulated knocking sounds by cracking their toe joints),[2] the "Rochester rappings" set off an international craze. Within months, people all over the United States were claiming to have received similar messages, and by the early 1850s the fad for seances and spirit communication had spread to England and through most of Europe.

Popular spiritualism borrowed much of its vocabulary and many of its

1

practices from other "isms" already long since at large in Western culture: occultism, Swedenborgianism, mesmerism, magnetism. But the phenomenon also quickly acquired its own distinctive, albeit ever evolving, characteristics. At first, spirit messages tended to arrive, like the Fox sisters' communications, in primitive written form: a sitter would call out the letters of the alphabet in order, and a rap, a knock, or the movement of a small table would signal that the correct one had been named. This was, clearly, a slow and laborious business; as Jean Gaudon notes of a similar method employed by Victor Hugo's seance circle in 1853, "It takes a long time for [the table] to say things, because there are more z's in the French language than one might think."[3] Within a few years, automatic writing and trance speaking began to replace table tilting as the most popular methods of spirit communication. Now, rather than merely facilitating the reception of rapped messages that everyone in the room could hear, spirit mediums entered a state akin to possession, becoming, they claimed, conduits for speech or writing not their own.

As the rage for spirit communication became increasingly widespread—and, for professional mediums, increasingly lucrative—it took on ever more spectacular and outlandish forms. By the 1860s and 1870s, one could sit for spirit photographs, attend spirit lectures on a range of progressive social and religious issues, and take part in carefully orchestrated seances at which ghosts materialized, voices spoke through levitating trumpets, messages wrote themselves on sealed slates, and mediums' bodies emitted disconcerting quantities of a strange, filmy substance known as ectoplasm. Not surprisingly, as the degree of showmanship involved in seances increased, so too did accusations of fraud. When a sheltered seventeen-year-old girl claims to speak with the voice of Abraham Lincoln or Charlotte Brontë, she may be doubted, but she cannot easily be disproved. By contrast, a professional materialization medium who produces flamboyant seance effects for profit is likely at some point to be caught red-handed engaging in acts of deliberate deception, as many well-known mediums eventually were. Informed skeptics such as Harry Houdini, the famous escape artist, and David P. Abbott, author of a 1909 book titled *Behind the Scenes with the Mediums*, dedicated themselves to discrediting spiritualism by exposing its most famous practitioners as charlatans.

Yet popular spiritualism persisted, as both a recreational pursuit and a quasi-religious belief, through the end of the nineteenth century and into the modernist era. (In the early twenty-first century, although New Age mysticism has by now largely taken its place, vestiges of spiritualist practice can still be found; for instance, a popular American cable television talk show, *Crossing Over*, features a professional spirit medium who claims to relay communications from audience members' deceased relatives.) With the advent of the Great War, the paradoxical practice of mourning the dead by refusing to let them die itself took a fresh lease on life, as millions of new clients flocked to spirit mediums in hopes of making contact with their dead. Widely read books such as Oliver Lodge's *Raymond* (1916) and Arthur Conan Doyle's *The New Revelation* (1918) brought further publicity and sanction to what was by then an already well-established and, in many circles, intellectually respectable cultural form.

Numerous historians have attempted to account for the astonishing rise and remarkable influence of popular spiritualism in nineteenth-century Britain and America.[4] Many of these scholars portray spirit mediumship as a self-empowering strategy enacted by specific oppressed or disenfranchised social groups such as African Americans (Baer), English plebians (Barrow), or women (Basham, Braude, Douglas, Owen). Spiritualism, however, was practiced at society's power centers—in aristocratic drawing rooms, in scientific laboratories, and even at the White House and Westminster—just as avidly as at its frayed edges, and the movement's allure extended to both men and women, to the socially privileged as well as to those struggling for cultural influence. Although it is certainly true that nineteenth-century spiritualism replicated problematic imperialist attitudes (by claiming to colonize new territories), class structures (by insisting simultaneously on the populist sympathies and the elitist insight of the spirit medium), and gender paradigms (by deploying traditionally "feminine" behavioral traits such as passivity, receptivity, and insensibility in the service of intellectual commodities typically coded as male, for example, knowledge, productivity, and reason), its widespread appeal seems to have depended, above all, on its elastic capacity to offer something for everyone, the empowered as well as the powerless.

Judging nineteenth-century spiritualism today is, as Cottom comments, "like trying to nail Jello to a tree."[5] But it would be difficult to overstate the movement's contemporary importance and influence. Spiritualism attracted social idealists who looked to the "other world" as a harmonious model for this one; religious reformers who were striving for a less hierarchical, more personal contact with God; and scientists who hoped to reveal material explanations for what they considered to be very real and plausible psychic phenomena. Public figures who are known either to have participated in seances themselves or to have taken an active interest in spiritualist investigations included prominent philosophers, psychologists, jurists, physical scientists, mathematicians, astronomers, evolutionary biologists, social reformers, abolitionists, journalists, religious leaders, theosophists, inventors, financiers, educators, politicians, royalty, and even a famous frontier hero.[6] Some of these individuals quickly rejected popular spiritualism, or accepted its premises but eschewed its vulgarity, or concerned themselves more with psychical research (the scientific study of unexplained phenomena) than with attempts to contact the dead. Others attended seances only to ridicule them—"the spirits . . . do not improve on acquaintance," scoffed Sir John Tyndall—or, like Thomas Henry Huxley, they dismissed the claims of spiritualists out of hand: "The only good that I can see in the demonstration of the truth of 'Spiritualism' is to furnish an additional argument against suicide. Better to live a crossing-sweeper than to die and be made to talk twaddle by a 'medium' hired at a guinea a *séance*."[7] All the same, hardly a leading intellectual of the late nineteenth century failed at least to register some comment on the subject. Karl Marx, for instance, makes explicit references to spiritualism in *Capital*, where, anticipating twentieth-century spiritualists' emphasis on the material aspects of spiritualism, he uses the example of table-turning seances to illustrate the transformative power of commodification:

> The form of wood, for instance, is altered, by making a table out of it. Yet, for all that the table continues to be that common, every-day thing, wood. But, so soon as it steps forth as a commodity, it is changed into something transcendent. It not only stands with its feet on the ground, but, in relation to all other commodities, it stands on its head, and evolves out of its wooden brain grotesque ideas, far more wonderful than "table-turning" ever was.[8]

Perhaps inevitably, the spiritualist movement proved particularly appealing to creative writers, who not only took part in spiritualist seances themselves but also wrote copiously about the subject. The catalog of late-nineteenth-century authors who dabbled (or, in some cases, wallowed) in spiritualism is lengthy and impressive. John Greenleaf Whittier, James Fenimore Cooper, Robert Dale Owen, Washington Irving, and Henry Longfellow all danced attendance upon the Fox sisters. Edward Bulwer-Lytton, Robert and Elizabeth Barrett Browning, William Thackeray, John Ruskin, and Leo Tolstoy were among the many eminent personages who participated in seances conducted by Daniel Dunglas Home, the famous materialization medium. Alfred Lord Tennyson, Lewis Carroll, John Addington Symonds, and John Ruskin were founding members of the London Society for Psychical Research. Harriet Beecher Stowe, Dante Gabriel Rossetti, Christina Rossetti, Laurence Oliphant, Rider Haggard, Rudyard Kipling, Andrew Lang, Maurice Maeterlinck, and J.-K. Huysmans all participated in spiritualist practices at one time or another. And Walt Whitman, although he left behind no explicit public commentary on spiritualism, produced a lusty, lyrical poem in which he praises spirit mediums as "complete women and men, their pose brawny and supple" who, like the Whitmanesque poet himself, possess the visionary ability to give voice and substance to "Death, the future, the invisible faith."[9]

Other well-known nineteenth-century writers, meanwhile, used the power of the pen to issue scathing attacks on popular spiritualism. Ralph Waldo Emerson called it "this rat-hole revelation" and remarked that "these adepts have mistaken flatulency for inspiration." Nathaniel Hawthorne professed to "a sluggish disgust, and repugnance to meddle with it." George Eliot declared that she would rather "be occupied exclusively with the intestinal worms of tortoises than with that." And George Bernard Shaw, in his 1920 preface to *Heartbreak House*, characterized Edwardian England's addiction "to table-rapping, materialization séances, clairvoyance, palmistry, crystal-gazing and the like" as a "drift to the abyss."[10]

"Hardly a major novelist of the period," notes Ann Braude, "could resist Spiritualism's dramatic possibilities."[11] Charles Dickens disdained spirit mediumship, but he published many articles on the subject in *Household Words* (1852–58) and *All the Year Round* (1859–66), and his fiction is liberally laced with allusions to ghosts and spirit communication. (As Elizabeth Barrett Browning drily noted, Dickens was fond of ghost stories, but only "so long as they are impossible.")[12] Robert Browning, Nathaniel Hawthorne, William Dean Howells, Henry James, Herman Melville, Leo Tolstoy, and Mark Twain were among those who used spiritualism as fodder for satire, a tradition still evident in twentieth-century works by authors as diverse as the comic novelist E. F. Benson, the playwright Noel Coward, the opera composer Gian Carlo Menotti, the short story writer Isaac Bashevis Singer, and the poet Stevie Smith.[13] Literary representations of seances and spirit mediums serve many different narrative purposes. They can wreak personal revenge on real-life spiritualists, as in Browning's "Mr. Sludge, 'The Medium,'" a dramatic monologue intended to expose the alleged chicanery of Daniel Dunglas Home. They can help establish an authentically Victorian atmosphere, as in A. S. Byatt's *Possession* or Joyce Carol Oates's *A Bloodsmoor Romance*, late-twentieth-century historical novels set in nineteenth-century Britain and America, respectively. They can be deployed strategically as a plot device, as in Dorothy Sayers's mystery novel *Strong Poison*, in which an amateur detective stages a fake seance to influence a suggestive witness. In some cases, they simply provide welcome comic relief, as in the 1990 movie *Ghost*, which accepts spiritualism's defining premise—that the dead survive and can communicate with the living—but nonetheless milks Whoopi Goldberg's character, a tawdry storefront medium, for every possible laugh.

Most frequently, however, spiritualist satire functions as social criticism, serving as a medium—pun intended—for humorous but nonetheless biting commentary on a range of cultural issues. From the first, popular spiritualism was associated by both its proponents and its detractors with anti-orthodox religious reform. Thus, one 1853 British commentator excoriated spiritualism as "an especially American plot" that had been exported to England from "the birth-place of Mormonism,'" while another described a "table-talking" seance at which the table moved slightly when the author asked if Satan's headquarters were in England, more violently when asked if they were in France and Spain, and more violently still when asked if they were in Rome.[14] Numerous nineteenth-century novelists published satirical attacks—often more melodramatic than humorous, and most by now deservedly forgotten—in which they lambasted spiritualism either for its "demonic causation" or because they regarded the movement "as a vulnerable symbol of the various radical and millenarian impulses of the time."[15] The most frequent targets of antispiritualist satire, however—and therefore, we can conclude, the objects of the greatest anxiety about changing social norms—were mediumistic women, whose quasi-priestly stature and pretensions to otherworldly knowledge were roundly deflated in fiction if not necessarily in real life. Priscilla in Hawthorne's *Blithedale Romance* (1852), Egeria in Howells's *Undiscovered Country* (1880), and Verena in James's *Bostonians* (1886) are all budding young mediums who, as Russell and Clare Goldfarb note, are ultimately "rescued" from the moral abyss of female self-determination by choosing a domestic role over their erstwhile spiritualist pursuits.[16] Even Herman Melville's 1856 story "The Apple-Tree Table," although less transparently about women's rights, has a similarly gendered valence; Ann Douglas sees this tale about mysterious rappings, seemingly delivered by spirits but in fact caused by a long-dormant insect, as enacting a struggle for interpretation between a rationalist father and his spiritualist daughters: "Who will determine the content and form of American culture?"[17]

Of course, not all nineteenth-century spiritualists were women. According to Ruth Brandon, "most of the really proficient conjuring was done by men," whose professional ethos emphasized masculine control rather than feminine passivity.[18] All the same, the fact that virtually all of spiritualism's leading satirists have been respected, highbrow male authors, whereas many of its literary proselytizers have been popular female writers of lyric poetry or romantic fiction—among them Elizabeth Barrett Browning, Elizabeth Stuart Phelps, Harriet Beecher Stowe, Marie Corelli, and, in the twentieth century, Edith Somerville, Ella Wheeler Wilcox, Catherine Dawson Scott, Rosamond Lehmann, and Taylor Caldwell[19]—has reinforced longstanding critical perceptions of spiritualists as blinkered, bathetic sentimentalists incapable of modernist irony. These gendered stereotypes are complicated, to be sure, by the fervent credulity of prolific and well-regarded male authors such as Sir Laurence Oliphant, Robert Dale Owen, Sir Arthur Conan Doyle, and W. B. Yeats. Yet all of these men relied, significantly, on female mediums (frequently their own wives) for spirit contact. "I have looked out of [the] eyes" of "the woman in me," wrote Yeats in 1936; "I have shared her desire." Perhaps this desire included a covert longing to achieve, like his own mediumistic wife, direct access to visionary perception, "that sudden miracle as if the darkness had been cut with a knife, [which] is mostly a woman's privilege."[20]

Writers of imaginative fiction and poetry have always functioned as spirit mediums of a sort: giving voice and substance to literary characters we cannot see but nonetheless believe to be real; ventriloquizing for the dead; penning elegies and requiems that celebrate the human soul's survival beyond death. Conversely, mediumship has always been closely allied with authorship. At least since the time of the Fox sisters, spirit mediums have typically regarded themselves as privileged recipients and interpreters of the written word. An astonishing number of their spirit communications, moreover, have arrived in written form, whether via automatic writing, through devices such as the planchette or the Ouija board, or by means of the old-fashioned alphabetic knockings and table-tipping seances favored by the Fox sisters. Even trance mediums who do not avail themselves of pen and paper frequently invoke literary personages, employ literary metaphors, and publish written accounts of their spirit communications. Despite their emphasis on the transcendental quality of their otherworldly vision, spiritualists have always relied heavily on written publications—books, periodicals, and the public press—for material dissemination of their messages.[21]

Literary scholars such as Cottom and Basham have noted that spiritualism's earliest practitioners, in drawing attention to the many connections between authorship and mediumship, stirred up a host of attendant cultural anxieties regarding literary authority, authenticity, inspiration, and the reliability of new communication technologies. Spirit mediumship was controversial in the nineteenth century, Cottom maintains, because it threatened "to expose language, behavior, character, individual persons, and the entirety of culture as unfounded representations." Imaginative writers, in particular, felt threatened by spiritualists' tendency to dwell on the inherent fragility and mendacity of language, laying bare, in effect, the tricks of the writer's trade: "By making the occult speak openly, spiritualism also made public the practices of interpretation that give words the effect of presence and materiality. . . . This is the reigning paradox of spiritualism: that its insistence on immediacy, on personal experience, was supported by reference to a compromising medium."[22]

The very characteristics that so discomfited nineteenth-century intellectuals, I argue here, can help to explain spiritualism's persistent, sometimes baffling appeal for twentieth-century writers. Even when they mocked its ludicrous lingo and derided its metaphysical excesses, modernist writers were intrigued and attracted by spiritualism's ontological shiftiness; its location of authorial power in physical abjection; its subversive celebrations of alternate, often explicitly feminine, modes of writing; its transgressions of the traditional divide between high and low culture; and its self-serving tendency to privilege form over content, medium over message. In the following chapters, at the risk of neglecting some of popular spiritualism's other important cultural manifestations, I focus on the forms of mediumship most closely allied with writing and the forms of writing most closely allied with mediumship. My aim is not to tout spiritualism as some kind of master key that will unlock all the nuances of literary modernism (or vice versa) but, more modestly, to suggest why twentieth-century rationalists steeped in an ironic sensibility and a materialist aesthetics might have been attracted to such a seemingly transcendental cultural discourse at all. Popular spiritualism, I hope to show, embraces rather than eschews paradox. Like modernism itself, it provides a fluid, often self-contradictory ideological space in which conservative beliefs can coexist with radical, even iconoclastic, thought and action.

CHAPTER ONE

Necrobibliography

"She had an idea that when people want to publish they are capable—." And then she paused, blushing.

"Of violating a tomb?"

Henry James, The Aspern Papers

I have sometimes dreamt . . . that when the Day of Judgment dawns and the great conquerors and lawyers and statesmen come to receive their rewards—their crowns, theirs laurels, their names carved indelibly into imperishable marble—the Almighty will turn to Peter and will say, not without a certain envy when He sees us coming with our books under our arms, "Look, these need no reward. We have nothing to give them here. They have loved reading."

Virginia Woolf, "How Should One Read a Book?"

Books in the Spirit World

"It is indeed impossible," contends Sigmund Freud in a 1915 essay, "to imagine our own death."[1] Imagining a continued existence beyond death is equally difficult, although many intrepid writers have attempted it. The most memorable of these—from Plotinus to Dante to Swedenborg—posit an oppositional cosmogony composed of both good and evil: an afterlife imbued with all the richness, texture, and complexity of this one. Modern spiritualists, however, have for the most part pictured instead a spirit world bathed only in sweetness and light, a heaven supposedly founded on spiritual values but in fact crammed with all the trappings of a deeply materialistic culture, from magnificent houses and priceless furnishings to exotic travel opportunities and even household help.[2] Nineteenth-century authors such as the popular novelist Elizabeth Stuart Phelps describe a sparkling domain of relentless domesticity, a sort of "celestial retirement village," in Ann Douglas's gloss, where "the chaos of productivity is eliminated in order to insure the pleasures of consumption."[3] Early-twentieth-century spirit mediums, similarly, promise a realm free of material discomfort and modernist angst, where worthy residents can enjoy fruits without peels, pets without fleas, sports without sweat, and sex without contraception.[4] And even today, among recent publications by spiritual seekers generally more concerned with recovering past lives and preparing for the New Age than with charting the topography of the afterlife, we can still find rapturous physical accounts of the spirit world, a sunny vacationland that is part Swiss Alps, part Key West, where one can stroll through etheric meadows discussing poetry with the spirit of John Lennon or sit under a palm tree typing earth-bound messages on a celestial computer.[5]

Since Blake's reading of Milton, of course, we have known that Paradise is boring. Such saccharine portrayals of the afterlife are thus likely to strike us not as fertile plumbings of the unimaginable but as symptoms of imaginative bankruptcy. And yet, while modern spiritualists' descriptions of the other world seemingly have little to teach us about the originality of their authors, they can often tell us a good deal about the social conflicts, ideological agendas, and even the imaginative innovations of the cultures from which they emerge, from the social progressivism of late-nineteenth-century Britain to the high-tech millennialism of our own recent fin de siècle.[6] In particular, otherworldly narratives from the modernist era, although largely devoid of formal experimentation and ironic self-consciousness, engage with many of the dominant tropes of literary modernism—linguistic playfulness, decenterings of consciousness, fracturings of conventional gender roles—and betray a characteristically modernist obsession with all things textual: reading, writing, literature, authorship, publication, libraries, and even the discourses and methodologies of literary criticism.

It seems no accident, in fact, that the very term "ghostwriting" originated, according to the *Oxford English Dictionary*, in the early years of the twentieth century. Whether it designates, as in standard dictionary definitions, the writing of a book for which someone else receives credit or, as in this book, a medium's publication of written messages supposedly authored in the spirit world, ghostwriting is an act that, although hardly unique to the modernist era, in many ways epitomizes its contradictions. Ghostwritten accounts of literary activities in the afterlife, even as they reflect the cultural pretensions and authorial aspirations of the mediums who communicate them, also call into question the timeless literary values they seem to celebrate, foregrounding the contingent nature of signification and the stubborn materiality of language. On a more terrestrial level, moreover, otherworldly narratives undermine the very institutions of authorship—copyright law, bibliographical conventions, the cult of the Great Writer—with which literate mediums have so eagerly sought to ally themselves. If the author is, as Michel Foucault puts it, "the ideological figure by which one marks the manner in which we fear the proliferation of meaning," then a spirit medium who claims to ghostwrite for the dead is that proliferation personified, the ideological figure for everything that, according to Foucault, the author-function holds in check: "the free circulation, the free manipulation, the free composition, decomposition, and recomposition of fiction."[7] Thus spirit mediumship enacts modernism's central paradox, exporting high literary culture to the spirit world only to subvert literature's most basic claims to ontological authority.

At first glance, to be sure, modernist-era accounts of the other world generally seem more reactionary than rebellious, more clichéd than controversial, putting a relentlessly happy face on human mortality. Dead families are reunited in breathtaking surroundings; higher astral planes promise even greater splendor for those who attain spiritual advancement; and friendly spirit guides—usually Native Americans, ancient Egyptians, or members of other "primitive," ostensibly death-affirming societies—facilitate communication with grieving relatives back on earth. As early as 1902, Frank Podmore observed that "these spirits have made heaven as familiar as a Yarmouth beach—and about as alluring." His complaint is a familiar one, echoed by twentieth-century commentators from Freud ("all their utterances . . . have been so foolish and so desperately insignificant that one could find nothing else to believe in but the capacity of the spirits for adapting themselves to the circle of people that had evoked them") to Theodor Adorno ("In pursuing yonder what they have lost, [spiritualists] encounter only the nothing they have. . . . The worthless magic is nothing other than the worthless existence it lights up. This is what makes the prosaic so cosy.").[8] On closer inspection, however, the domestic sphere evoked by modern spiritualists often turns out to be not so much cozily *heimlich* as eerily *unheimlich*. How else can we describe a place where human bodies dry instantly after bathing, where hidden music (heavenly Muzak?) plays constantly in the background, where people can go fishing but the fish never die, where gustatory consumption is encouraged yet defecation is unnecessary?[9] In fact, reading several otherworldly narratives in quick succession leads not to reassurance or temptation but to a kind of metaphysical vertigo. Spiritualist apologists concoct ingenious responses to accusations of inconsistency or illogic, but their explanations, shoring fragments of reason against the potential ruins of a precarious metaphysics, often threaten to plunge believers and skeptics alike into an intellectual abyss, a crisis of detail that is characteristically modernist in its effects if not its causes.

Contributing to the destabilizing effect of modernist-era spirit narratives is the fact that, although most of the spiritualist publications cited in this book chronicle the words and actions of male spirits, the majority were written by or communicated through female mediums: male voices mouth a distinctively female agenda. Following a pattern already set in the second half of the nineteenth century, many of the early twentieth century's best-known spiritualist proselytizers were men of high social and intellectual standing—Sir Oliver Lodge, Sir Arthur Conan Doyle, William Butler Yeats, Lord Hugh Dowding—yet mediumship itself remained very much the province of women, offering one of the relatively few means by which women of virtually any social or educational background could earn money, engage in high-profile careers, lay claim to otherworldly insight, and subvert male authority, all while conforming to normative ideals of feminine passivity and receptivity. But whereas nineteenth-century mediums pursued a primarily religious and domestic agenda, organizing the realm of the dead according to the family-centered principles that they hoped to promote on earth,[10] modernist-era mediums pursued instead an intellectual one, appropriating imagery, themes, techniques, and even personalities from the realms of literature and literary studies.

Not coincidentally, many of the best-known female mediums of the modernist era either came from literary backgrounds or undertook literary careers quite separate from their mediumistic vocations. Hester Dowden (aka Hester Travers Smith), one of London's preeminent professional writing mediums, was the daughter of the distinguished Irish literary critic Edward Dowden, the mother-in-law of the Abbey playwright Lennox Robinson, and a close acquaintance of numerous other literary luminaries, from W. B. Yeats to Bram Stoker. Having grown up watching the literary elite of Dublin pass through her house, Hester

Dowden would later claim to have communicated with, among others, the spirits of Oscar Wilde, Francis Bacon, and William Shakespeare. Dowden was close friends with Geraldine Cummins, another London medium of Irish origins, who, in addition to authoring dozens of widely read books and articles on spirit communication, was also a successful biographer, novelist, and playwright. Cummins worked for a time in Dublin's National Library, saw her early work performed at the Abbey Theatre, and in later years produced two novels and a literary biography of novelist Edith Somerville. Eileen Garrett, an Irish medium who eventually rose to prominence in American parapsychology circles, directed a publishing firm, founded a New York literary magazine that attracted contributions from such highly regarded authors as Robert Graves, Klaus Mann, and Aldous Huxley, and published several novels under the pen name Jean Lyttle. Catherine Dawson Scott, who published several books of spirit messages from the likes of W. T. Stead and Woodrow Wilson, was a popular novelist and the founder of P.E.N., the international writers' association. Elsa Barker, whose 1915 spirit communications from a deceased judge were still being read and cited by spiritualists decades later, and Winifred Graham Cory, who published two books of "letters from Heaven" dictated by her late father, were both successful novelists as well. And Rosamond Dale Oliphant, an American spiritualist who for a time devoted eight hours of each day to automatic writing, was the granddaughter of the social reformer Robert Owen, the daughter of Robert Dale Owen (himself an avid spiritualist), and the second wife of the British novelist and philosopher Laurence Oliphant. Her communications came, she believed, from a literary consortium of familial spirits that included her famous father and grandfather, two late husbands, and even her first husband's first wife.[11]

Typically, these mediums received most if not all of their spirit communications via automatic writing, a method of transmission particularly well suited to their literary interests and agendas. ("It is unfortunate I happen to be a writer of fiction," notes Cory ingenuously, "for I know well people who scorn the possibility of communication, will think I have invented the wording of this book.")[12] In some cases, ghostwriting for the dead served as a logical extension of their own authorial talents; in others, no doubt, it served as a substitute. But these women were not the only spiritualists interested in the intellectual life of the dead. Even mediums with no apparent literary connections of their own often went out of their way to extol the pleasures, both worldly and otherworldly, of books. Indeed, the very fact that spirit mediums of the modernist era wrote and published so prolifically—the years between and during the two World Wars saw an unprecedented boom in otherworldly messages and books about spirit communication—marks them as active and eager participants in a bibliophilic culture.

Nowhere is this fascination with books, authorship, and textuality more evident than in modernist-era descriptions of the other world. Again and again, literature classes, poetry readings, and famous writers are invoked as metonyms for the discursive authority and cultural empowerment desired, no doubt, by the mediums themselves. Predictably, many spiritualist narratives enact stock middlebrow fantasies of intellectual egalitarianism, promising the hoi polloi a chance to rub shoulders with the famous. Oliphant's ghostly communicators report, for instance, that the souls of the dead quickly drift into affinity groups—"into the Rossetti group, or the George Eliot group, or the group of Orthodoxy, or the Salvation Army group"—where, if "the lover of George Eliot wishes to hear a sequel to Adam Bede," he or she can do so through thought waves.[13]

Other accounts move beyond heavenly autograph seeking to describe a much more active participation in literary pursuits. The desire to communicate one's otherworldly experiences in writing is a hallmark of numerous spiritualist narratives, including some communicated by spirits who showed no particularly lyrical inclinations while on earth. "I would like to have been a poet at that moment [of arrival in the spirit world]," proclaims the spirit of the journalist W. T. Stead (via medium Pardoe Woodman) in one fairly typical effusion, "but as it was I just wanted to express myself with pen and ink." Likewise, the spirit of T. E. Lawrence confesses (via medium Jane Sherwood) that he has been able to fulfill in the spirit world "an urge I never fully satisfied on earth," producing "a scanty output of what I hope is poetry."[14] A similar poetic imperative persists even today, incidentally, in another literary genre concerned, like spirit narratives, with describing unknown worlds. In the 1997 film version of Carl Sagan's 1985 science fiction novel *Contact*, the astronaut Ellie Arroway, upon catching her first ecstatic glimpse of an alien planet, murmurs, "They should have sent a poet!"[15]

To some extent, this emphasis on reading, writing, and intellectual community in the other world merely echoes the evolutionary meliorism already evident in much nineteenth-century spiritualist rhetoric. In particular, educational metaphors—whereby the passage from one sphere of human existence to the next is depicted as a kind of graduation or matriculation—invoke lofty Victorian ideals of eternal self-improvement, expressed via detailed descriptions of otherworldly schools, universities, and even scholarly research projects undertaken by the dead.[16] Many spiritualist testimonies, in fact, take the notion of higher education to its literal extreme: one medium reports on a series of educational lectures delivered by visitors from Neptune to "Professors and students from Colleges in higher Astral-States"; another extols the pedagogical benefits of taking students on cosmic field trips via instantaneous thought travel ("the whole class can go and see the thing for itself"); another describes "an ancient city where are seats of learning; not an exact replica of my own Oxford but a university town of widely-spaced buildings of noble aspect"; another relays messages from a young World War I pilot who announces that he is now happily studying, appropriately, "the higher mathematics"; and still another relates that even psychoanalysis finds its counterpart in the world of the dead: every newly arrived spirit "is interviewed by one of the Advanced Spirit Instructors and the whole record of earth is discussed and analysed. Reason, motive and result. The full and detailed record contains everything, there is nothing overlooked, and this is the time for paying the bill."[17] Besides undoubtedly reflecting modernist-era mediums' own considerable intellectual ambitions and desires to advance to a better station in life, such accounts seem to have appealed to a wide range of spiritualist readers, including not only disappointed underachievers longing for a fresh start but also overachievers seeking new challenges. For instance, Lord Hugh Dowding, who as a famous war hero might have been content to spend eternity resting comfortably on his laurels, confesses in *Many Mansions* his desire to pass the afterlife studying such arcane subjects as wave mechanics and atomic physics: "It would be pure pleasure to go to school again with a new-model brain and satisfy all my perplexities."[18]

Books, the cornerstones of educational institutions both otherworldly and terrestrial, represent this progressive zeal reduced to its smallest, most compact unit. In the other world just as in this one, it seems, a well-made book embodies the ultimate academic fantasy, an idealized union of intellectual stimulation and tactile pleasure. (At least one medium insists, to be sure, that the binding on otherworldly books, although it "looks like, and feels like, a very good leather," is actually a sophisticated synthetic product instead, since there is no slaughtering of animals in heaven.)[19] Thus, when T. E. Lawrence's spirit reports (via Jane Sherwood) that he now divides his time between studying "the higher philosophy" and learning the fine art of book making—itself a balancing act between intellectual and material pursuits—he fulfills the bibliographic fantasies of such creative writers as the French poet Stéphane Mallarmé, who describes how a beautifully made book can invoke "that ecstasy in which we become immortal for a brief hour," or Virginia Woolf, who speculates that those who love books on earth will have a special place in heaven.[20] The notion of cheating death through literature is, of course, an old and familiar trope, promising eternal life both to the poet and to the poet's subject. Mallarmé's and Woolf's formulations are notable, however, in that they add the reader to the pantheon. If books ensure immortality to virtually everyone who comes in contact with them—indeed, if a lifetime of reading makes even God envious—it is little wonder that a former man of action such as T. E. Lawrence should choose to spend immortality making books.

In some modernist-era spiritualist testimonies, books serve not only as metonyms for cultural empowerment and self-improvement but also as metaphors for the afterlife itself: "We are not merely short stories on the pages of earth," as the spirit of F. W. H. Myers puts it (via Geraldine Cummins); "we are a serial, and each chapter closes with death."[21] At the same time, however, the role of books in spiritualist discourse is very much at odds with their function as deathless symbols of intellectual authority and spiritual fulfillment. A number of scholars have noted that spirit communication itself, with its many rules, quirks, and foibles—its dependence on darkened rooms, specialized props, credulous participants, pliant mediums, obliging spirit guides, favorable atmospheric conditions, and so on—calls attention to the fragility and tenuousness of all human intercourse; it conveys, in Daniel Cottom's words, "the extreme difficulty—even the utter improbability—of communication."[22] Descriptions of otherworldly books have a similar effect, for they reify the material nature of literary discourse: the dependence of mortals and spirits alike on contingencies of language and signification. Spiritualist testimonies characteristically emphasize the spirits' ability to communicate telepathically, without words. Yet otherworldly books, by their very nature, contradict and undermine this supposed obviation of language.

Thus they enact modern spiritualism's central metaphysical conflict: its paradoxical proclivity to materialize the spirit world even while trying to spiritualize the material one.

Spirit mediums approach this paradox in a variety of ways, whether by subverting it, ignoring it, or, most frequently, by embracing and manipulating it to their own purposes. Catherine Dawson Scott's spirit messages from a "clever, but tiresome" great uncle, for instance, both magnify and collapse traditional distinctions between spirit and matter by insisting that "thoughts are things": "If I make, that is, think, a poem, it is a shining brilliance, and every spirit in my neighborhood is able to enjoy it." In the dead uncle's account, reading as well as writing becomes a material process, a kind of intellectual equivalent to the ectoplasmic evulsions so popular in late-nineteenth-century mediumship: "You do not read here, but the story flows before you from its inception to its finis."[23] Similarly, Hester Dowden's spirit communicators in *One Step Higher* assign physical qualities to thought, noting that they can read lengthy books in a single day thanks to the "immense increase in vibration" of their brain waves. Dowden's account of the other world differs significantly from Dawson Scott's in that it insists on the physical existence of otherworldly books, which provide the dead with a material link to the living: "Our books are bound as yours are and are cared for by special persons who have had their training on the earth sphere." But her vivid description of heavenly libraries stocked with "endless books on colour, sound and perfume, which are all three the expression of what is divine in different keys," echoes Dawson Scott's "shining" visual poems. Both mediums invoke a synesthetic idyll of glowing words, vibrating thoughts, musical colors, and flowing stories.[24]

On one level, such linguistic fantasies reflect mankind's age-old desire to transcend human discourse altogether and learn to speak the language of God—or, in this case, the next best thing, the language of the spirits. On another level, however, they demonstrate the mediums' powerful awareness of the material, physical nature of language. Like mystics lamenting that they can never fully describe their union with the divine, spiritualists frequently complain about the inadequacy of human language to provide an accurate picture of the other world. Yet often their solution is to resort to the linguistic trope of metaphor, mustering similes drawn from the discourses of literary translation and cross-cultural encounter: "Even in our own world," one commentator reminds us, "the African Chief who came to England in a big liner and stayed at Buckingham Palace with the 'Great White King' found it quite impossible by picturesque language or other method to convey to his people any conception of what he had seen and experienced, so different was life in Central Africa from life in a great city like London, though in the same world."[25] Ironically, some spiritualists even invoke language itself as a metaphor for the transcendence achieved when material form is rendered into pure idea. For instance, the educational reformer Rudolf Steiner, in a 1914 talk titled "The Presence of the Dead in Our Life," uses the mechanics of reading to explain why the dead do not always appear to clairvoyants exactly as they looked when alive:

> The individual's appearance in the clairvoyant sphere seems to resemble a physical figure but can be as different from the being really present as the signs for the word "house" are from the actual house. Since we can read, we do not concentrate on the signs that make up the word "house" and do not describe the shape of the letters, but instead we get right to the concept "house." In the same way, we learn in true clairvoyance to move from the figure we perceive to the actual being. That is why we speak of reading the occult script, in the true sense of the word. That is, we move inwardly and actively from the vision to the reality it expresses just as written words express a reality.[26]

Differentiating between "the figure" of a person (i.e., the physical body) and the "actual being" (the spirit or soul), Steiner echoes in his terminology Ferdinand de Saussure's famous distinction, formulated just a few years earlier, between the signifier and the signified: between the word itself and the idea or object for which it stands. But whereas Steiner, in describing the mystic's visionary apprehension of "the occult script," assumes that the signifier is transparent and Adamic—"Since we can read, . . . we get right to the concept 'house'"—Saussure emphasizes its intractable opacity. In doing so, he anticipates not only a major principle of modernist poetics but also the spiritualist narratives of literate mediums such as Dowden and Dawson Scott, whose synesthetic fantasies, despite their sometimes transcendental vocabulary, evince a keen awareness of the essentially arbitrary and unstable nature of the signifier. In the late nineteenth century, many prominent spiritualists—among them Charles Beecher, Robert Owen, and Victoria Woodhull—were deeply involved in language reform movements, translating their desire for a socially progressive afterlife into a commitment to develop a universal language here on earth.[27] By the twentieth century, however, such linguistic idealism had largely faded (although the April 1943 issue of the *Psychic Review* does include a report on "the first official Esperanto-Spiritualist séance ever publicly held," moderated by the spirit of W. T. Stead).[28] Instead, modernist-era spiritualists seem almost to revel in the fact that the dead, like us, are mired in the materiality of the written word.

Because the spirits' very ability to communicate, as we are reminded again and again, depends on the emotional willingness, intellectual aptitude, and physical stamina of the mortals through whom they speak or write, otherworldly authors are predictably full of praise for those rare mediums who are intelligent enough, gifted enough, but also passive and pliant enough to act as their amanuenses: "You are a perfect aeolian lyre that can record me as I think" (Wilde's spirit to Hester Dowden); "It is no easy matter to attain and retain that combination of self-control, combined with the sensitiveness of the visionary and idealist. All this is essential, however, before a perfectly attuned instrument opens to receive the perfect message" (Conan Doyle's spirit to Grace Cooke); "Thou art a harp all finely strung and tuned by God's own hand; / An instrument the like of which none own in spiritland!" (Shakespeare's spirit to Sarah Taylor Shatford).[29] Significantly, in all three of these examples the medium is compared not to a writing instrument but to a musical one. The words of writers such as Wilde, Conan Doyle, and Shakespeare, when transmitted through a medium's mind and body, themselves become veritable works of synesthetic art: language rendered as pure musical sound. Far from promising a simple escape from or glib transcendence of language, however, such instrumental metaphors point to the emphatic physicality of spirit communication, which depends for its efficacy on the medium's delicate vibrations, careful attunement, and exquisite self-control.

It hardly requires a cynic, of course, to perceive the motivation and self-interest involved when a medium transmits messages in which she herself is lavishly lauded by the ghosts of famous men. Yet mediumistic self-acclamation is fed as much by analogy as by egotism. If a spirit medium wants to call attention to the importance of her own profession, it behooves her to foreground the ways in which that other kind of medium, language, bridges the gap between idea and expression much as she herself bridges the gap between the dead and the living. Spirits who speak in human language, in other words, necessarily require human mediums through whom to speak. The spirits' dependence on material signifiers guarantees an equivalent dependence on human bodies and minds.

This formulation helps to explain why otherworldly narratives from the modernist era so frequently emphasize the mediated nature not only of speech and writing but of the seemingly more passive act of reading as well. Although some spirit communicators claim that all the books ever written, including those published after their own deaths, are readily available for otherworldly perusal, others admit that they depend on human readers for their enjoyment both of new books and, more surprisingly, of older ones, including sometimes their own. The spirit of T. E. Lawrence, for example, reports that he can read the books he wrote while on earth only via his medium, Jane Sherwood: "I saw afresh through her eyes the records of campaigns I had myself written." Elsewhere we are told that famous writers "cannot even read the works they once committed to paper save through the spectacles of some human mind"; the living, it seems, serve not only as the spirits' writing instruments but also as their reading glasses. Indeed, according to the spirit of Oscar Wilde (communicating via Hester Dowden), reading is just one aspect of his continuing dependence on human vision: "Over the whole world have I wandered, looking for eyes by which I might see. . . . Through the eyes out of the dusky face of a Tamal girl I have looked on the tea fields of Ceylon, and through the eyes of a wandering Kurd I have seen Ararat and the Yezedes. . . . It may surprise you to learn that in this way I have dipped into the works of some of your modern novelists."[30]

Such confessions as these reverse the traditional spiritualist hierarchy of spirit and matter, which privileges the former and denigrates the latter. The visionary power of the spirits, we learn, depends on rather than supersedes the visual capabilities of ordinary mortals. Wilde's spirit goes so far as to hint that human vision is superior to his own precisely because of its limitations: "we get confused by seeing into each other's thoughts."[31] Paradoxically, this kind of radical intersubjectivity, which disorients the spirits and makes them long for the physical anchor of human embodiment, frees human mediums and their imitators into new possibilities of discourse. In fact, when Wilde's spirit laments that he has wandered all over the world "looking for eyes by which I might see," he articulates a central principle of modernist poetics, whereby writers seek to look through the eyes and speak with the voices of numerous speaking subjects, often shifting, like a medium during a seance, from one voice to another with little or no warning.

This is not to say that spiritualism itself consistently enacts the discursive innovations or ideological reversals for which it provides such a compelling model. Despite their out-of-this-world subject matter, spiritualist publications from the first half of the twentieth century often resemble nothing so much as stuffy academic treatises, complete with scholarly introductions, footnotes, appendixes, illustrations, name-dropping, and the inevitable impenetrable jargon. However, their pseudoscholarly packaging plays an importantly subversive role, for even as it attempts to enhance the intellectual credibility of spiritualism, it masks, just as crucially, the female authorship of many otherworldly narratives, placing upon them the imprimatur of male academic authority. More often than not, the spirit messages relayed by female mediums have supposedly been dictated by men (frequently famous writers) now residing in the spirit world; they are said to have been transmitted via male "spirit guides" or "controls," who serve as the mediums' point men in heaven; and they have been edited, introduced, and/or interpreted by male "experts," who vouch for their authenticity by using tactics borrowed from such male-dominated fields of endeavor as science, psychology, and, most notably, literary criticism.

In particular, spiritualist commentators delight in employing the time-honored literary-critical technique of stylistic analysis. A 1926 book of spirit communications from Jack London (via Margaret More Oliver), for instance, is prefaced by a letter from Sir Arthur Conan Doyle, who dismisses out of hand the possibility of mediumistic fraud: "No one who has any instinct for literature or ear for the rhythm of prose could deny that some of these [messages] possess the graphic, explosive force which was so characteristic of Jack London at his best." Years later, Conan Doyle's own posthumous communications (via Grace Cooke) are said by W. R. Bradbrook to exhibit "the force of a powerful mind charged with fresh and virile conception, endeavoring to break through the limitations of the gentler nature and less trained mentality of the medium."[32] In both cases, the clarity and vigor of a female medium's language—"explosive force," "virile conception"—serve for a male commentator as clear internal evidence of a male writer's psychic presence.

Even female-authored spiritualist testimonies that have not been edited or glossed by men often assume a protective cloak of male authority. In some cases, that authority is conveyed institutionally, as when Perky Bysshe Shelley's medium, Shirley Carson Jenney, proudly informs her readers that her previous book of Shelley's spirit poems "has been placed in the Shelley Memorial Library, Rome, Italy," as if its mere presence in such an august edifice guaranteed its respectability.[33] In other cases, masculinity becomes a stylistic attribute, as when the spirit of Mark Twain warns the two genteel ladies through whom he is dictating an otherworldly story, "Dear ladies, when I say d-a-m-n, please don't write d-a-r-n. Don't try to smooth it out." The two women dutifully restrain themselves—"We held ourselves passive, ready to fall in with the humor or whim of our astonishingly human though still intangible guest"—with the happy result that Twain's new story "bristles with profanity."[34]

Such stratagems of legitimization, although they seemingly validate male-dominated cultural institutions, in fact call into question the authorial conventions on which those very institutions are founded. When a female medium claims to speak with the voice (or write with the pen) of a man, she does more than merely stake out her own position among the literary elite. She rewrites traditional definitions of authorship, suggesting that a famous writer's literary oeuvre, far from being limited and determinable, can be added to or subtracted from long after the writer's death. What Michel Foucault calls the author-function[35]—the use of a given author's name to bestow authority and value on a text—is therefore simultaneously appropriated and undermined by any medium who signs a famous writer's name to words penned by her own hand. Paradoxically, by calling dead authors back to life, she brings about the death of the Author, or at least of the author-function as defined by Foucault. By insisting on the existence of physical books in the afterlife, the ghost-writing medium casts doubt on the transcendent power of language. By filling the spirit world with libraries and poetry readings, she tosses high-brow literature into the maw of popular culture. And by revering and fetishizing famous dead writers, she exposes the precariousness of their authorial identities and the instability of their literary oeuvres. Thus she anticipates the central innovations not only of modernist literary aesthetics—its fragmentations of identity, subversions of literary tradition, and celebrations of intersubjectivity—but of postmodern textual criticism as well, which teaches that literary masterpieces once considered eternal and immutable are in fact indeterminate, endlessly malleable, and circumscribed by contingencies of production, editing, reception, and interpretation.

GHOSTS IN THE LIBRARY

Ghostwriting is an act of more than merely symbolic or aesthetic importance for twentieth-century literature. Indeed, mediumistic appropriations of literary identities can have very real and concrete consequences for those institutions charged with protecting the property rights of authors and the integrity of their work. For instance, copyright law, which was formulated with living writers and their heirs in mind, has little to say about the legal status of literary texts supposedly authored in the spirit world. Similarly, library card catalogs, which codify and legitimize the institution of authorship, are not generally designed to accommodate books attributed to spirits. Thus, by publishing written accounts of their communications with the dead, spirit mediums trouble the living stream of human discourse in some very material ways.

This is not to say that mediumistic practices always shake up the status quo. On the contrary, some modernist-era ghostwriters proved remarkably adept at invoking legal protection for their spiritualist pursuits when it served their interests to do so. The novelist Radclyffe Hall, for instance, threatened in 1919 to sue for slander when a young woman named Cara Harris tried to block publication of the otherworldly communications she had allegedly received from Harris's mother, who had been Hall's lover. Harris was eventually forced to withdraw her contention that Hall was an unreliable psychic investigator who had misrepresented her mother's words. Later, when St. George Lane Fox-Pitt, who openly disapproved of Hall's lesbianism, tried to block her appointment to the Society for Psychical Research council on the grounds that she was a "grossly immoral woman," Hall brought a successful slander lawsuit against him as well; the jury refused to accept Fox-Pitt's insistence that his accusation referred only to Hall's research paper, which promulgated what he considered to be a false and misleading belief in spirit survival, and not to her personal morals.[36] Both Harris and Fox-Pitt clearly regarded Hall's spiritualist involvement, and particularly her publication of messages from Harris's mother, as a weakness in her armor, a vulnerable opening through which to attack her sexual conduct. Their gambit backfired, however, for despite her undeniable transgressions of numerous laws both written and unwritten—authorial conventions, standards of sexuality, and gendered dress codes, among others—Hall was able to make aggressive use of the British courts to protect herself from claims of impropriety.

In another celebrated court case from the 1920s, medium Geraldine Cummins sued a client, Frederick Bligh Bond, who had published automatic scripts communicated via Cummins's hand from an otherworldly spirit called the Messenger of Cleophas. Arguing that the scripts, which he had typed, punctuated, and paragraphed, were authored by the Messenger of Cleophas and addressed to him, Bond insisted that the copyright should be his as well, to which Cummins's council archly retorted "that it might just as well be said that the copyright in Keats's *Ode to the Nightingale* [*sic*] was vested in the Nightingale."[37] After two days of testimony, a High Court justice ruled in favor of Cummins, declaring the scripts to have been coauthored by the medium and the Messenger together but assigning the copyright to the medium alone. "As he (his Lordship) had no jurisdiction beyond the country in which he lived," the *London Times* reported, "he was obliged, having regard to the Copyright Act of 1911, to confine the copyright to the plaintiff."[38] The justice's tongue-in-cheek ruling rendered explicit what spiritualists had already long since known and used to their own advantage: earthly laws have no power in the spirit world. At the same time, according to Cummins, the case established an important precedent in British law: "A lawyer informed me that if I had lost the case, any author's typist could claim, and might successfully establish, that he was the exclusive owner of the book he was employed to type."[39]

Cummins's typist analogy is problematic, of course, given that mediums often justify the importance of their own profession by describing themselves as secretaries taking cosmic dictation from dead authors. For instance, Hester Dowden referred to herself as W. T. Stead's amanuensis ("In writing the book which follows, my sensations have been those of a secretary who is taking down intricate and difficult ideas"); Catherine Dawson Scott called herself Woodrow Wilson's "stenographer—or should the word be dictaphone?"; and the real-life secretary of the novelist Edgar Wallace even claimed to have received spirit messages from his recently deceased employer via dictaphone records.[40] If an author's typist cannot assert ownership of "the book he was employed to type," one might ask why a medium should be allowed to profit from books supposedly authored by someone other than herself. The answer, as Cummins herself notes, is that "a spirit has no property rights in this world."[41] The nonexistent legal status of the dead puts the ownership of a spirit text up for grabs by anyone bold enough to lay claim to it. Thus, even if it goes against a medium's professional interests to claim authorship of the otherworldly messages she relays, it often serves her legal and pecuniary interests—not to mention, as in the case of Radclyffe Hall, her reputation and personal honor—to do so.

In most instances, to be sure, mediums benefit from insisting on the authorial integrity of their communicating spirits. Take the case of the popular novelists known as Somerville and Ross (Edith Somerville and Violet Martin), who coauthored some thirty widely read novels about life in the Irish countryside. Only an alert reader who perused the birth and death dates at the bottom of a card catalog entry or consulted a literary reference book would be likely to notice that nearly half of those books were published after Martin's death; Somerville, who reported that her beloved cousin collaborated with her from the spirit world via automatic writing, insisted that both names should continue to appear on each book's title page. Although her motivation was most likely sentimental rather than financial, there can be little doubt that the fourteen collaborative novels published by Somerville after Martin's death sold more briskly under the familiar moniker "Somerville and Ross" than they would have under Somerville's name alone.

Somerville's attributional imperative still carries force today: even in recently compiled electronic card catalogs, Somerville and Ross are almost invariably listed as coauthors, with no mention of Violet Martin's problematic status as a spirit. (Indeed, bibliographers seem far more concerned with Martin's pseudonymousness than with her posthumousness.) The most practical challenges posed by spirit authorship, in fact, affect the daily work not of lawyers and judges but of librarians and bibliographers, who have often been stymied when asked to catalog novels and other literary works ostensibly written by the dead. The bibliographic information for such books varies considerably from one cataloger or cataloging system to the next, with every solution suggesting a different understanding of what constitutes an author. Consider *The Blue Island*, a 1922 record of communications received from the spirit of W. T. Stead, a well-known Victorian journalist, via medium Pardoe Woodman in sittings with the dead man's daughter, Estelle.[42] The British Library Catalog names Woodman (the medium) and Estelle Stead (the recipient of the messages) as the book's coauthors, whereas the National Union Catalog contains a separate author entry for each; both catalogs also include a cross-reference to W. T. Stead. But the OCLC (Online Computer Library Center) electronic catalog, which draws its entries from libraries all over the world, contains no less than seven different listings for the book: three under Woodman, two under "W. T. Stead, Spirit," and two simply under W. T. Stead, making no attempt to differentiate the flesh-and-blood Stead from his ghost. In each case, a different cataloger has apparently made his or her own decision about the ontological status of both W. T. Stead and the narrative ascribed to him.

One reason for such apparent inconsistencies is that over the years the cataloging conventions followed by librarians have changed significantly, and with them the rules regarding mediumistic writings. During the first four decades of the twentieth century, no major cataloging code in English offered any guidelines whatsoever for classifying books supposedly authored by spirits. Librarians had either to rely on their own instincts or to adapt the rules pertaining to "joint author entries" or "pseudonymous and supposititious books."[43] Not until 1941 did the American Library Association (ALA) code add specific instructions for cataloging "mediumistic writings," perhaps due to the rising popularity of such books in the 1920s and 1930s: "Enter a work received through a medium (automatic writing, table-rapping, ouija board, etc.) under the medium with added entry for the purported author."[44] These new rules were part of a more general trend, as James Tait notes in his study of the author function in changing cataloging codes, toward assigning authorship to the person deemed "intellectually responsible" for a book rather than relying primarily on information from its title page. The resulting "proliferation of rules to cover specific cases" led to an "almost complete absence of any principles of entry," a frustrating state of affairs that Tait illustrates by invoking, significantly, the new rule on mediumship:

Rule 11, for example, directs that mediumistic writings are to be entered under the medium rather than the supposed spirit whose alleged messages he transmits, in spite of the fact that the spirit is nearly always given greater prominence on the title-page. Is this rule consistent with that for "Ghost writings" (rule 3E) which are entered under the name of the original talker? Is the catalog-using public going to appreciate the distinction between the two types of authorship? [45]

Tait's anguished queries about the contradictions of the new code go to the heart of the dilemma posed by any mediumistic writing: cataloging rules that rigidly adhere to the intellectual-responsibility model of authorship subvert the very institution they ostensibly seek to uphold, for they grant the real power of authorship, the power of naming, not to the writer who produces a book but to the librarian who catalogs it.

The most recent development in the bibliographical status of ghosts and mediums occurred in 1978, when the ALA code was revised again. This time the heading "Mediumistic Communications" was eliminated, and new rules were listed under the separate categories of "Spirits" and "Spirit Communications": "Add to a heading established for a spirit communication the word [spirit]. . . . Enter a communication presented as having been received from a spirit under the heading for the spirit. Make an added entry under the heading for the medium or other person recording the communication."[46] Thus, whereas the drafters of the 1941 ALA code assumed that a medium bears the intellectual responsibility for the spirit messages he or she communicates and is therefore their real author, the 1978 rules—which are still in effect today—seek only to differentiate the author-function of the spirit communicator (e.g., "W. T. Stead, Spirit") from that of the historical figure with whose voice he or she supposedly speaks (e.g., "William Thomas Stead, 1849–1912"). In doing so, the new rules could be said to legitimize the spiritualist principles so adamantly rejected in the 1941 code: for how can a book be ascribed to a spirit unless spirits really exist and are able to communicate with the living? At the very least, the 1978 code suggests that the spirit medium's word is more authoritative than that of the cataloger. Such validation of spirit authorship comes too late, however, for the many mediumistic communications cited in this book, most of which were published between 1914 and 1945 and so were cataloged using the 1941 rules or, more likely, no rules at all. (Some, to be sure, have since been entered into electronic databases under the 1978 code.) Their ideological content, which insists on the reality of spirit survival, is therefore likely to remain forever at odds with their catalog information, which usually designates the spirit mediums rather than the spirits as their principle authors.[47]

By introducing over the years such mutable and contradictory cataloging rules—providing, for instance, one set of rules for "ghost writings" and another for writing ghosts—the ALA code has rendered the author concept itself into a kind of ghost, a murky shadow of something that was once seemingly clear, comprehensible, and familiar. "It is one of the unformulated assumptions of most discussions of cataloging that we all know what is meant by authorship," notes cataloging expert Leonard Jolley. "[But] the concept of personal authorship . . . becomes more and more tenuous as it is pursued through joint authorship, multiple authorship, corporate authorship, and, finally, if it does not vanish completely as a reliable guide, it is so metamorphosed as to be hardly recognizable."[48] Authorship itself having become an elusive specter, the library catalog—the agent of the author concept's ghostly attenuation—in turn takes on a function akin to that of a spirit medium, relaying, as the principal librarian of the British Museum assures us in his 1965 preface to the British Library Catalog, "tales of possessions" from the mysterious other world of bibliographers and catalogers to the more down-to-earth realm of the reading public: "The catalog becomes, in fact, a major means of communication with the outside world."[49]

For many spiritualists, of course, this state of affairs is not necessarily unwelcome. The confusing bibliographic status of ghostwritten books has in fact been exacerbated, often deliberately, by the mediums, editors, and publishers who produce them. Sometimes messages received from famous authors via female mediums are sandwiched into books narrated by men, with the medium's name divulged so deep inside the book that even the most assiduous cataloger would be hard put to discover it: "Payne, Edward Biron. *The Soul of Jack London*" (the name of the medium, Margaret More Oliver, does not appear until the last page); "Cooke, Ivan. '*Thy Kingdom Come* . . . ' *A Presentation of the Whence, Why, and Whither of Man. A Record of Messages Received from One of the White Brotherhood, Believed to Have Been Known on Earth as Arthur Conan Doyle*" (the author's wife, medium Grace Cooke, is referred to throughout most of the book only by her spiritual name, Minesta).[50] In other cases, only the name of the purported spirit author appears on the cover and title page, and the medium's name is disclosed in an introduction or preface, if at all. Spiritualists, after all, have a vested interest in making it difficult for bookshelf browsers to differentiate spirit texts from those more conventionally authored. For instance, the numerous books posthumously published under the name of W. T. Stead not only validate the spiritualist beliefs of the historical Stead but consolidate his author-function as well, for they make it seem that he wrote far more books, especially on the subject of otherworldly communication, than he actually did.[51]

Whereas some spirit mediums duck the responsibilities of attribution to increase the authorial value of their ghostwritten texts, others do so for opposite but equally self-serving reasons, endowing their otherworldly narratives with the pseudoscientific authority of an author-function cut loose from its moorings. Medium Hester Dowden, for example, wrote only one book under her own name, but she assisted in the production and publication of at least a dozen more, most of which were published, edited, and presumably financed by her professional clients.[52] Taken together, these books encompass a wide range of literary genres, including interviews, conversational fragments, historical narratives, philosophical treatises, political ruminations, critical essays, short stories, and even several full-length children's novels. They are credited, moreover, to an impressive array of otherworldly authors, from eminent men of letters—Bacon, Plotinus, Shakespeare, Stead, Wilde—to the otherwise unremarkable friends and spouses of several of Dowden's clients.[53] Nonetheless, despite their seeming heterogeneity, these texts together present a fairly consistent view of the other world, a place where Dowden's own interests, hobbies, and ideological preferences (literature, music, religious heterodoxy, animal rights) play, not coincidentally, a central role. Much as scientists assert the truth of their research claims by employing passive, universalizing verb tenses and avoiding the naked pronoun *I*, Dowden lends her mediumistic messages the authority of anonymity, or at least of multiple authorship, when she underplays and disguises her own role in their production and transmission.

In exploiting bibliographic conventions to her own ends, a medium such as Hester Dowden becomes a ghostwriter in two senses: ostensibly allowing ghosts to write through her, she in fact writes through them. She embodies, in fact, the fertile paradox at the heart of all modern mediumship: her claim to intellectual passivity belies a creative agency and an iconoclastic impulse very much at odds with her seeming cultural conservatism. Insisting on the truth of spirit survival even while robbing the dead of their previously stable identities, she seemingly defies yet irresistibly enacts the disintegration of the speaking self in a complex, heteroglossal, stubbornly materialistic modern world.

CHAPTER TWO

The Undeath of the Author

Not only the best, but the most individual parts of [a poet's] work may be those in which the dead poets, his ancestors, assert their immortality most vigorously. . . . No poet, no artist of any art, has his complete meaning alone. His significance, his appreciation is the appreciation of his relation to the dead poets and artists. You cannot value him alone; you must set him, for contrast and comparison, among the dead.

T. S. Eliot, "Tradition and the Individual Talent"

And what the dead had no speech for, when living,
They can tell you, being dead: the communication
Of the dead is tongued with fire beyond the language of the living.

T. S. Eliot, *Four Quartets*

Apophrades

At least since T. S. Eliot published "Tradition and the Individual Talent" in 1917, it has been a critical commonplace that all authors are haunted by their most famous precursors and that every literary text is inhabited, as J. Hillis Miller puts it, "by a long chain of parasitical presences, echoes, allusions, guests, ghosts of previous texts."[1] In *The Anxiety of Influence*, Harold Bloom seemingly builds on this notion when he names "*apophrades*, or the return of the dead," as one of the six "revisionary ratios" that mark the inevitably agonistic struggle between creative writers and their literary ancestors. But Bloom's version of *apophrades*—a word referring to "the Athenian dismal or unlucky days upon which the dead returned to reinhabit the houses in which they had lived"[2]—invokes not the haunting power of the dead over the living but an opposite trajectory of influence. Only by calling the dead back to life, Bloom suggests, can living poets appropriate their literary masters' voices and usurp their authorial powers.

Bloom characterizes *apophrades* as a purely metaphorical process, a

32

drama of authorial one-upmanship enacted in and through literary texts. Numerous modern writers, however, have envisioned a much more literal "return of the dead" than Bloom presumably had in mind. Some have addressed the issue thematically, composing stories, poems, and plays in which famous dead authors speak and write from beyond the grave. Others have actually attempted to make direct contact with literary figures from the past, overcoming their anxieties of influence not by overtly attacking the authoritative ancestors who haunt their own work but by transforming the mighty dead into docile, tractable spirits. In doing so, these writers affirm and imitate the mechanics of mediumship, with all its Oedipal posturings and gendered power plays, even while spiritualist ghostwriters attempt to imitate the mechanics of authorship.

Needless to say, the notion that the great authors of the past might return to inhabit the minds and the Ouija boards of the living is one with which literary skeptics and satirists have had a veritable field day at least since the mid-nineteenth century. In James Russell Lowell's "The Unhappy Lot of Mr. Knott"(1851), for instance, some fifty-three famous spirits with conveniently rhyming names, from Cicero and Defoe to Rousseau and Poe, assemble at a seance to give nonsensical advice to a befuddled father seeking the right husband for his daughter. Mark Twain's unfinished novel, *Schoolhouse Hill* (1898), includes a riotous parody of a seance at which Napoleon, Shakespeare, Lord Byron, and other notable spirits are summoned to speak via a tapping table:

> Byron was the most active poet on the other side of the grave in those days, and the hardest one for a medium to get rid of. He reeled off several rods of poetry now, of his usual spiritual pattern—rhymy and jingly and all that, but not good, for his mind had decayed since he died. At the end of three-quarters of an hour he went away to hunt for a word that would rhyme with silver—good luck and a long riddance, Crazy Meadows said, for there wasn't any such word.[3]

Literate spirits have even been known to play a role in literary hoaxes. In 1872, the eminent classicist Robert Scott (a colleague of H. G. Liddell, the father of Lewis Carroll's Alice) published an article in *Macmillan's Magazine* under the pseudonym Thomas Chatterton, whom any educated reader would have recognized as the perpetrator of an infamous authorship hoax a century earlier.[4] According to the article, the "true source" of Carroll's highly original poem "Jabberwocky"—which Carroll allegedly cribbed from an old German ballad, "Der Jammerwoch"—was revealed at a seance by the spirit of one Hermann von Schwindel.[5]

For Scott, spirit communication serves as a metaphor for (and unsubtle signifier of) spurious authorship. Robert Browning's dramatic monologue "Mr. Sludge, 'The Medium'" satirizes spiritualism in a more serious and bitter vein; but here, too, mediumship and authorship share symbolic space. Browning's unscrupulous Mr. Sludge, modeled after the famous Victorian medium D. D. Home (who deeply impressed Elizabeth Barrett Browning and deeply irritated her husband), insists that he should not be blamed for manufacturing spirit messages from the famous dead because he does so in response to his gullible clients' own secret desires:

> Who was the fool
> When, to an awe-struck wide-eyed open-mouthed
> Circle of sages, Sludge would introduce
> Milton composing baby-rhymes, and Locke
> Reasoning in gibberish, Homer writing Greek
> In naughts and crosses, Asaph setting psalms
> To crochet and quaver?

Sly Sludge goes so far as to argue that when he invents an idyllic spirit world in which "Bacon advises [and] Shakespeare writes you songs," he is merely emulating the great poets of his own age:

> So, Sludge lies!
> Why, he's at worst your poet who sings how Greeks
> That never were, in Troy which never was,
> Did this or the other impossible great thing!
> He's Lowell—it's a world (you smile applause)
> Of his own invention—wondrous Longfellow,
> Surprising Hawthorne! Sludge does more than they,
> And acts the books they write: the more his praise![6]

Thus, even while attacking spirit mediums, Browning admits to a distant kinship. Famous himself for his dramatic monologs, the poet was clearly well aware that, like Sludge, he earned his living by inventing new worlds, pleasing a fickle public, and making the dead speak.

Nineteenth-century authors such as Lowell, Twain, Scott, and Browning tend to explore the relationship between ghostwriting and legitimate authorship in satirical terms, representing spiritualism itself as either silly or sinister. A number of twentieth-century writers, by contrast, have produced quite serious and sober-minded representations of such situations, thereby suggesting that spiritualism can provide a productive and compelling paradigm for imagining the haunting effects of dead poets upon the living. For modern authors from Rudyard Kipling to A. S. Byatt, spirit communication does more than merely provide, in Yeats's phrase, "metaphors for poetry." It *becomes* a metaphor for poetry: that is, for the inscrutability of poetic inspiration, the frustrations of poetic production, and the death-defying power of words.

Kipling's 1902 short story "Wireless," for instance, brings spiritualism into the new century by explicitly associating the mysteries of poetic influence with the wonders of technology. The story presents two parallel events: while a radio operator attempts to receive Marconi signals from a distant transmitter, a consumptive chemist in the next room receives broken fragments of John Keats's poetry. Weak, coughing blood, obsessed with a fleshly young woman named Fanny Brand (after Keats's Fanny Brawne), young John Shaynor falls into a drug-induced sleep and becomes the mediumistic vessel, although he has never read Keats, for verses that fit perfectly his own physical and emotional circumstances. The narrator explains this enigma by using the vocabulary of electrical induction: "It's the . . . Hertzian wave of tuberculosis, *plus* Fanny Brand and the professional status which, in conjunction with the main-stream of subconscious thought common to all mankind, has thrown up temporarily an induced Keats." When the wireless operator, Mr. Cashell, reports that he has been intercepting Marconi signals from two ships at sea—"Neither can read the other's messages, but all their messages are being taken in by our receiver here"—the relationship between these fragmentary transmissions and Shaynor's unwilled channeling of Keats is made explicit: "Have you ever seen a spiritualistic seance?" Cashell asks. "It reminds me of that sometimes—odds and ends of messages coming out of nowhere—a word here and there—no good at all."[7]

Numerous scholars have noted the historical and thematic parallels between the rise of spiritualism in the late nineteenth century and the simultaneous development of new communications technologies, including mass-circulation newspapers, the telegraph, and wireless radio.[8] The Society for Psychical Research (SPR) was founded by scientists who hoped to find material explanations for spiritualist phenomena, and spiritualists typically employed (and employ to this day) scientific, highly technical language to explain the mechanics of spirit communication. "The quest for a hidden pattern, a unifying framework, a fundamental theory, to bring together every diverse particle and force in the cosmos," notes historian Janet Oppenheim, "was intrinsically the same, whether one stressed the links between heat, electricity, magnetism, and light, or looked for connections between mind, spirit, and matter."[9] In the twentieth century, as radios became an increasingly affordable household item, the notion that the dead can communicate via "etheric vibrations," using a special frequency undetectable by the living, became a spiritualist commonplace.[10] By the time H. D. claimed in the late 1940s to have received seance messages from dead R.A.F. airmen, radios were such unremarkable domestic objects that her conflation of radio communication and spirit communication emphasizes quotidian ignorance rather than scientific knowledge: "It seemed in the end, as natural as receiving a letter or a telegram. . . . I don't know how a telephone does work, nor wireless nor radio."[11]

When Kipling published "Wireless" in 1902, however, radio signals were still considered an exotic, mysterious, and by no means a "natural" way of transmitting messages across vast distances. Kipling's story highlights the uncertainty of modern communication networks, which at best require skillful interpretation—the decoding of dots and dashes—and at worst reduce meaningful discourse to unintelligible fragments. More importantly, Kipling uses the spiritualism/technology analogy to remind us that poetic inspiration, like the misdirected Morse code messages and scrambled poetry fragments in his story, can arrive via unseen channels from often inscrutable sources. Kipling's sister, Alice Fleming, was an avid spiritualist who was to spend the next several decades involved in the SPR's famous "cross-correspondence" experiments, in which four writing mediums with no knowledge of one another's work took down thousands of spirit messages that, when collated by an independent group of investigators, demonstrated "an astonishing inter-connectedness and consistency of theme and imagery."[12] Both in Kipling's story and in his sister's later SPR experiments, terrestrial interpreters re-assemble and give coherent meaning to communiqués from famous dead writers. Yet that meaning remains forever implicated in the fragmentary nature of its transmission and reception. Interpretation—itself a mediumistic mode—trumps information.

In "Wireless," Kipling portrays poetic influence as unconscious and for the most part ineffectual. Whether he has been fed lines of poetry directly by Keats's spirit or, as the narrator speculates, indirectly via a common "main-stream of subconscious thought," Shaynor himself is clearly no Keats. Nor does he even recognize his own achievement as a medium: "But mediums are all imposters," he declares at the end of the story, ignorant of the evening's mystifying events ("Wireless, 40). A similar dynamic informs W. B. Yeats's *The Words upon the Window Pane*, a 1930 play about a female trance medium who speaks with the voices of Jonathan Swift and the two women Swift loved, "Stella" and "Vanessa." Although the play's Mrs. Henderson is a seasoned professional medium, she, too, like Kipling's unwitting Mr. Shaynor, transmits famous poetry—in this case, lines written to Swift by Stella—that she claims never even to have read. ("Is he a popular writer?" inquires Shaynor when asked if he has heard of Keats; "Swift? I do not know anybody called Swift," Mrs. Henderson insists.)[13] John Corbet, a skeptical young Cambridge postgraduate, gleans from Mrs. Henderson's seance messages hitherto unknown personal details about Swift, which just happen to confirm exactly his own hypothesis that Swift eschewed sex and marriage because he feared passing his madness on to his children. In contrast to Kipling's narrator, who entertains no doubt regarding Mr. Shaynor's mediumistic ignorance and innocence, Yeats's Corbet believes, at least at first, that Mrs. Henderson is "an accomplished actress and scholar" who feigns mediumship for profit (*Words*, 14). By the end of the play, however, both he and the audience are left with little doubt that her possession by the restless spirit of Swift was real, made possible because Stella herself had once etched a poem into the windowpane of the house in which the seance takes place.

Any resemblance between Yeats's "Mrs. Henderson," an Irish-born medium who plies her thriving spiritualist trade in London, and the real-life Mrs. Hester Dowden, an Irish-born London medium whom Yeats knew and admired, is probably not accidental. Dowden's mediumistic daughter, too, may well have informed the character of Mrs. Henderson; Dolly Robinson was a frequent houseguest of Yeats and his wife in the late 1920s and is reputed to have had a brief affair with her obliging host around the time the play was being written.[14] But Yeats's most important mediumistic model was no doubt found even closer to home: until just a few years previously, his wife Georgie had been involved in transmitting spirit messages so symbolically rich and philosophically complex and that they could not, Yeats believed, possibly have originated in her own consciousness. Yeats downplays the intellectual acumen and academic background of literate mediums such as Hester Dowden, not to mention those of his own wife, when he portrays Mrs. Henderson as an ignorant, money-grubbing simpleton. (To be sure, he at least covertly acknowledges the possibility of female intellectual accomplishment when one of his characters calls Stella "a better poet than Swift" [*Words*, 230].) Indeed, Yeats focuses not on Mrs. Henderson's mediumship so much as on the intellectual struggles of earnest young John Corbet, who gives voice to Yeats's own burning desire, evident everywhere in his *Vision* papers, to communicate directly with the great minds of the past. *The Words upon the Window Pane* is in fact a work of scholarly wish fulfillment: none of the frustrations that characterized Yeats's real-life spirit communications via Georgie, which unfolded over a period of several years and were marked by maddening reversals, frequent backtrackings, and deliberate obfuscations,[15] mars the words of Swift, who delivers to Corbet a neatly packaged confirmation of the earnest young student's own doctoral thesis. The play is by no means without humor; on the contrary, Yeats demonstrates a healthy capacity for self-parody when he offers us one character who fervently believes that there are "race horses and whippets in the other world" (*Words*, 227) and another who declares herself "utterly lost" if her dead husband does not offer her daily counsel (230). All the same, one suspects it would have been a far richer and more compelling work had Yeats endowed his medium with the intelligence of Georgie Yeats and her communications with the complexity, inscrutability, and suggestive power of his own *Vision* messages.

Although *The Words upon the Window Pane* offers us little understanding of Mrs. Henderson's mediumistic motivations, the play provides a powerful lesson about the capacity of great authors such as Swift to haunt the minds of the living. John Corbet is a literary critic, not a poet, but he longs as much if not more so than does Yeats himself to speak directly with the dead. A. S. Byatt, writing more than half a century after

Yeats, offers a cautionary corrective to this desire; her 1992 novella *The Conjugial Angel* tells the story of Emily Tennyson Jesse, the erstwhile fiancée of Alfred Tennyson's friend Arthur Hallam, whose tragic early death the poet so famously mourned in his 1850 elegy "In Memoriam A. H. H." Tennyson's poem gives life to the dead not only through its conventional assertion that Hallam's spirit lives on in nature—"Thy voice is on the rolling air; I hear thee where the waters run"[16]—but also by enshrining Hallam's memory in deathless words. Mrs. Jesse, we learn, is haunted at least as much by her brother's poem as by Hallam's mouldering ghost; both berate her for her faithlessness in having married someone else rather than mourning her lost fiancé forever.

Like Kipling and Yeats, Byatt emphasizes the literary valences of spiritualism and the spiritualist valences of literature, intimating that the dead live on not only in our memories but also and especially in our words. Her story turns on its head the familiar, supposedly comforting trope of immortality achieved through art; instead, exploring the dark side of authorial power and textual longevity, Byatt maps out some of the ways in which literary texts, like ghosts that refuse to die, can constrain our lives and truncate our imaginative powers. She ends her novella by granting to spiritualism a redemptive quality lacking, paradoxically, in Kipling's and Yeats's more credulous mediumistic fables: after finally confronting Hallam's visible ghost at a seance, Emily Jesse is at last able to banish him from her imagination and fully embrace her life with her husband. Thus, like T. S. Eliot in *Four Quartets* (in which the appearance of a "familiar compound ghost," reminiscent of Swift and Yeats, validates Eliot's own literary enterprise) or Seamus Heaney in "Station Island" (in which the ashplant-waving ghost of James Joyce affirms his Irish descendant's poetic calling), Byatt hints at the emancipatory potential of haunting.[17] But ghosts, she suggests, must be rendered visible and material—at least imaginatively, as in Eliot's and Heaney's poems—before they can be exorcized. Ghostwriting spirits, which manifest themselves purely in and through language, remain a different and more complex matter altogether.

SPIRIT MEDIUMS AND DEAD WHITE MEN

Noting the many analogies between mediumistic communication and "the traditional literary concept of inspiration," Daniel Cottom points out that "this parallel could be extended to encompass all the ills to which texts are heir, from stupidity to cupidinous irresponsibility to the ghostly abyss of false personation, which literary language would term 'plagiarism.' "[18] Certainly, as we have seen, ghostwriting can engender a raft of authorial anxieties concerning originality, authenticity, and authority. But popular spiritualism can also provide a useful paradigm for probing the mechanics of Bloom's Oedipal *apophrades*, a return of the literary dead that ultimately empowers rather than diminishes the living. For professional spirit mediums, after all, appropriating the voices of the dead—including famous dead authors—is all in a day's work.

This is not to suggest, however, that most ghostwriting mediums can be classified as "strong poets" in Harold Bloom's sense of the term. Ghostwritten texts are notorious for their stylistic shortcomings, and even literate mediums with authorial aspirations of their own, such as Geraldine Cummins or Catherine Dawson Scott, would hardly qualify for Bloom's exclusive pantheon of Great Writers. Moreover, as Sandra Gilbert and Susan Gubar have noted, Bloom's characterization of literary history as a generational struggle between powerful fathers and interloping sons leaves little room for female agency: "Where, then, does the female poet fit in? Does she want to annihilate a 'forefather' or a 'foremother'? What if she can find no models, no precursors? Does she have a muse and what is its sex? Such questions are inevitable in any female consideration of Bloomian poetics." What Bloom's Oedipal model of authorship does provide, however, as Gilbert and Gubar go on to argue, is a useful model for understanding "the patriarchal poetics (and attendant anxieties) which underlie our culture's chief literary movements."[19] Whatever their relationship to or putative place within literary tradition, all writers—including women writers, including even ghostwriters—inevitably work in the shadow of powerful father figures whose textual authority they long to make their own.

For the ghostwriting mediums of the modernist era, those fathers are often literal rather than literary, returning from beyond the grave to apologize to daughters whose spiritualist pursuits they once disparaged. Shirley Carson Jenney claimed to have coauthored an entire book with the spirit of her previously agnostic father. Bessie Clarke Drouét and Gladys Osborne Leonard recall how their formerly skeptical fathers spoke to them in seances to admit the existence of life after death. Novelist Winifred Graham Cory's father remembers "how difficult I found it on earth, to be sure that the automatic messages really came from the other world," and he confesses through his daughter's mediumship the inaccuracy of his heavenly vision: "I believed in the future life, but I did not dream it would be like this, so full of wonder, interest, and charm." And although Hester Dowden never attempted direct communication with the spirit of her distinguished father, Professor Edward Dowden, she did report that her longtime spirit control, Johannes, bore an uncanny physical resemblance to him: "A grave face with a broad, fine forehead, the thick hair sweeping backwards. The face of a scholar. I asked Johannes to explain this: His reply was, 'I am connected with Edward, your father, in a long line of ancestry.'" Dowden was thus able to spend much of her mediumistic career in intimate collaboration with a handsome male spirit who looked like her father's "twin brother" but who exhibited none of Edward Dowden's inconvenient standoffishness or skepticism. Instead, Johannes resided inside Hester's own Ouija board, came whenever he was called, and provided unstinting praise of her mediumistic talents.[20]

In other cases, the paternal relationship between a spirit and his medium is professional rather than personal. Mediumistic aptitude is often described as an inherited trait, passed down via cultural heritage— Irish spiritualists, for instance, frequently credit their supernormal sensitivity to their upbringing in the land of faeries and leprechauns—or directly from parents to children, as when Hester Dowden's daughter Dolly took over her mother's role as one of W. B. Yeats's favorite mediums.[21] An avid belief in the afterlife, likewise, tends to run in families; thus the daughters of Sir Arthur Conan Doyle and W. T. Stead became passionate champions of their fathers' spiritualist cause (as did Conan Doyle's son), devoting much of their energy later in life to documenting their beloved fathers' survival. Not surprisingly, then, many of the same modernist-era mediums who claimed to have received conciliatory messages from their real-life fathers also transmitted messages from famous dead spiritualists—admiring and supportive father figures who lavished paternal praise upon their professional offspring.[22]

Although such mediumistic appropriations of famous spiritualists' voices may seem rooted in daughterly devotion, they often contain competitive overtones, as when Hester Dowden usurps the privileged filial role once held by W. T. Stead's daughter Estelle, who recalls nostalgically how in "the old days" her father "would walk up and down in his sanctum dictating and talking to me when I acted as his secretary." Now it is Dowden, we learn, whose "sensations have been those of a secretary" as she takes down Stead's dictations from the spirit world.[23] The extent to which virtually all mediumship involves a generational struggle for expressive authority becomes particularly evident when, in the second half of the twentieth century, admiring male mediums begin to publish revisionist spirit communications from their spiritualist foremothers. David Kendrick Johnson records a mediumistic interview with the spirit of Eileen Garrett, who discusses at length the erotic aspects of mediumship, a subject not touched on at all in the staid autobiography that she wrote while still alive. Similarly, Percy Allen, one of Hester Dowden's professional clients, reports that he began communicating with Dowden via automatic writing almost immediately after her death, tapping into mediumistic talents he had not known he possessed. Allen's opening comment contains more than just a hint of triumph: "Now Hester, our positions are reversed. *I* become the medium, *you* the communicator."[24]

The Oedipal dimensions of ghostwriting are thrown most clearly into relief, however, when writing mediums claim to take up the pens (or, as spiritualists frequently put it, *become* the pens) of their literary forebears—authoritative father figures such as Robert Browning, Arthur Conan Doyle, Joseph Conrad, Stephen Crane, T. S. Eliot, T. E. Lawrence, Jack London, Edgar Allan Poe, William Shakespeare, Percy Bysshe Shelley, Ivan Turgenev, Mark Twain, H. G. Wells, and Oscar Wilde.[25] Although otherworldly messages have also been received from the spirits of female authors (for example, Charlotte Brontë, Elizabeth Barrett Browning, and Marie Corelli) and/or transmitted via male mediums (for example, A. P. Sinnett, Charles Tweedale, and Cyril Wild),[26] a substantial majority of the ghostwritten spirit communications published in English between 1914 and 1945 involve literary texts and/or spiritualist musings transmitted via female mediums from the proverbial company of "dead white men" whose works make up the bulk of the Western canon.[27] The mediums' daughterly revolt can manifest itself rather subtly, to be sure. Ghostwriting mediums typically express great admiration and awe for their spirit collaborators, as when Shirley Carson Jenney confesses that Percy Bysshe Shelley "had always been a family idol," or when Margaret More Oliver enthuses in a tone of almost sexual ecstasy about her otherworldly intercourse with Jack London: "Can you know what it means to associate for months closely engaged with another soul in a great task and to communicate entirely by means of thought? To have your own thoughts answered swiftly without any physical or material means being brought into use? A super-earthly comradeship resulted." More modest mediums may even describe their work as an act of otherworldly charity, as when Hester Dowden declares of a benighted Oscar Wilde, "If it relieves him to let fly his bitter shafts of wit once more, I feel, in mere courtesy, I must permit him to relieve his mind."[28]

Such a rhetoric of esteem or generosity belies, however, the revisionist agenda at the heart of all spirit communications with the famous dead, who are often made to issue statements through their mediums that they would surely never have ventured while alive. In numerous ghostwritten texts, for instance, a famous author's well-known disapproval of spiritualism becomes, after death, apologetic approbation. The spirit of Jack London publicly renounces, via Margaret More Oliver, "my old materialistic yawp," speaking out in favor of spiritualism instead. George Eliot, who once called spiritualism "that odious trickery," confesses after her death via Susan Horn that, "in the inmost recesses of my nature," she had in fact believed in immortality all along. And Robert Browning's spirit ruefully informs poet Vera Staff, via Staff's mediumistic mother, that he wishes he had never published his bitterly satirical poem, "Mr. Sludge, 'The Medium'": "It was written in a moment of haste and anger. If it has been misunderstood, then I am sorry and I do regret having written it."[29]

Even when they do not explicitly disavow their antispiritualist prejudices, moreover, the spirits of famously skeptical writers offer implicit recantations whenever they deliver new manuscripts to the public via ghostwriting mediums. Despite Mark Twain's disgust during his lifetime at spiritualists' tendencies to charlatanism, for example, his spirit turns to two admiring female mediums for help in transmitting a new novel, *Jap Herron,* from the other world. H. G. Wells dictates a 283-page account of his posthumous adventures inside medium Elizabeth Hawley's body, in direct contradiction of Wells's public assertion, while alive, that mediumistic communication with the dead is impossible. The spirit of T. S. Eliot transmits a lengthy series of poems and New Age sermons via automatist P. M. Doucé—"A Nobel Prize winner, seen or unseen, was an astounding plus to have as a counsel!" she boasts—despite the scathing dismissals of spiritualist pursuits contained in some of Eliot's most famous poetic works. And the spirit of Charles Dickens dictates a lengthy conclusion to his unfinished novel *Edwin Drood*, even though, while alive, Dickens had publicly derided popular spiritualism and all its trappings. "If it was a true communication," notes Arthur Conan Doyle, one of the ghostwritten novel's few defenders, "it must have been intensely galling to the author that his efforts should have been met with derision." Indeed, Conan Doyle can hardly disguise his glee at the prospect of Dickens's spirit being thus forced to eat crow: "There would however, be a certain poetic justice in the matter, as Dickens in his lifetime, even while admitting psychic happenings for which he could give no explanation, went out of his way to ridicule spiritualism, which he had never studied or understood."[30]

Conan Doyle's response to Dickens has a double edge: he speaks not only as a spiritualist but also as a successful author in his own right, a literary latecomer intent on besting his famous predecessor. Although Conan Doyle does not claim to have conversed with Dickens directly, he would have been in good company had he done so. Since the rise of popular spiritualism in the mid-nineteenth century, a remarkable number of eminent authors have quite literally sought to communicate— usually with the help of a trusted medium, occasionally on their own— with some of their most influential literary predecessors. Victor Hugo spent two years of exile on the Isle of Jersey in rapped conversation with William Shakespeare, who dictated a new play in which animated furniture, not unlike Hugo's own turning table, comes to life and utters spiritual profundities. Harriet Beecher Stowe conducted an automatistic interview with the spirit of Charlotte Brontë, who obligingly described the fates of various other literary inhabitants of the spirit world: William Thackeray, for instance, has lost his "slight savageness" and "is very lovable now." Conan Doyle was importuned by the spirit of Joseph Conrad "to finish a book of [Conrad's] about French history." André Gide conversed briefly via a writing medium with the ghost of Oscar Wilde. Novelist Taylor Caldwell received welcome literary encouragement from the spirit of George Eliot, who told her, via a male medium: "I want you to know I have been inspiring your writing, and there are times when I have helped you over difficult passages." And Sylvia Plath and Ted Hughes, while vacationing with poet Thomas Kinsella near Yeats's Thoor Ballylee in Ireland, were emboldened to conjure vaguely Yeatsian spirits via a Ouija board.[31]

Few if any such attempts at spirit communication have resulted in memorable new works of imaginative literature. Nonetheless, all of these writers clearly turned to popular spiritualism in search of specifically literary commodities: inspiration, advice, authority, ancestral approbation. Others have gone a step further, seeking otherworldly approval for spiritualist pursuits that their most influential mentors would surely have derided. H. D., for instance, was urged in a 1943 seance by the spirit of Sigmund Freud, with whom she had undergone psychoanalysis a decade earlier, to continue with the spiritualist researches that he had once dismissed as a "dangerous symptom" of psychic derangement.[32] Her spirit communications from the man she privately called Papa thus provided the means by which she was finally able to master the Master and supplant his ideas with her own: "Respect for you—attached—mind keen at end—you are placing yourself at disposal of a greater mind—you are the instrument—you will prove the work of this Master (Freud) did not represent a finality but a THRESHOLD . Not science, only lever that opened door—way cleared, then work begins."[33]

Similarly, James Merrill recounts in *The Changing Light at Sandover* how he summoned the spirit of W. H. Auden, who sardonically confesses (using the uppercase letters that mark all of Merrill's spirit communications) that he too should have conjured spirits with an overturned teacup and Ouija board rather than devoting his life to organized religion:

> I COULD CURSE MY HIGH
> ANGLICAN PRINCIPLES . . . THE CHURCH
> MY DEARS THE DREARY DREARY DEAD BANG WRONG
> CHURCH & ALL THOSE YEARS I COULD HAVE HELD
> HANDS ON TEACUPS[34]

Like so many other literate mediums who claim to speak with or for the dead, both H. D. and Merrill bring famous literary father figures back to life not to honor them but to supplant them. Reverential in their rhetoric but patricidal in their aims, they enact Bloom's *apophrades* in the most literal possible way: "The mighty dead return, but they return in our colors, and speaking in our voices."[35]

Freud himself would probably have had no argument with the notion that spirit mediumship—whether performed by professional mediums or by mediumistic authors—inevitably plays out an Oedipal drama of textual patricide and generational succession. "Our unconscious," as he sagely observes, "will murder even for trifles." In *The Future of an Illusion,* Freud even goes so far as to assert that all religion originates "in the Oedipus complex, the relation to the father" and that spiritualism enacts, accordingly, the infantile ambivalence of any child toward a powerful parent.[36] Other psychoanalytical theorists have offered their own variations on Freud's formulation that spiritualist belief finds its genesis in family conflict. Carl Jung links a primitive belief in spirits to the parent/child relationship: "As the origin of pathogenic conflicts frequently goes back to early childhood and is connected with memories of the parents, it naturally follows that the spirits of relatives are particularly revered or feared by primitives." Nicolas Abraham regards ghosts as psychopathological symptoms of repressed ancestral sins: "The phantom is a formation of the unconscious that has never been conscious—for good reason. It passes—in a way yet to be determined—from the parent's unconscious into the child's." Psychic investigator Théodore Flournoy, one of Freud's earliest disciples, explains medium Hélène Smith's apparitional visions of Marie Antoinette as hysterical manifestations of an unconscious hostility toward her parents, thereby anticipating, as Terry Castle has noted, Freud's 1907 essay "Family Romances," which argues that the common childhood fantasy of having descended from royalty has its origins in a similar resentment. And psychologist Wilfred Lay, in a 1921 book subtitled *The Psychoanalysis of Spiritism,* locates spiritualism's Oedipal axis not, like Freud, in the true believer's relationship to a fictive paternal God; not, like Jung, Abraham, or Flournoy, in the medium's relationship to dead parents or dead ancestors; but rather in the spiritualist sitter's relationship to the medium. Unconsciously, Lay writes, the sitter "identifies the medium with the most omnipotent being he conceived of in his infancy—his father."[37] Lay's assignment of paternal identity to the spirit medium is somewhat surprising, given the preponderance in 1920s Britain of female mediums. All the same, for Lay just as for Freud, Jung, and others, spiritualism always reenacts on some level the struggle for authority between a rebellious child and his or her parents.

Despite such apparent unanimity on the psychoanalytic front, however, it would be a mistake to explain all attempts at spirit communication in terms of infantile aggression against (or even repressed erotic attraction to) powerful elders. Much of popular spiritualism's staying power throughout the first half of the twentieth century—a period when declining mortality rates and rising religious skepticism might otherwise have been expected to spell the movement's demise—can be attributed to the two world wars, which produced countless grieving parents desperate for emotional succor. Sir Oliver Lodge's enormously influential *Raymond* (1916), which details the eminent physicist's spirit messages from a young son recently killed in battle, was only one of the dozens of such books published during or just after the First World War, many of which sport titles that emphasize their historical specificity.[38] Soon after the Great War, Sir Arthur Conan Doyle published an account of the spirit conversations he had been holding with his son Kingsley, who had died after being wounded in the Somme.[39] And during the Second World War, former Air Chief Marshal Hugh Dowding, a national hero widely credited with having helped win the Battle of Britain, wrote several books in which he detailed his new-found conviction that dead soldiers can communicate with the living. A generation after Conan Doyle's and Lodge's personal family tragedies helped to fan the flames of wartime spiritualism, Dowding's loss of numerous symbolic sons—the R.A.F. airmen who died under his command—served a similar function.[40]

Of course, young men who have died in battle hold no monopoly on inducing parental grief. Poet Ella Wheeler Wilcox first turned to spiritualism when she tried to make contact with her stillborn baby. Novelist Rosamond Lehmann became a believer in psychic phenomena following the death of her beloved young daughter.[41] Surviving husbands have sought to converse with dead wives, brothers with dead sisters, even animal lovers with beloved pets. Most such attempts, clearly, are rooted in primal sorrow rather than in patricidal revenge. Yet even resurrections of dead children or animals serve a revisionist function not unlike that performed whenever a spiritualist ghostwrites for a famous author or, more generally, when any figure of parental authority is made to relinquish his or her voice to a living medium. Communication with the dead is always, on some level, a repudiation of history, a rebellious attempt to repair the past at the cost of denying the present. Thus popular spiritualism seeks to slay not only the Author and the Father—authoritative absolutes writ large—but also that biggest bogey of them all, Death.

The work of mourning, notes Jacques Derrida, "consists always in attempting to ontologize remains, to make them present," a task in which "all semanticization—philosophical, hermeneutical, or psychoanalytical—finds itself caught up."[42] Spiritualists aspire to neutralize grief by naturalizing haunting. Yet their efforts to "ontologize remains" result, paradoxically, in a radical subversion of the ontological stability they seemingly seek to recover. Indeed, the very process of "semanticization" itself, whereby sorrow is transformed into language, charts the spirit medium's path to discursive power. For if reading affords one method by which humans traditionally evade mortality ("We die with the hero with whom we have identified ourselves," notes Freud, "yet we survive him, and are ready to die again just as safely with another hero"), while writing makes possible another ("My love looks fresh, and Death to me subscribes,/Since, spite of him, I'll live in this poor rhyme"), ghostwriting offers a third and even more triumphant means of cheating death through language.[43] By rendering formerly physical entities into creatures that, like literary characters, cannot exist outside of human discourse, ghostwriters reify and ratify the life-giving power of words—especially their own.

CHAPTER THREE

Necrobardolatry

Glendower: I can call spirits from the vasty deep.
Hotspur: Why, so can I, or so can any man:
But will they come when you do call for them?
William Shakespeare, *Henry IV*

Ghost: I am thy father's spirit,
Doomed for a certain term to walk the night,
And for the day confined to fast in fires,
Till the foul crimes done in my days of nature
Are burnt and purged away. . . . List, list, O, list!
If thou didst ever thy dear father love—
William Shakespeare, *Hamlet*

SPECTERS OF SHAKESPEARE

William Shakespeare haunts English-speaking culture like the
ghost of Hamlet's father, forever accusing us, his wayward descendants,
of failing to rise to his own formidable standard of literary achievement. Shakespeare troubles our collective imagination in other, more
complex ways as well. Our greatest writer is our greatest enigma, a historical personage about whom less is known but more has been specu-
lated than virtually any other figure in Western literary history. Jorge
Luis Borges, in a 1960 prose poem, calls him "Everything and Nothing":

History adds that before or after his death he found himself facing
God and said: *I, who have been so many men in vain, want to be one man,
myself alone.* From out of a whirlwind the voice of God replied: *I am
not, either. I dreamed the world the way you dreamed your work, my Shakespeare: one of the forms of my dream was you, who, like me, are many and no
one.*[1]

49

Although Borges's Shakespeare is a mortal man with thoughts and feelings of his own, his epistemological status, the poet suggests, is comparable to that of God.

As both Everything and Nothing, both many and no one, Shakespeare raises the dual hermeneutic specters of overdetermination and indeterminacy. His murky features mirror the interpretive paradoxes of every age or culture that has tried to lay claim to his image. Throughout much of the eighteenth century, for instance, England's struggle to establish a coherent national identity found simultaneous expression in the canonization and bowdlerization of Shakespeare's plays, seemingly contradictory symptoms, as Michael Dobson has argued, of a single appropriative impulse. Victorian England's troubled obsession with erosions of religious and patriarchal authority led, similarly, both to the rise of empiricist biography and to a compensatory proliferation of alternate authorship theories. Most recently, postmodern America's tendency to counter deconstructive impulses with commodity fetishization has resulted in a radical disjunction between scholarly and popular representations of the Bard: "Ironically," notes Linda Charnes, "at the very moment that textual scholars have come to understand 'Shakespeare' to be a speculative appellation attached, uncertainly, to multiplicitous texts that have fragmented and unstable production histories, American culture has hypostatized Shakespeare's 'identity' into a form of symbolic capital that circulates in the culture like unalloyed gold coin."[2]

For modernist writers, the Shakespearean paradox itself—Shakespeare's dual role as both the symbolic Father whose burdensome influence must be overcome and the ultimate site of textual ambiguity—forms part of his enduring fascination. Shakespeare embodies and thereby validates the central contradiction at the heart of modernist ideology, which seeks to embrace both the cult of the Author and the death of the Author, both tradition and radical rupture. Predictably, modernist literature is replete with attempts to make "Everything and Nothing" into something new: *The Tempest* alone, for instance, has been recast, reimagined, or otherwise intertextualized in works as diverse as T. S. Eliot's *Waste Land*, W. H. Auden's *The Sea and the Mirror*, Aldous Huxley's *Brave New World*, and H. D.'s *By Avon River*. But nowhere is Shakespeare's iconic status within modernist discourse more vividly enacted than in those instances in which Shakespeare the literary ghost is represented literally as a ghost, an articulate otherworldly spirit who speaks to or through living authors from beyond the grave. Given voice and substance as a ghost, Shakespeare functions as a prototypical modernist text in his own right, imbued with cultural authority, deeply invested in literary tradition, yet aggressively, transgressively multivocal and multivalent.

Conjurations of Shakespeare's ghost are not, of course, unique to modernism. The annals of literary history and popular spiritualism alike are filled with Shakespearean possessions and hauntings. Throughout the eighteenth century, spectral appearances by the Bard typically served a clearly fictionalized, satirical function. In an anonymous pamphlet published in 1755, for instance, Shakespeare's spirit returns to the world of the living to chastise the Shakespearean actor David Garrick for his involvement in a theatrical scandal. In a 1796 poem by George Woodward, similarly, the playwright's ghost rebukes Sammy Ireland for digging up Stratford relics—"He'd never give his deep researches up, / Until he'd found my spoon and christ'ning cup"—and warns him against the cardinal sin of forgery.[3]

With the advent of popular spiritualism in America and Europe, however, communications with Shakespeare's spirit frequently came to be represented as matters of historical fact, as when Victor Hugo quite earnestly asserted that he had conversed via a tapping table with the Bard. By the early twentieth century, published accounts of mediumistic communications with Shakespeare had become even more frequent and more credulous, if not necessarily more creditable. Medium Sarah Taylor Shatford published several volumes of Shakespearean poetry, allegedly received via clairaudient dictation, in the 1910s and 1920s. Bessie Clark Drouét reported that her brother spoke briefly with Shakespeare during a seance in the early 1930s. Hester Dowden claimed to have received Shakespearean communications via a Ouija board in the late 1930s and early 1940s. Daisy Oke Roberts conversed with Shakespeare and other Elizabethan notables in the early 1950s. Robert Leichtman "interviewed" Shakespeare via medium David Kendrick Johnson in the 1970s. And the poet James Merrill, although he did not profess to have spoken directly with Shakespeare, was told by Ouija board spirits in the 1970s that the former playwright was now a teenage nuclear physicist living somewhere on earth.[4]

As part of their narratives involving Shakespeare's afterlife, spiritualists often take pains to assert a personal proclivity for Shakespearean drama, a privileged connection to which they attribute their mediumistic affinity. Hester Dowden's biographer, for example, who supplies Shakespearean epigraphs for every chapter of his hagiographical book, repeatedly notes Dowden's familial and social connections to Shakespearean scholars and actors. Geraldine Cummins, whose passion for Shakespeare absorbed much of her childhood, describes *Richard III* as "an ABC of Spiritualism" and recalls in her autobiography how she and her brother used to obsessively reenact the drama's ghost scene, playing the parts of all eleven ghosts. A number of spiritualists even go so far as to argue that Shakespeare himself was a psychic, thereby claiming him as one of their own. Austin O. Spare, an automatistic artist, told journalist Hannen Swaffer in an interview that "*Hamlet* was the result of a psychical experience of Shakespeare's, which found expression in the art form he had adopted; otherwise you cannot explain him." Similarly, Daisy Roberts, after an illuminating conversation with the spirit of Sir Philip Sidney (who, she says, inspired Shakespeare to write *Hamlet*), concludes that Shakespeare was "extremely psychic" and "could have written automatically or through telepathic communications."[5]

Such enthusiastic spiritualist appropriations of Shakespeare find an imaginative foil, to be sure, in various twentieth-century works of fiction that hearken back to the admonitory tradition of eighteenth-century satire. Perhaps the best known of these, especially to American readers, is Isaac Asimov's "The Immortal Bard," a 1954 short story in which a physicist named Dr. Phineas Welch tipsily confesses to a young English professor that he once brought Shakespeare back from the dead and enrolled him in an evening literature course. "What happened?" asks the professor uncomfortably, suddenly recalling a bald man in his own Shakespeare class who had "a queer way of talking." "I had to send him back to 1600," Welch replies indignantly: "How much humiliation do you think a man can stand? . . . Why, you poor simpleton, you *flunked* him."[6]

A similar conceit is developed at considerably greater length in Hugh Kingsmill's 1929 novella *The Return of William Shakespeare*, in which an eccentric young scientist manages to import Shakespeare into the present day by means of a technique called reintegration. Unfortunately, despite elaborate plans for a lecture tour (on topics such as "My Methods: How I Wrote *Hamlet*" and "Girls, Elizabethan and Modern"), Shakespeare's health proves too fragile for public appearances. While debates rage in the newspapers as to whether it is morally right to resuscitate the dead, and while a clever impersonator attempts to fill the poet's place at a party that includes such eminent intellectuals of the day as George Bernard Shaw, H. G. Wells, Alfred Bennett, Lord Balfour, J. C. Squire, Desmond MacCarthy, and John Middleton Murry, Shakespeare himself fades quietly away, dying, in effect, a second death.[7]

In Kingsmill's novella as in Asimov's story, the historical Shakespeare turns out to be an ordinary sort of bloke, a figure of pity rather than of awe, a man who cannot withstand the weight of his own reputation. Yet although both tales make use of certain spiritualist tropes—not least among them an almost unbounded faith in the power of science to overcome the accepted limitations of human existence—neither is really a ghost story. Instead, Shakespeare is shown to be one of us, a mortal man who just happens to have been temporarily temporally displaced. Only brainy, out-of-touch literary types, the stories impute—the fictional English instructor portrayed in Asimov's tale, the real-life intellectuals satirized in Kingsmill's—would refuse to be consoled by the moral of these fables, which is that the inflationary power of the human imagination can best be brought to heel by a good dose of scientific cleverness and down-to-earth reality.

For many modernist writers, however, that inflationary power is precisely the point of any creative endeavor. Shakespeare can be either ephemeral or all powerful, but he can never be merely ordinary. For that very reason he must be conceived of as a ghost rather than a flesh-and-blood mortal. Ghosts are not just dead people transported through space or time into the quotidian realm of the here and now. They are symbolic entities, objects of admiration and dread, emblems of literature's capacity to haunt our imagination and disturb the status quo. Freud, in his 1919 essay "The 'Uncanny,'" uses examples from Shakespeare's plays to argue that true uncanniness resides in "the world of common reality" rather than in spooky literary texts: "The souls in Dante's *Inferno*, or the supernatural apparitions in Shakespeare's *Hamlet*, *Macbeth* or *Julius Caesar*, may be gloomy or terrible enough, but they are no more really uncanny than Homer's jovial world of gods."[8] Freud's observation is belied, however, both by his own use of a literary text to illustrate the psychological workings of the uncanny (he cites at length E. T. A. Hoffmann's story "The Sand-Man") and by the many Freud-influenced psychoanalytic theorists who have used figures and scenes from Shakespeare's plays to demonstrate precisely the kinds of uncanny effects that Freud describes. Marjorie Garber, for instance, focuses on the very plays singled out by Freud as lacking in uncanny affect—*Hamlet, Macbeth,* and *Julius Caesar*—to show how writing and haunting are inextricably linked in Shakespeare's work.[9]

Similarly, in *Specters of Marx,* Jacques Derrida invokes one of Shakespeare's most famous ghosts, Prince Hamlet's murdered father, as his prime exemplar of a spectral subject who haunts future generations by disrupting linear conceptions of history and reminding us, through his uncanny revenance, that "the time is out of joint." Derrida justifies his persistent focus on Shakespeare's paternal ghosts by noting both that Marx's *Communist Manifesto* (first published in 1848, the year that many historians identify with the birth of modern spiritualism) opens with a scene of ghostly return—"A specter is haunting Europe"—and that Marx himself regarded Shakespeare as one of the fathers of modern-day economic theory, which is premised on the "phantomalization of property."[10] Shakespeare's haunting influence on Derrida's own imagination, meanwhile, is made evident by the renegade philosopher's virtual obsession with the psychological, linguistic, and historical import of the ghost scenes in *Hamlet.* Visual images not of Marx but rather of King Hamlet's ghost grace both the front and back covers of Derrida's book; quotations from *Hamlet* serve as book and chapter epigraphs; and numerous lines and stage directions from the play are excerpted, explicated, deconstructed, and etymologized throughout the text in ingenious and exhaustive detail.

Derrida joins a long line of thinkers—psychologists, social critics, creative writers, literate spiritualists—who have, as Michael Dobson puts it, imagined Shakespeare's authorship as "a form of fatherhood, with Shakespeare himself regularly and pervasively identified with the most powerful fathers in his own *oeuvre*—whether those who refuse to die (King Hamlet, Julius Caesar), or the magician Prospero, able to raise the dead."[11] In particular, Hamlet's murdered father—a stage role played, according to tradition, by William Shakespeare himself[12]—has served numerous commentators besides Derrida as a potent symbol of Shakespeare's own capacity to haunt, trouble, and admonish his literary descendents. Sigmund Freud mentions in a footnote to his 1925 autobiography that Shakespeare composed *Hamlet* immediately after his own father's death in 1601. Jacques Lacan equates King Hamlet's ghost with the phallus, which Hamlet "cannot strike . . . because the phallus, even the real phallus, is a ghost." Nicolas Abraham invokes Hamlet's father as an illustration of his theory that we are always already haunted by the unknown misdeeds of our ancestors, which reside in our psyches like vengeful poltergeists unless driven away through the psychoanalytic process. And Sylvia Plath, whose original title for *The Colossus* was *Full Fathom Five* (a line that refers to Ferdinand's allegedly drowned father in *The Tempest*), implicitly compares herself to a haunted Prince Hamlet when she wonders in a 1958 journal entry to what extent her Ouija board experiments with her husband, Ted Hughes, involve "our own intuitions working, and how much queer accident, and how much 'my father's spirit.' "[13]

Derrida's call in *Specters of Marx* for a new "hauntology"—a "logic of haunting" that would be "larger and more powerful than an ontology or a thinking of Being"—thus seems particularly appropriate for the study of Shakespeare's haunting presence in literary modernism, a period marked both by a vexed fascination with ghosts and by a persistent foregrounding of the temporal instability that ghostliness calls into play. Scholars of modernism, to be sure, tend to downplay if not to deny outright modernism's spiritualist subtext, in keeping with Derrida's assertion that "a traditional scholar does not believe in ghosts—nor in all that could be called the virtual space of spectrality."[14] Even those critics, moreover, who focus on the mystical, occult, and theosophical elements of modernist literature or who survey modernist tropes of haunting are often unwilling to accord equal attention to modernist writers' real-life fascination with the historical phenomenon of popular spiritualism. Leon Surette, for instance, whose 1994 book *The Birth of Modernism* breaks important new ground in tracing hitherto unacknowledged occult influences on the works of Pound, Eliot, and Yeats, dismisses "conversing with ghosts" as a frivolous, disreputable offshoot—akin to "transmigrating from Dublin to Tibet, running naked in the moonlight, or signing pacts with the devil"—of more erudite occultist pursuits. Jean-Michel Rabaté, who attempts in his 1996 study *The Ghosts of Modernity* to "sketch a symptomatic history of modernity" through figures of haunting and failed mourning, evinces little interest in the actual spiritualist experiments of writers such as Yeats (who is barely mentioned in the book), Pound, or H. D. And Terry Castle, in her brilliant essay "Phantasmagoria: Spectral Technology and the Metaphorics of Modern Reverie," traces what she calls a "metaphoric shift" from early-nineteenth-century representations of ghosts as something real, external, and visible to early-twentieth-century, Freud-inspired notions of specters as purely imaginative entities:

> Even as we have come to discount the spirit-world of our ancestors and to equate seeing ghosts and apparitions with having "too much" imagination, we have also come increasingly to believe, as if through a kind of epistemological recoil, in the spectral nature of our own thoughts—to figure imaginative activity itself, paradoxically, as a kind of ghost-seeing.

Although modernists are no doubt more likely than their literary predecessors to represent haunting as a purely psychological process, Castle fails to acknowledge the ways in which a real belief in ghosts and spirits continues to motivate much twentieth-century imaginative production.[15]

A related occlusion occurs, despite Shakespeare's own frequent figuration as a modernist ghost, in the realm of recent Shakespeare studies. In his 1991 book *The Modernist Shakespeare*, Hugh Grady credits the Shakespeare critic G. Wilson Knight with the development of a spatial hermeneutic, later appropriated with great success by the New Critics, that privileges thematic unities over temporal concerns such as historical difference, chronological sequence, and mechanical causality. By employing interpretive methods unconsciously modeled on the aesthetic innovations of literary modernism in the 1920s and 1930s, Grady argues, Knight effectively "refunction[ed] the Shakespearian play as a Modernist text" and transformed Shakespeare himself into a "Modernist icon," a practitioner *avant le lettre* of what Joseph Frank would later identify as modernism's privileging of "spatial form."[16] Unfortunately, Grady laments, Knight's considerable influence on twentieth-century literary criticism has been obscured and qualified by

> a growing eccentricity in Knight's later work, an eccentricity linked with Knight's growing interest in Spiritualism. In his later work, Knight [who died in 1985] has claimed to have communicated with his dead brother, constructed a theory of acting linked to Spiritualism through the nineteenth-century figure François Delsarte, [and] argued for the presence in Shakespeare of various Spiritualist and even Buddhist ideas.

What Grady fails to recognize, however, is that Knight's "distinctly Modernist and spatial" mode of reading Shakespeare, which isolates the text "from any evolutionary stream" and analyzes it instead in terms of "structures conceived as unified in a single instant of time,"[17] has much in common not only with modernist literary aesthetics but also with the "hauntological" disturbance that occurs whenever a ghost confounds history by bringing the past to life and giving absence itself a spatial form. Knight's eventual turn to spiritualism, in other words, far from being merely a bizarre symptom of a personal pathology, can be read as a logical extension of his atemporal, spatializing critical mode.

By the same token, we can regard the spiritualist pursuits of modernist writers and intellectuals as central rather than aberrational elements of their modernist aesthetics. Like modernist writers, spirit mediums frequently subvert their own invocations of eternal truths by means of an endlessly shifting subjectivity. Conversely, like spirit mediums, modernist writers counter a sense of ontological crisis with fragments of history—dead ancestors, ancestral texts—shored against the ruins of an alienating, disjointed present. In a historical era marked by loss, alienation, and a literal fragmentation of bodies, the ghosts of the dead trouble the texts of modernism like the plaintive whisper of Hamlet's father ("Remember me"), pleading for a literary re-membering of the bodies whose loss their spectral presence so eloquently signals.

JOYCE, DOWDEN, AND THE FATHER'S SPIRIT

Nowhere are the links between modernist aesthetics and popular spiritualism more subtly yet strikingly articulated than in the intertextual interactions of James Joyce, one of modernism's most influential writers, and Hester Dowden, a prominent and prolific spirit medium with literary pretensions of her own. During a period that neatly spanned most of the modernist era, from 1922 through Joyce's death on the eve of the Second World War, these two Irish stepchildren of Shakespeare played out a lively intellectual drama worthy of the Bard himself, complete with colorful characters, unexpected plot twists, erudite spooks, and the obligatory cross-dressing. The fact that Joyce was not a practicing spiritualist heightens rather than diminishes the significance of these exchanges, for it confirms my contention throughout this book that spiritualist tropes play a vital role in the thematic and aesthetic innovations of a wide range of modernist writers, the skeptical as well as the credulous. Joyce's apparent lack of belief in the main premises of the spiritualist movement—the survival of the soul after death, the possibility of spirit communication, the presence of the dead among the living—did not stop him from employing such concepts in the service of his art. Ghosts, after all, including those of the literary variety, often haunt most effectively where they are least expected.

In the writings of both Joyce and Dowden, ghostly manifestations of Shakespeare and other dead authors are primarily verbal rather than visual, taking the form either, for Dowden, of mediumistic messages from beyond (that is, statements from the dead communicated by means of automatic writing) or, for Joyce, of textual hauntings. Joyce's *Ulysses*, for instance, is riddled with ghostly returns, references to Hamlet's dead father, and Shakespearean allusions, yet Shakespeare's ghost makes only one visual appearance in the novel, when, "rigid in facial paralysis," he gazes back at Stephen Dedalus and Leopold Bloom from a Nighttown mirror.[18] This emphasis on Shakespeare's words rather than his visual image reflects a more general shift in spiritualist practice from the Victorian public's fascination with spirit photographs, materialization, and other "phantasmagoria"—phenomena deftly explored in recent essays by Terry Castle, Cathy Davidson, Andrew Miller, and others—to a twentieth-century focus on the affinities between otherworldly communication and such voice-and text-based technologies as the telephone, the telegraph, and the radio.[19] More significantly, it also indicates a growing awareness, among modernist writers as well as modernist-era spiritualists, of writing as an act of mediumship and of mediumship, conversely, as an act of authorship.

Marjorie Garber notes that "the appearance of ghosts within [Shakespeare's] plays is almost always juxtaposed to a scene of writing," signaling a host of interlocking concerns about "authority, legitimacy, usurpation, authorship, and interpretation."[20] In the writings of Joyce and Dowden, similarly, spectral presences are almost always linked to anxieties about textual authority, intellectual legitimacy, and the equivocal role of Irish writers in the British literary tradition. This is particularly true of *Ulysses*, which was first published in 1922 under the imprimatur of Sylvia Beach's Paris bookstore, Shakespeare and Company; thus, on the first edition's title page, Joyce's name shares pride of place with that of his formidable forebear, indicating both a family connection and an act of usurpation on the part of the literary latecomer. Shakespeare plays a central role in the novel, serving as a prism for Joyce's dazzling reflections on an astonishing range of subjects, from the status of biography in literary history to the consubstantiality of Father and Son in the doctrine of the Holy Trinity. But it is when references to Shakespeare and ghosts appear together—and especially when Shakespeare himself is represented as a spectral, haunting presence—that the authorial and filial anxieties of Joyce and his fictional alter ego, young Stephen Dedalus, manifest themselves most persistently.

Most of the novel's allusions to Shakespeare occur in the "Scylla and Charybdis" chapter, the episode in the Dublin public library where Stephen becomes involved in a lively debate about Shakespeare's life and character. Loosely based on the episode of Homer's *Odyssey* in which Odysseus's sailors must navigate between rocky shoals and a sucking whirlpool, "Scylla and Charybdis" is generally taken by commentators to find its Joycean parallel in Stephen's attempt to cling to the rock of Aristotelian philosophy even while surrounded by "the swirling deeps of Platonist metaphysics."[21] But the chapter's lengthy Shakespeare debate—in which both real-life characters (the poet Æ, the essayist John Eglinton, and the "Quaker librarian" T.W. Lyster) and literary inventions (Stephen Dedalus and Buck Mulligan) vigorously take part—suggests another analogy as well: Shakespeare himself represents both Scylla and Charybdis, both the immovable rock of literary tradition against which Stephen continually bangs his head and the vertiginous whirlpool of ambiguity and unknowability that threatens to overwhelm him.

The perils of the latter are demonstrated through the many contradictory views of Shakespeare that emerge in the course of the debate. George Russell (Æ), whom Stephen derisively identifies with the "astral levels" and "lotus ladies" of the theosophical doctrine that informed much of this real-life figure's poetry (*Ulysses*, 157), is the first to praise Shakespeare's universality: "The words of Hamlet bring our minds into contact with the eternal wisdom, Plato's world of ideas" (152). Mr. Best, a librarian, reminds us that "Coleridge called him myriadminded" (168), and Eglinton, too, emphasizes Shakespeare's all-encompassing nature: "He is the ghost and the prince. He is all in all" (174). Buck Mulligan, on the other hand, tries to burst the bubble of Shakespeare's mystified appeal by dubbing him "the gaseous vertebrate" and, in an even more damning slight, "the chap that writes like Synge" (162–63).

Stephen, characteristically, prefers to dwell on the paradoxes of Shakespeare's identity, calling him in turn "the deathsman of the soul" (154), "a ghost by absence" (155), and "a lord of language" (161). At one point he even intimates that Shakespeare is a more successful creator than God, "the playwright who wrote the folio of this world and wrote it badly" (175). Stephen's English flatmate Haines, meanwhile, derisively borrows a metaphor from popular spiritualism (or, more accurately, from spiritualist appropriations of Native American lore) when he registers his contempt for these wildly disparate views: "Shakespeare is the happy huntingground of all minds that have lost their balance" (320).[22]

Motifs of ghostliness, haunting, and resurrection echo throughout *Ulysses*, from Stephen's guilty memories of his dead mother—"Her glazing eyes, staring out of death, to shake and bend my soul" (9)—to Leopold Bloom's morbid musings on death and corpses at Paddy Dignam's funeral: "Give you the creeps after a bit. I will appear to you after death. You will see my ghost after death. My ghost will haunt you after death. . . . Let them sleep in their maggoty beds. They are not going to get me this innings" (94). But it is in "Scylla and Charybdis," where Stephen identifies Shakespeare with King Hamlet's ghost and Prince Hamlet, in turn, with the playwright's dead son Hamnet, that Joyce most explicitly interweaves images of haunting with another major theme of *Ulysses*—the centrality, both personal and religious, of the father-son relationship. Again and again, references to ghosts prompt Stephen's meditations on paternity, inheritance, filial indebtedness, and the burden of performative anxiety placed on him by such literary father figures as Yeats, Eglinton, Russell ("A.E.I.O.U.," Stephen reminds himself ruefully), and, of course, Shakespeare himself: "He is a ghost, a shadow now, the wind by Elsinore's rocks or what you will, the sea's voice, a voice heard only in the heart of him who is the substance of his own shadow, the son consubstantial with the father" (156, 162).

Commenting on some of the alternate authorship theories that have identified the "real" author of Shakespeare's plays as, variously, the Earl of Rutland, Sir Francis Bacon, and the Earl of Southampton, Stephen tries to overcome his anxieties of influence by insisting that a powerful son can, in effect, give birth to his own father: "When Rutlandbaconsouthamptonshakespeare or another poet of the same name in the comedy of errors wrote *Hamlet* he was not the father of his own son merely but, being no more than a son, he was and felt himself the father of all his race, the father of his own grandfather" (171). Buck Mulligan's mocking paraphrase—"he proves by algebra that Hamlet's grandson is Shakespeare's grandfather and that he himself is the ghost of his own father" (15)—hints that Stephen's position, seemingly grounded in logic, is little more than the wistful fantasy of a paranoid son. Yet in the Nighttown episode of *Ulysses*, Stephen does momentarily become the ghost of his own father—the ghost, that is, of his literary ancestor Shakespeare— when he and Leopold Bloom, a far less threatening surrogate father, together gaze into a "mirror [held] up to nature" and behold, instead of their own faces, that of William Shakespeare, crowned "by the reflection of the reindeer antlered hatrack in the hall" (463).

Stephen, who fears cuckoldry by his muse nearly as much as Bloom fears his wife Molly's infidelities, is not the only literary son whose authorial anxieties vis-à-vis Shakespeare haunt the pages of *Ulysses*. Joyce, too, notes Vincent Cheng, felt himself to be "in a father-son relationship with Shakespeare," and Stephen's Viconian fantasy in "Scylla and Charybdis," whereby "the son becomes a rival to his father, overthrows him, and rises to replace him," reflects Joyce's own wishful thinking as much as Stephen's.[23] Joyce positions himself throughout *Ulysses* as the knowing, usurping son not only of Shakespeare but also—by means of appropriation, allusion, and merciless parody—of a host of real-life Shakespearean scholars and speculators. These include Georg Brandes and Sidney Lee (160), from whose popular biographies Joyce drew most of his information about Shakespeare's family;[24] Frank Harris, author of an erotically tinged biography titled *The Man Shakespeare* (161); Judge D.P. Barton, who wrote a book on links between Ireland and Shakespeare (163); Edward Vining, who proposed in his 1881 *The Mystery of Hamlet* that Hamlet was a woman (163); Karl Bleibtreu, a proponent of the Rutlandian authorship theory (176); George Bernard Shaw, who wrote a play titled *The Dark Lady of the Sonnets* (161); and, most significantly, Oscar Wilde, who advanced, in an 1889 novella titled *The Portrait of Mr. W. H.*, a lively but historically unfounded theory that Shakespeare wrote his sonnets for a man named Willie Hughes.[25] Wilde's book is praised by one of the librarians in "Scylla and Charybdis" as a "brilliant" story told with a characteristically "light touch," a description that adds fuel to the flame of Stephen's already well-developed sense of authorial anxiety: "His glance touched faces lightly as he smiled, a blond ephebe. Tame essence of Wilde" (163). Yet Joyce's clever compatriot, as we shall see, receives his comeuppance in *Finnegans Wake*, where Wilde appears, tamed, as a ghost who returns from the depths not to haunt but to supplicate: "Pity, please, lady, for poor O.W. in this profundus snobbing I have caught."[26]

Another Irish Shakespeare scholar who arouses Stephen's filial anxieties in "Scylla and Charybdis" is Edward Dowden, a distinguished professor at Trinity College who produced a number of widely read books on Shakespeare, including an 1877 school primer that would remain in print for more than a hundred years.[27] A decade after *Ulysses* was published, John Eglinton explicitly contrasted Dowden's scholarly demeanor with the relatively unimpressive figures cut by Irish contemporaries such as Yeats and, presumably, the young Joyce: "No one caught a more respectful attention from the Dublin citizen, who would muse on him wistfully for a moment, hurrying to his tramcar with an armful of books, his looks emanating a kindly radiance. It was with a far more quizzical eye that the same citizen would glance at Yeats himself or any other poet." It was not, however, Dowden's professorial appearance so much as his critical output that accounted for his local and international prestige: "*his* name more than any," Eglinton averred, "carried the repute of Trinity College about the world."[28] Dowden's division of Shakespeare's life and work into four distinct periods provided structure and coherence for generations of schoolchildren and scholars. Indeed, wrote S. Schoenbaum as recently as 1991, "Dowden's Shakespeare . . . has after almost a century not entirely taken leave of the academy; from time to time he still returns to haunt the classroom, like the ghost of Hamlet's father stalking the battlements of Elsinore."[29]

In Schoenbaum's description, significantly, it is not Shakespeare but rather Dowden's version of him who takes on the haunting, admonitory, disquieting role of King Hamlet, the imperious dead father who refuses to leave his son in peace. Certainly Edward Dowden's role as one of Dublin's foremost men of letters haunted a number of his Irish contemporaries, including not only Joyce but also Yeats, who devoted part of a 1916 memoir, *Reveries over Childhood and Youth*, to a description of his dealings with the recently deceased professor, one of his father's closest friends. As a very young man, Yeats recalled, he had admired Dowden as "an image of romance" and a "sage." By 1916, however, he had come to regard him as an impediment to intellectual progress.[30] In several letters to his father, Yeats apologized at length for his unsympathetic portrayal of Dowden, whose public disparagement of the Irish Literary Movement had bitterly disappointed the young poet:

> I couldn't leave Dowden out, for in a subconscious way, the book is a history of the revolt, which perhaps unconsciously you taught me, against certain Victorian ideals. Dowden is the image of those ideals and has to stand for the whole structure in Dublin, Lord Chancellors and all the rest. . . . It is difficult for me to write of him otherwise; at the start of my movement in Dublin he was its most serious opponent, and fought it in ways that seemed to me unfair. He was always charming in private but what he said in private had no effect upon his public word.[31]

Despite certain attempts to distinguish Edward Dowden from his father—"he had already, when both men were in their twenties, decided it is plain that Dowden was a Provincial"—several passages in the younger Yeats's memoir make it clear that the two men played similar, even overlapping, roles in the poet's conception of his own intellectual development. "It was only when I began to study psychical research and mystical philosophy that I broke away from my father's influence," Yeats writes at the beginning of one chapter. He immediately goes on to relate an anecdote about an awkward meeting at Edward Dowden's house with his former headmaster, yet another outspoken adversary of the young man's newfound mysticism. Invoked together in the same paragraph, father, headmaster, and Dowden all merge into a single figure of oppositional paternal authority.[32]

Late in his life, Yeats would describe his relationship to Shakespeare's work, and indeed to the entire English literary tradition, in terms laden with a love/hate ambivalence reminiscent of his portraits of both Dowden and his father: "Then I remind myself . . . that I owe my soul to Shakespeare . . . and to the English language in which I think, speak, and write, that everything I love has come to me through English; my hatred tortures me with love, my love with hate."[33] As early as 1901, Yeats had written an essay on Shakespeare in which he had attacked Dowden as a representative of the "middle class" intellectual values he abhorred: "The more I read," he wrote to Lady Gregory from the Shakespeare Hotel in Stratford, "the worse does the Shakespeare criticism become and Dowden is about the climax of it. I[t] came out [of] the middle class movement and I feel it my legitimate enemy." Yet in 1910 the poet briefly came to harbor hopes of inheriting Dowden's chair at Trinity College after the professor's retirement: "There is a question of my some day taking Dowden's place," he confided to his father.[34] Thus, even while he worked to overthrow the conservative Dublin literary establishment that Dowden (and Dowden's "middle class" Shakespeare) epitomized, Yeats also quite literally longed to take his place.

For Joyce, similarly, Edward Dowden represented, like Shakespeare himself, one of the intellectual father figures whose power and influence he would struggle in *Ulysses* to overcome. In 1903, a young, impecunious James Joyce had asked Professor Dowden to recommend him for a position at the National Library, the very institution in which the "Scylla and Charybdis" episode takes place.[35] Dowden had refused, calling Joyce "extraordinary" and "quite unsuitable" for the job. Clearly this rejection weighed on Joyce's mind, for more than a decade later he wrote a letter to Karl Bleibtreu (whose theory that Shakespeare's plays were written by the Earl of Rutland is mentioned briefly in "Scylla and Charybdis") asking Bleibtreu's opinion of Dowden and his work.[36] Bleibtreu's reply—he called Dowden a "fool" whose "polemics in defence of the Stratford clown" revealed his "colossal ignorance"—may well have added fuel to the flame of Joyce's animosity toward the man who had once refused to help him get a job.[37] Joyce probably felt that he was merely paying the professor back in kind when he included in *Ulysses* several references to Dowden, whom Buck Mulligan describes as a rather stuffy academic with a particular squeamishness regarding imputations (such as Oscar Wilde's) that Shakespeare was a homosexual:

O, I must tell you what Dowden said!
—What? asked Besteglinton.
William Shakespeare and company, limited. The people's William. For terms apply: E. Dowden, Highfield house. . . .
—Lovely! Buck Mulligan suspired amourously. I asked him what he thought of the charge of pederasty brought against the bard. He lifted his hands and said: *All we can say is that life ran very high in those days.* Lovely! (*Ulysses*, 168)

While Buck publicly mocks Dowden's professorial mannerisms, Stephen's private thoughts—"Shakespeare and company, limited. . . . For terms apply: E. Dowden"—link the name of Edward Dowden with that of Joyce's publisher, Shakespeare and Company, thereby identifying Shakespeare's ghost, "the people's William," as a commercial product bought and sold by booksellers and academics alike. (As early as 1884, upon being commissioned to write an essay for a popular magazine, Dowden himself had facetiously written to a friend, "I have had a board put up over our hall door, *Dealer in words, licensed to sell polysyllables.*")[38] Later in the chapter, when Stephen admits to not really believing his own psychobiographical reading of Shakespeare, John Eglinton condemns young Dedalus's apostasy with words that once again associate Dowden with the commodification of Shakespeare scholarship: "Well, in that case, he said, I don't see why you should expect payment for it since you don't believe it yourself. Dowden believes there is some mystery in *Hamlet* but will say no more" (176). In both passages, Joyce subtly impugns Dowden for treating Shakespeare less as a national literary treasure than as a going concern.

Although Edward Dowden was still very much a part of the Dublin intellectual scene on Bloomsday, June 16, 1904, he had been dead for nearly a decade by the time *Ulysses* was published; thus he was in no position to rebut Joyce's unflattering portrayal of him. That task fell instead to Dowden's daughter Hester, a charismatic hostess and talented musician whose influential friends and close acquaintances included such notable figures as Yeats, Æ, Bram Stoker, and the Shakespearean actress Ellen Terry (all four of whom, incidentally, are alluded to in *Ulysses* or *Finnegans Wake*). Indeed, when Yeats published the 1916 memoir in which he included an unsympathetic portrayal of Edward Dowden, his greatest concern, aside from offending his own father, was that Hester Dowden (still known at the time under her married name, Hester Travers Smith) might cast him out of her spiritualist circle: "I wonder if Mrs. Smith, Dowden's daughter, whom I like . . . will invite me to any more seances at her house."[39] Yeats's apparent admiration of Hester Dowden's mediumistic talents was, it seems, well justified; by 1922, the year that *Ulysses* was published, she was well on her way to becoming one of London's preeminent professional spirit mediums, a position that she would maintain until her death in 1949. Certainly Joyce himself, with his fondness for themes of death, resurrection, and spectral apparitions, could hardly have come up with a more inventive plan than hers for avenging her slighted father: in a series of otherworldly interviews conducted in 1923 by means of a Ouija board and published in 1924 as *Psychic Messages from Oscar Wilde*, she called up the ghost of Wilde to pronounce judgment on Joyce's scandalous novel.

As an Irishman and a would-be Shakespeare scholar whose theories are mentioned in "Scylla and Charybdis," Wilde serves as a metonymic stand-in for Edward Dowden, whom Hester, in a career that would involve some forty thousand spiritualistic sittings, never attempted to contact directly.[40] Presumably Professor Dowden—the kind of man, at least in Joyce's characterization, who threw up his hands at the mere mention of "the charge of pederasty brought against the bard"—would not have been wildly pleased by his daughter's choice of surrogate. Be that as it may, in *Psychic Messages from Oscar Wilde*, the ghost of Wilde essentially takes on Edward Dowden's role as Professor of English Literature, offering his criticisms and insights regarding a wide range of authors both new and old. One of these, inevitably, is Shakespeare, whose use of the phrase "old mole" to describe King Hamlet marks him, Wilde tells us, as a protospiritualist: "[The expression] was well chosen and should be of interest to the Society for Psychical Research, as it displays an inward knowledge of the state over here."[41] But Wilde, with the anachronistic hubris typical of ghosts, does not limit himself to discussing only authors whose works he had read during his lifetime. Announcing that "I have dipped into the works of some of your modern novelists," he also offers his opinions concerning a number of contemporary writers, from Bennett, Philpotts, and Galsworthy to Shaw and the Sitwells. Most of these he gently disparages with the kinds of barbed, witty aphorisms characteristic of Wilde while he was still alive, declaring, for instance, that Bennett "has conjured so long with the wand of his master Flaubert that he has really succeeded in persuading himself and others that he has learnt the trick" and that Philpotts, despite his beautiful depictions of natural scenes, suffers from "nature's lack of variety": "One wishes that spring would sometimes forget to come to Dartmoor" (*Psychic Messages*, 18–19).

Yeats, who admired Hester Dowden but publicly criticized her father, receives somewhat harsher treatment from Wilde: "I knew Yeats very well—a fantastical mind, but so full of inflated joy in himself that his little cruse of poetry was emptied early in his career. . . . He will not be interested to know that I have still the voice to speak and the mind to put my thoughts on paper. He is too full of his own literary salvation to worry over a brother in art who fell from too much beauty, or rather, the desire for beauty" (14). But it is not until Hester Dowden hazards the question, "What is your opinion of 'Ulysses,' by James Joyce?" that the ghost of Wilde finally exchanges wit for passion, unleashing a veritable flood of abuse that goes on for several paragraphs:

> Yes, I have smeared my fingers with that vast work. . . . It gives me the impression of having been written in a severe fit of nausea. . . . I feel that if this work has caught a portion of the public, who may take it for the truth, that I, even I, who am a shade, and I who have tasted the fulness of life and its meed of bitterness, should cry aloud: "Shame upon Joyce, shame on his work, shame on his lying soul."

Denouncing his countryman's novel, which had been published just one year previously, as a "great bulk of filth" and a "heated vomit," Wilde describes Joyce as "a monster who cannot contain the monstrosities of his own brain." He even provides a fiendish twist on Joyce's favorite theme of father-son conflict, suggesting that Joyce has been defiled by his own literary offspring: "the creatures he gives birth to leap from him in shapeless masses of hideousness, as dragons might, which in their foulsome birth contaminate their parents" (38–40).

An editorial note, meanwhile, assures us that these deprecatory remarks must surely have come from Wilde himself, because they could not possibly have originated in the consciousness of his medium; Hester Dowden, we are informed, had once "glanced at a copy of 'Ulysses' for a few minutes in Ireland," but "out of seven hundred pages she could not have read more than half a dozen, nor had she read reviews of this work. She was not in a position to criticize it" (42–43).[42] Given, however, Joyce's treatment in *Ulysses* of Dowden's father—whose name, position, and personal connection to herself she mentions nowhere in her Wilde book—this disclaimer seems at best disingenuous and at worst downright deceptive. Wilde's seemingly impartial criticism of Joyce is clearly intended to obscure the medium's own ferocious partiality. Like Shakespeare's ghost throughout "Scylla and Charybdis," in fact, Wilde is invoked here as a figure of inviolable otherworldly authority, yet his very existence as ghost—the fact that his voice and even his vocabulary depend on the mediumistic offices of Hester Dowden—marks him instead as an emblem of the multiple perspectivism, textual precariousness, and shifting subjectivity that characterize, paradoxically, the Joycean prose style he so vehemently attacks.

That Joyce himself was aware of such potential alliances between spirit mediumship and modernist literary aesthetics is made evident by his wholesale appropriation of spiritualist tropes in the pages of *Finnegans Wake*. Joyce had, of course, already mocked the theosophical pretensions of Æ, Eglinton, Yeats, and other members of the Irish Literary Renaissance in "Scylla and Charybdis," and in the "Cyclops" chapter of *Ulysses* he had offered a hilarious parody of spiritualist rhetoric:

> In the darkness spirit hands were felt to flutter and when prayer by tantras had been directed to the proper quarter a faint but increasing luminosity of ruby light became gradually visible, the apparition of the etheric double being particularly lifelike owing to the discharge of jivic rays from the crown of the head and face. Communication was effected through the pituitary body and also by means of the orange-fiery and scarlet rays emanating from the sacral region and solar plexus. (*Ulysses*, 247–48)

In *Finnegans Wake*, however, spiritualism becomes more than just fodder for satire; it comprises a major theme of the novel, even providing one of the book's main structural principles. James Atherton notes that "details and methods from dozens of books about spiritualism are used in the *Wake*" and that the entire third book is, at least on one level, "a report of a spiritualist séance."[43] Throughout the *Wake*, in fact, as in a seance, the living enter a dreamlike state that corresponds at least briefly to death, while the words of the dead are filtered through a living medium—in this case, Joyce himself—into a discourse of almost vertiginous intersubjectivity.

In a 1925 letter to Harriet Weaver about the "Work in Progress" that would eventually become *Finnegans Wake*, Joyce revealed that "a book of spirit talks with Oscar Wilde . . . will explain one page of it." Not only had Joyce read *Psychic Messages from Oscar Wilde*, but he was clearly well aware of the identity (and presumably of the critical agenda) of its author: "Mrs. Travers Smith, the 'dear lady' of the book, is a daughter of professor Dowden of Trinity College, Dublin."[44] Atherton contends that

Joyce's "pardonable annoyance" at Hester Dowden's book finds expression between pages 419 and 424 of the *Wake*. "'Oscar Wild . . . Puffedly offal tosh' (419.24), 'properly spewing' (421.27), and 'Obnoximost posthumust!' (422.12) are samples of it."[45] A far more explicit set of references to Hester Dowden's conversations with Wilde occurs, however, somewhat later in book 3, where Wilde speaks from beyond the grave to or through a spirit medium:

> —Is that yu, Whitehed?
> —Have you headnoise now?
> —Give us your mespilt reception, will yous?
> —Pass the fish for Christ's sake!
> —Old Whitehowth he is speaking again. Ope Eustace tube! Pity poor whiteoath! Dear gone mummeries, goby! Tell the woyld I have lived true thousand hells. Pity, please, lady, for poor O.W. in this profundust snobbing I have caught. Nine dirty years mine age, hairs hoar, mummeries failend, snowdrift to my elpow, deff as Adder. I askt you, dear lady, to judge on my tree by our fruits. I gave you of the tree. I gave two smells, three eats. My freeandies, my celeberrimates: my happy bossoms, my all-falling fruits of my boom. Pity poor Haveth Childers Everywhere with Mudder! (*Finnegans Wake*, 535.22–535.35)

This passage alludes, among other things, to the ear trumpets ("Ope Eustace tube!") and complaints about bad reception ("Have you headnoise now?") that were common features of spiritualist seances; to Wilde's partial deafness, acquired during his years in prison ("deff as Adder"); to the prison stay itself and Wilde's account of the experience in *De Profundis* ("my celeberrimates," "this profundust snobbing"); and, of course, to Hester Dowden, the "dear lady" whom Wilde had asked in *Psychic Messages* to "Pity Oscar Wilde" (*Psychic Messages*, 12, 5). A careful reading shows, moreover, that it is Wilde rather than Humphrey Chimpden Earwicker, the *Wake*'s central character, who pronounces the phrase "Haveth Childers Everywhere," which not only encodes Earwicker's important initials (HCE, as in "Here Comes Everybody") but also invokes the themes of generation and regeneration that permeate the novel. Thus Wilde serves for Joyce as well as for Hester Dowden as an otherworldly spokesman who is also—somewhat paradoxically, given Wilde's homosexuality—a prolific if problematic father figure.

A subsequent paragraph in *Finnegans Wake*, similarly, is riddled with allusions to spirit communication, poor reception, the survival of souls after death, and the skepticism of nonspiritualists:

> That was Communicator, a former colonel. A disincarnated spirit, called Sebastion, from the Rivera in Januero, (he is not all hear) may fernspreak shortly with messuages from my deadported. Let us cheer him up a little and make an appunkment for a future date. Hello, Commudicate! How's the buttes? Everscepistic! He does not believe in our psychous of the Real Absence, neither miracle wheat nor soul-surgery of P. P. Quemby. He has had some indiejestings, poor thing, for quite a little while, confused by his tonguer of baubble. (*Finnegans Wake*, 535.36–536.8)

"Tonguer of baubble" refers, perhaps, to the role of the spirit medium in "tonguing," or giving utterance to, a confusing babble of spirit voices. At the same time, the phrase could allude to the ghost of Wilde, who confesses to Hester Dowden in his *Psychic Messages* that he longs for "an occasion on which I may reasonably babble about my lost illusions" (*Psychic Messages*, 44). Yet "tonguer of baubble" also serves as an appropriate appellation for Joyce himself, who, as the *Wake*'s "tonguer of babble," produces many ephemeral bubbles of meaning, many playful linguistic baubles.

If Oscar Wilde's cameo appearance in *Finnegans Wake* can be read on one level as Joyce's mischievous response to Hester Dowden's immoderate attack on *Ulysses*, on another level the *Wake* itself validates and perhaps even self-consciously imitates the multivocality and otherworldly "hauntology" of Dowden's mediumistic discourse. Grace Eckley, who has noted a number of parallels between Joyce's narrative mode and "the 'after death' communications that were popular at the time of Joyce's writing," goes so far as to contend that *Finnegans Wake* is, fundamentally, a spiritualist text: "Literary criticism lacks terminology for this, which may be called an afterlife above-earth dual narration."[46] Eckley's reading of the *Wake* largely depends, however, on her own controversial theory that the "biographical original" of Earwicker was the journalist W. T. Stead, whose public championing of spiritualism made it virtually inevitable that numerous mediums would claim after his death to have received spirit communications from him. (Hester Dowden was one of those mediums; in 1912, just after Stead's death in the *Titanic* disaster, she reportedly received several brief messages from him, and in 1933, with the blessing of Stead's daughter, Estelle, she published a book supposedly ghostwritten by Stead via the Ouija board.)[47] Earwicker's concealed identity as Stead, Eckley contends, is Joyce's much-vaunted "weapon of silence," the key that neatly unlocks all the secrets of an otherwise enigmatic novel. Eckley offers substantial archival evidence for reading certain passages in the *Wake* as allusions to Stead's life and work, and she points out some intriguing parallels between the structure of *Finnegans Wake* and Stead's spiritualist interests: his fascination, for instance, with automatic writing; his belief in multiple personalities; his definition of the unconscious as "the ghost that dwells in each of us"; and his advocacy of a "prayer telephone" by which one might converse directly with the other world.[48]

Unfortunately, however, Eckley's critical methodology—she reads even the most trivial details as evidence of encoded textual secrets and gives the same authoritative weight to spirit messages from Stead and Wilde as she does to more conventionally reliable literary sources—bears an all-too-uncanny resemblance to that of the numerous anti-Stratfordians who have deployed anagrams, cryptograms, rearrangements of key passages, and even communications from the dead to "prove" that the true author of Shakespeare's plays was someone other than Shakespeare. Indeed, almost as if to anticipate approaches and claims such as Eckley's, *Finnegans Wake* contains numerous references to Shakespearean cryptograms, forgers, claimants, imitators, and alternate authorship theories. Sir Francis Bacon, for instance, together with Delia Bacon (no relation), a nineteenth-century proponent of the Baconian theory who reportedly received confirmation of her hypothesis from Francis Bacon's ghost,[49] accounts for at least twenty such allusions, providing material, moreover, for a whole series of Shakespearean breakfast puns involving "Hamlet and Bacon."[50] Where Eckley tries to decode *Finnegans Wake* by means of a single skeleton key, Joyce himself invokes cryptic specters and closeted skeletons that are clearly meant to raise multiple interpretations rather than to lay them comfortably to rest.

Among these literary specters, predictably, is King Hamlet's ghost—a metonym, as we have seen, for Shakespeare himself—who, even more so than in *Ulysses*, plays a crucial role in the *Wake* in linking Joyce's central themes of paternity, authorship, and filial anxiety with tropes of textual instability. King Hamlet's exhortation to his son to "List, list, O, list!" for instance, becomes Earwicker's far more feeble "Ear! Ear! Weakear!" (*Finnegans Wake*, 568.25), a commentary both on the unreliability of verbal communication (including, presumably, spirit communication) and on Earwicker's own weakening role as paternal lawgiver. The ghost's plaintive "Remember me," meanwhile, becomes Anna Livia Plurabelle's echoing "mememormee" ("me, me, more me"?), an utterance that dismembers even while preserving a faint memory trace of its original (628.14). Shakespeare's voice surely echoes in these lines, yet one could equally well argue that the appropriated phrases mock the original texts to which they bear at most a ghostly resemblance. Parody, Joyce suggests, is not only a haunted literary form but also, perhaps, a form of haunting.

Although it seems unlikely that Hester Dowden ever read *Finnegans Wake*, she too, like Joyce, would ultimately use the figure of Shakespeare to question and subvert the very notion of paternal authority. Indeed, Dowden's later work as a medium would put a whole new spin on the Shakespearean authorship controversy, Joyce's privileged locus of precarious textuality and authorial uncertainty, by even more explicitly linking Shakespeare's ghost to Joyce's master plot of literary patricide. In the late 1930s, Dowden hired out her services as a professional medium to a man named Alfred Dodd, who had already written several books proselytizing for the Baconian authorship theory. Bacon, Dodd believed, had woven into Shakespeare's plays an elaborate network of "numbers, anagrams, purposeful printing errors, special type-setting, hieroglyphics, allegorical pictures, emblematic head and tail-pieces, water-marks, etc" revealing his true identity. In his spare time, moreover, when he was not busy writing the plays usually credited to Shakespeare or translating the King James Bible, Bacon had set up "an ethical, secret school whose members could communicate with each other, among themselves and down the ages by private methods, even in published books. . . . In short, he was a Psychic, so sensitive that he was constantly attuned to the higher vibrations of the Great Invisibles."[51] And how better to prove the psychic prowess of the "Immortal Master," Dodd reasoned, than to communicate with his spirit by means of seances and mediums?

Dodd sought (and for the most part received) confirmation of his Baconian theory from a number of prominent mediums, among them Hester Dowden, whose involvement in Dodd's project would clearly have appalled her famous father. Much of Edward Dowden's career as a Shakespeare scholar had, after all, been devoted to debunking alternate authorship theories: "My own notion," he humorously averred to a colleague who proposed to solve the mystery by opening Shakespeare's tomb, "is that Bacon after his decease made away with Shakspere's skull, & then having forgotten which was his own & which Shakspere's & being ashamed of what he had done, he never returned to his grave; which accounts for no remains having remained in St. Michael's Church."[52] For Dodd, Hester Dowden's divided loyalties served as the primary guarantee of her veracity; why, after all, would she contradict her father unless she had genuinely received otherworldly assurances convincing her that the Baconian theory was true? But the medium's own words hint at other possible motivations. Dodd reports Dowden's chagrined reaction when she first began to receive messages confirming that Bacon was the author of Shakespeare's plays: "Do you know who I am?" she asked; "*I am Professor Dowden's daughter, the Shakespearean scholar. He went into the matter thoroughly, and I therefore know there is nothing in it.*"[53] Dowden protests loudly here on her famous father's behalf, but her syntax is revealing: "I am Professor Dowden's daughter, the Shakespearean scholar." Just as Oscar Wilde's ghost once spoke through her to defend her slighted father, now Shakespeare's ghost—or, more accurately, the spirit of Francis Bacon—speaks through her to undermine that same father's intellectual legacy. In doing so, he establishes Hester Dowden, not Edward Dowden, as the true "Shakespearean scholar," the one whose work is sanctioned, as the professor's was not, by otherworldly authority.

Nor did Hester Dowden's daughterly insubordination end there. In 1942, in the employ of a different amateur Shakespeare scholar, Dowden revealed through a new series of spirit communications that Dodd's Baconian theory was false and that Shakespeare's works were composed instead by the Earl of Oxford—a discovery, coincidentally enough, that exactly confirmed the hypothesis of her new client, Percy Allen. When asked to explain the apparent discrepancy between the two sets of messages, the spirit of Francis Bacon replied through Hester Dowden's Ouija board that he had been misrepresented by an uninformed "spirit deputy" who had claimed responsibility on his behalf for Shakespeare's plays. This deputy, Bacon complained, "is firmly convinced that I wrote the plays and sonnets, and took no trouble to have a direct message from me." Mrs. Dowden, Bacon emphasized, was in no way to blame for the communicative glitch: "She is my pen. . . . My *pen* is not responsible for what I say."[54]

Through Hester Dowden's mediumship, Bacon and other spirits revealed to Allen that most of the works commonly attributed to Shakespeare were in fact composed by a consortium of authors, led by Lord Oxford but also including John Fletcher, Francis Beaumont, Ben Jonson, Christopher Marlowe, Sir Walter Raleigh, Sir Philip Sidney, and even Shakespeare himself, a rough countryman with just enough literary talent to concoct dramatic plots and add some colorful touches. "Shakespeare," in other words, was the work of a committee, the composite creation of a group of men whose intellectual sum was greater than their parts. In the course of transmitting these revelations, meanwhile, "Professor Dowden's daughter, the Shakespearean scholar" was in fact permitted to become a Shakespearean scholar in her own right, offering original interpretations of this composite Shakespeare's works, delineating the authorship of each play, and divulging some astonishing biographical secrets, such as the little-known fact that Oberon in *A Midsummer Night's Dream* was modeled on the real-life Earl of Southampton, "Lord Oxford's son by Queen Elizabeth." Cunningly, Hester Dowden even used her father's role as an eminent Shakespearean to validate her own usurpation of that role, reminding Allen's readers—through Francis Bacon's voice rather than her own—that she possessed a "direct line of ancestry" with the great Elizabethans "through the knowledge and inclination of her father."[55]

For psychoanalytic theorists of the uncanny such as Freud, Lacan, and Derrida, ghosts represent the unwilled return of something deeply familiar but previously repressed: "the gaps," in Nicolas Abraham's words, "left within us by the secrets of others."[56] For Dowden and Joyce, in contrast, the spirits of Wilde, Shakespeare, and other famous authors are neither psychic gaps nor unwelcome revenants; instead, they are literary entities strategically employed not only to haunt the living but also to goad, unsettle, and ultimately redefine the dead. Indeed, had Joyce lived long enough to read and satirize Allen's and Dodd's anti-Stratfordian tomes, he might well have been forced to recognize that Hester Dowden's Shakespeare was in certain respects very closely akin to his own, a phantom father who loomed so large that he had to be broken up in order to be contained. For Joyce, Shakespeare's ghost offered a spectral reminder of his authorial belatedness vis-à-vis a number of literary father figures. For Dowden, he personified the Shakespearean father whose formidable shadow had for so long eclipsed her own. And how better to lay such a powerful ghost to rest than by calling him first to life? How better to escape the father's tenacious whisper—"Remember me"—than by filling the air with dismembering echoes? Resurrected by Joyce and Dowden as a ghost, feted yet hopelessly fractured, Shakespeare becomes an emblem of modernism itself: the tradition that can ever be written anew, the authoritative voice that fragments, ecstatically, into a liberating polyphony.

CHAPTER FOUR

Metaphorical Mediumship

T. S. Eliot writes with such fluidity, you would think that he was inspired by spirits, who, by virtue of being dead, have all the time in
the world to come up with such eloquence.
                    Amazon.com reader's review of Eliot's *Selected Poems*

I am afraid of the life after death.
        T. S. Eliot (alias Arnaud), quoted by Ezra Pound in Canto 29

To be modern is to live a life of paradox and contradiction. . . . It
is to be both revolutionary and conservative: alive to new possibilities for experience and adventure, frightened by the nihilistic
depths to which so many modern adventures lead, longing to create and to hold on to something real even as everything melts.
                    Marshall Berman, *All That Is Solid Melts into Air*

LOW HAUNTS, HIGH ART

In 1923, Thomas Mann wrote an apologetic essay titled "An Experience in the Occult," a theme that he called "preposterous, and, indeed, suspect":

But do people choose their subjects, I ask? No, they write and they talk
of what they are ridden by, and nothing else. . . . And all my good, respectable ideas have been vitiated by personal contacts and observations, which are at once so puerile, and yet to such a degree unex-
plainable (if I may talk about degrees of unexplainableness), that I
cannot get away from them, and find myself, for the moment at least,
spoilt for the contemplation of those more unsullied, those saner,
chaster realms of thought where I could move with so much honour
and credit to myself. I say spoilt. And truly it is a sort of corruption
which breathes from the region I have in mind: that probably not
deep, yet subterranean region, that turbid and equivocal plane of ex-

istence, with which, in my folly, I have put myself in touch; it lures me astray from my lawful concerns to those which I know full well are none of mine, though they exercise upon my fancy and my brain a pungent attraction, like the fumes of wood-alcohol (by contrast with the bouquet from the pure wine of the spirit of civilization).

Confessing that he had recently joined the ranks of prominent "university professors, . . . philosophers and psychologists, . . . natural scientists, physicists, physiologists, and physicians, who take advantage of the bad street-lighting in Munich to steal like conspirators" to evening sittings at the home of the noted psychical researcher Dr. Albert Freiherr von Schrenck-Notzing, Mann recounts his attendance at a seance in which a young dentist named Willy S., possessed by a spirit control called Minna, had caused lights to hover, music to play, furniture to tremble, and a typewriter to produce garbled messages tapped out by unseen hands. "I love that which I call the moral upper world," Mann assures us; "I love the human fable, and clear and humane thought. I abhor luxations of the brain, I abhor morasses of the spirit." The "undignified" and "trivial" phenomena of the seance room, he acknowledges, "are well calculated to be offensive to our proud aesthetic sense." Yet he concludes by asserting that "to deny their abnormal reality would be nothing less than unreasonable obstinacy."[1]

A year later, Mann would elevate his "subterraneous" seance experience to a more respectable aesthetic level, publishing the memorable chapter in *The Magic Mountain* that ends with Hans Castorp, the novel's impressionable young protagonist, coming face to face with the materialized ghost of his dead cousin. Like Yeats, who would justify similar seance involvements by comparing his muse to a high-society woman who "gives herself to unknown sailors,"[2] Mann thus transformed low cultural experience into high cultural expression, transporting insights gleaned in what Yeats called the "low haunts" of popular spiritualism to "the moral upper world" of literature, home of the "pure wine of the spirit of civilization." Mann's enological metaphor is not as explicitly erotic as is Yeats's fable of the slumming muse, but it implicates spiritualist experience in a similarly charged drama of forbidden, sexualized desire. The "pungent attraction" of the occult "lures" the author away from the "chaster" realms of high culture, begetting guilty pleasure as well as new art.

Mann was representative rather than aberrational among literary modernists in his vexed attraction to popular spiritualism, that disreputable site of forbidden desire. A striking number of his literary contemporaries similarly recognized in spiritualist discourse a compelling model—albeit, in Mann's words, a "suspect" and even "preposterous" one—for some of their most significant thematic and aesthetic innovations: displacements of authorial voice; subversions of spatial and temporal conventions; deliberate confusions of gender roles; elisions of high and low culture. I certainly do not intend to make the claim here that all modernist writing is deeply indebted to popular spiritualism, or even that every reference to ghosts and haunting betrays a conscious engagement with the spiritualist movement. I will argue, however, that spiritualism acquired a sometimes surprising metaphorical currency among early-twentieth-century intellectuals, including many who eschewed its claims and mocked its vulgarity. Whether viewed seriously or satirically, spirit mediumship illuminates the foibles of written and verbal communication and the paradoxes of modernist thought. Thus, even avowed skeptics were not above seeking in the "low haunts" of spiritualism fresh material for their art.

D. H. Lawrence, for instance, eschewed "the Oliver Lodge spiritualism" that he associated with spirit messages about lost "hotel bills and collar-studs": "The passionate dead act within and with us," he insisted, "not like messenger boys and hotel porters. Of the dead who really live, whose presence we know, we hardly care to speak—we know their hush." Yet elsewhere, even while rejecting spiritualism's forms, he acknowledged the validity of its claims: "It is true, as William James and Conan Doyle and the rest allow, that a spirit can persist in the after-death. Persist by its own volition."[3] An obsession with this "after-death" informs and complicates some of Lawrence's most powerful works: fiction and poetry in which he laments his mother's posthumous influence; ghost stories that point to the discomfiting presence of supernatural forces in everyday human experience; poems from the Great War that invoke the "unassuaged and angry" spirits of dead soldiers.[4]

For the most part, Lawrence's ghosts appear in his work without the benefit of mediums, darkened rooms, or the other trappings of popular spiritualism. Instead, the poet himself serves as the medium who communicates, often unwillingly, between the worlds of the living and the dead. In an early poem titled "The Inheritance," for example, the "gift of tongues" bequeathed to him by his deceased but still powerful mother—"You sent me a cloven fire/Out of death"—allows him not only to write about the dead but also to see right through living people as though they were transparent spirits: "people waft/Like candid ghosts"; "Form after form, in the streets/Waves like a ghost along"; "the town/Glimmers with subtle ghosts"; "I move among a townfolk clad/With words, but the night shows through/Their words as they move" (*Complete Poems*, 108–9). Speaking in tongues, possessed by his mother's language and vision, the poet perceives living people as ghosts even while his mother, the real ghost, remains vividly and persistently alive.

Elsewhere, in a wartime poem titled "We Have Gone Too Far," Lawrence suggests that "the ghosts of the slain," "the cold ghosts that homeless flock about/Our serried hearts," need only to be offered a peaceful final resting place in the hearts of the living (736). But in another poem from the same period, "Erinnyes," he recommends a far grimmer form of dispatch for the restless spirits who still wander the earth. Arguing that the "insistent ghosts" of dead soldiers—"Victorious, grey, grisly ghosts in our streets,/Grey, unappeased ghosts seated in the music halls"—make those who survive them seem "pale and bloodless" in comparison, Lawrence urges the living to stop allowing themselves to be possessed by the dead:

> For one year's space, attend on our angry dead,
> Soothe them with service and honour, and silence meet,
> Strengthen, prepare them for the journey hence,
> Then lead them to the gates of the unknown,
> And bid farewell, oh stately travellers,
> And wait till they are lost upon our sight.

> (740)

This theme is picked up again in "Glad Ghosts," a 1926 short story in which Lawrence explicitly criticizes popular spiritualists for letting the dead rule the living. "I think it makes a horribly depressing atmosphere, spiritualism," complains the story's narrator; "I want to kick." And kick he does, convincing a houseful of people he describes as "the living dead"—"They all seemed awkward, as if I had interrupted them at a

séance"—to banish their angry, energy-sapping ghosts and "come to life"
once again.[5]

Works such as "Erinnyes" and "Glad Ghosts" anticipate Lawrence's ad-
monition, in a draft of his famous poem "The Ship of Death," that the
dead should fully abandon themselves to their fate:

> Oh pity the dead that are dead, but cannot take
> the journey, still they moan and beat
> against the silvery adamant walls of this our exclusive existence.
> They moan and beat, they gnash, they rage
> they fall upon the new outcoming souls with rage
> and they send arrows of anger, bullets and bombs of frustration
> over the adamant walls of this, our by-no-means-impregnable
>   existence.
> Pity, oh pity the poor dead that are only ousted from life
> and crowd there on the grey mud beaches of the margins,
> gaunt and horrible,
> waiting, waiting till at last the ancient boatman with the common
>   barge
> shall take them aboard, towards the great goal of oblivion.
>
>   (962)

Written shortly before his own death in 1930, "The Ship of Death"
makes clear why Lawrence urged so vehemently in his earlier poems that
the dead be put in their place. Ghosts disrupt ontological certainties,
calling into question the comforting finality of death. They lob "arrows
of anger, bullets and bombs of frustration" over the walls of human existence, bombarding the living with unresolved emotions until the living
themselves become ghostlike. Crowding "gaunt and horrible" on "the
grey mud beaches of the margins," they remain relentlessly material
presences, memories clothed in a ghastly fleshly form. No wonder
Lawrence eschewed popular spiritualism, with its promises of otherworldly communication. It took him many years, as his early poetry and
fiction attest, to lay his own mother's memory to rest. Understandably,
he had no desire to resurrect her, or any other ghost.

Surprisingly, however, in a draft of the introduction to his 1928 *Collected Poems*, Lawrence explicitly invokes ghosts and apparitions to describe the workings of his own poetic imagination:

I used to feel myself at times haunted by something, and a little guilty about it, as if it were an abnormality. Then the haunting would get the better of me, and the ghost would suddenly appear, in the shape of a usually rather incoherent poem. Nearly always I shunned the apparition once it had appeared. From the first, I was a little afraid of my real poems—not my "compositions," but the poems that had the ghost in them. . . . To this day, I still have the uneasy haunted feeling, and would rather not write most of the things I do write—including this note. (849–50)

Yet Lawrence's apparent aversion to any form of haunting remains evident even here. Indeed, his self-professed feelings of guilt, abnormality, and uneasiness recall Mann's descriptions, in his 1923 essay, of spiritualist experience as corrupt and suspect. This admitted "uneasiness" might help explain why, in the published version of this same essay, he eventually omitted all references to ghosts and haunting, substituting instead his well-known formulation that all true poetry springs from one's "demon," a repressed version of one's self: "A young man is afraid of his demon and puts his hand over the demon's mouth sometimes and speaks for him. And the things the young man says are very rarely poetry. So I have tried to let the demon say his say, and to remove the passages where the young man intruded" (28).

A decade later, W. B. Yeats would posit otherworldly spirits and personal demons as interactive, cohabitative entities: "Spirits do not tell a man what is true but create such conditions, such a crisis of fate, that the man is compelled to listen to his Daimon."[6] For Lawrence, in contrast, external and internal inspiration would remain metaphorically incompatible concepts. Haunting, as he describes it here, sounds a lot like ghostwriting: possession by an explicitly literary spirit. But whereas writing mediums frequently relish their intercourse with famous dead authors, famous living authors such as Lawrence are seldom quite so eager to abandon themselves to the uncertainties and the passivity of mediumship. Lawrence's demon, however disconcerting, is clearly a version of himself, a manifestation of his own unconscious, the id in Freud's psychic constellation. The ghost or apparition, by contrast, which produces in the poet such an "uneasy haunted feeling," suggests a less welcome psychic presence, a powerful external Other.

Virginia Woolf, even more so than Lawrence, was content to portray

ghosts as internal psychological entities so long as she did not have to acknowledge them as real. She "liked talking to Yeats," for instance, but
found his spiritualist anecdotes difficult to stomach: "after an hour's
hard work," she reported of one conversation with the credulous poet,
"the occult appeared—an illuminated coat hanger, a child's hand, and a
message about an unborn baby in Greek—at which I gasped, like a dying
alligator."[7] And although she had little patience for Yeats's spectral the-
atrics, Woolf was deeply interested in what she called the "psychical
ghost story." In 1918 she wrote a largely sympathetic review of Dorothy
Scarborough's *The Supernatural in Modern English Fiction*, singling out
Henry James for special praise:

> [To make our flesh creep] the author must change his direction; he
> must seek to terrify us not by the ghosts of the dead, but by those
> ghosts which are living within ourselves. . . . The horror of [*The Turn
> of the Screw*] comes from the force with which it makes us realize the
> power that our minds possess for such excursions into the darkness;
> when certain lights sink or certain barriers are lowered, the ghosts of
> the mind, untracked desires, indistinct intimations, are seen to be a
> large company.[8]

James's haunting spirits, Woolf notes elsewhere, "have nothing in common with the violent old ghosts—the blood-stained sea captains, the
white horses, the headless ladies of dark lanes and windy commons.
They have their origin within us."[9]

Woolf's own fiction, although less explicitly concerned with gothic at-
mospherics, is full of such "psychical ghosts" or "ghosts of the mind." In
Night and Day (1919), as George M. Johnson notes, Woolf subverts "the
materialism of the classical novel" by creating a pervasively "supernatural aura," with allusions to ghosts—usually as metaphors for memory or
as indications of a character's emotional insubstantiality—occurring on
practically every page.[10] In "Kew Gardens" (1919)—"certainly a ghost
story," in Nicholas Royle's assessment—an old man's seemingly nonsensical ramblings about "spirit matter . . . rolling between the hills like
thunder" ultimately help to explain and structure the story's temporal
telescopings, perceptual distortions, and transmissions of disembodied
voices.[11] In *Jacob's Room* (1922), haunting takes on a teleological twist, as
the life story of a fairly ordinary young man, modeled after Woolf's own

dead brother Thoby, becomes charged with existential significance, a kind of advance haunting effect created in anticipation of his untimely death. And in *Mrs. Dalloway* (1925)—another story pre-haunted by the main character's imminent but unspoken demise—Clarissa Dalloway develops a "transcendental theory" that explains her mysterious mental alliance with Septimus Smith, a suicidal, shell-shocked ex-soldier:

> Odd affinities [Clarissa] had with people she had never spoken to, some woman in the street, some man behind a counter—even trees, or barns. It ended in a transcendental theory which, with her horror of death, allowed her to believe, or say that she believed (for all her skepticism), that since our apparitions, the part of us which appears, are so momentary compared with the other, the unseen part of us, which spreads wide, the unseen might survive, be recovered somehow attached to this person or that, or even haunting certain places, after death.[12]

Clarissa's beliefs, as Johnson remarks, bear a "striking affinity" with those of contemporary psychical researchers and spiritualists, who frequently describe an "unseen world" contiguous with the visible world.[13] Woolf herself, like Mrs. Dalloway, was indubitably a skeptic; yet she clearly absorbed—and deployed more often sympathetically than satirically—a good deal of the spiritualist language and thought so prevalent in Britain during and just after the Great War. Characteristically, however, Woolf alters what she appropriates. The word "apparition," for instance, usually used to describe a ghost, designates in *Mrs. Dalloway* the physical body of the living: "the part of us which appears," as opposed to the part of us that remains unseen. Life, in other words, takes on an insubstantial, ghostly quality, as in Woolf's snail's-eye view of people walking through Kew Gardens: "Thus one couple after another with much the same irregular and aimless movement passed the flower-bed and were enveloped in layer after layer of green-blue vapour, in which at first their bodies had substance and a dash of colour, but later both substance and colour dissolved in the green-blue atmosphere."[14] Ghosts, meanwhile, become endowed with an agency that the living sometimes seem to lack. Thus, in a 1921 short story titled "The Haunted House," although there are no visible spirits in evidence ("we see no lady spread her ghostly cloak"), the narrator and her partner learn to value the comfort and security of the home that they share with a "ghostly couple" who, although separated on earth, are now joined in eternal love.[15] Far from inducing supernatural terror or even psychic discomfiture, haunting enriches the narrator's life.

Woolf's "The Haunted House" brings to mind a similarly titled short story by Lennox Robinson, the Irish dramatist and close friend of Yeats who would eventually marry medium Hester Dowden's daughter, Dolly Travers Smith. In Robinson's tale "The Unhaunted House," a writer and his superstitious wife go to great lengths to rent a house that contains no ghosts whatsoever. Once they move in, however, the writer finds himself unable to write:

> He explained what "unhaunted" pushed to its ultimate conclusion meant. It meant a total absence of association, it meant something vital was lacking, it meant that something had died out of everything in the house. There was nothing there that could not be seen with the eye and touched with the hand. . . . In that house you experienced nothing good or bad, you felt nothing, could imagine nothing.[16]

Like Woolf, Robinson posits haunting as a necessary condition of living, and especially of living as a writer: a world without ghosts would be a world without memories, associations, imagination. Woolf differs significantly from Robinson, to be sure, in that she refused to traffic with real (as opposed to merely metaphorical) spirits. Yet her novels and short stories bear everywhere the mark of spiritualist speculation. Woolf's ghosts, like Henry James's, are "ghosts of the mind," but they are not merely mental artefacts. Whereas James's stories question the reality of ghosts, Woolf's expose the inherent ghostliness of reality.

Despite her apparent aversion to spiritualist practice, Woolf sometimes described herself in mediumistic terms: "I think writing, my writing, is a species of mediumship. I become the person."[17] Other modernist writers, similarly, have granted metaphorical approbation to spirit mediums even while abjuring spiritualism itself. Surrealist André Breton, for instance, took part in 1922 in so-called seances with his friends but refused to countenance the possibility of communicating with the dead: "It goes without saying that at no time, from the day we first consented to [undertake] these experiments, did we adopt a spiritualist point of view. As far as I'm concerned, I formally refuse to admit that a communication of that sort can exist between the living and the dead."[18] Yet Breton recognized and even highlighted similarities between surrealist writers' "automatisme psychique" and the spiritualist phenomenon of automatic writing: "We flatly denied the tenets of spiritualism (no possible communication between the living and the dead)," he later explained, "all the while maintaining a keen interest in some of the phenomena it had helped bring to light."[19] In a sympathetic 1925 paean to female fortune-tellers, he goes so far as to explicitly liken surrealists to spirit mediums, liberators of human consciousness whom a craven public desires "to submit to the observations of doctors, 'scholars,' and other illiterates."[20] Years later, in 1952, he would found a newsletter titled *Médium: Informations surrealistes.*[21]

The Italian Futurists, like Breton and the surrealists, frequently drew upon mediumistic metaphors without necessarily believing in spirit survival. Filippo Marinetti's early Futurist manifestoes, notes Lawrence Rainey, are informed by "a complex of critical metaphors . . . that involves mediums and automatic writing, analogies between the body and language, and . . . a metaphorics of shock, trauma and pathology—a complex that Marinetti mobilizes in the service of an anxious engagement with questions about identity and authority, the self and technology, and the possibilities of representation under the regime of modernity." In a 1910 essay titled "Multiplied Man and the Reign of the Machine," for example, Marinetti compares human transformations occasioned through technological violence with "the phenomena of externalized will that continually reveal themselves at spiritualist seances"— that is, the ectoplasmic heads and hands produced by materialization mediums. Modern man, he promises, will soon "externalize his will and make it into a huge invisible arm . . . he will be endowed with surprising organs"—what Rainey calls "the somatic counterpart of automatic writing." Rainey goes on to contend that Italian Fascist iconography, like Italian Futurist imagery, is indebted to mediumistic prototypes:

Some critics have urged us to see the "doubled" heads and ectoplasmic limbs of spiritualist mediums as part of a protofeminist language of the body, a somatic expression of all that has been repressed by patriarchal culture, a mirror image of libidinal desire. Yet most of us viewing the ubiquitous multiplication of Mussolini's head [on postcards from the 1920s and 1930s] will doubtless think of the head's traditional association with reason and control, and especially here, with notions of seeing and surveillance, notions most typically linked with patriarchal ego or superego. Perhaps we err in supposing that we must choose one view over the other.

Fascism, Futurism, and popular spiritualism, Rainey argues, share in "a paradox central to modernity itself": although all three movements promise "to enhance (in part through technology) individual autonomy . . . that promise has inexorably given way to a disturbing practice of collective conformity and increasing enthrallment."[22]

Yet spiritualism also enacts an inverted and potentially liberating paradox, equally "central to modernism itself": spirit mediums' supposed thralldom to the voices of the dead is precisely what enables their individual autonomy, cultural authority, and literary productivity. Thus, for modernist writers such as Rainer Maria Rilke, mediumship provided a model for creative power achieved through apparent passivity. In 1912, at the urging of his close friend and patron the Princess Marie von Thurn und Taxis, Rilke took part in a series of seances with the princess's son, Pascha, who used a planchette, a device designed to aid in automatic writing, to answer the poet's concealed written questions. (The princess, although a corresponding member of the London Society for Psychical Research, declared herself to be "absolutely not a medium" and merely observed the proceedings.)[23] Rilke was excited and intrigued by the resulting communications, and particularly by his written conversation with the spirit of someone identified only as *die Unbekannte*, "the unknown woman," who successfully convinced him to undertake a long-contemplated journey to Spain. Several months later he wrote to ask the princess where he could acquire a planchette of his own: "I am drawn to the unknown," he confessed.[24] Soon thereafter he reported that his attempts to contact the spirit world had been unsuccessful: "Apparently the Spirits wanted nothing to do with me." An encounter with a medium in Munich left him, like Mann in similar circumstances a decade later, "disgusted" (*dégouté*), and he thereafter abandoned spiritualist pursuits for good.[25] Yet nearly ten years after his first experiments with the planchette, during another period of creative fallowness, he published a group of poems that he claimed had been "dictated" to him by the ghostly figure of a man in eighteenth-century dress, "Count C. W.": "He composes many poems that I myself would never have approved of."[26]

Toward the end of his life, Rilke would pronounce himself, like the Princess Marie, "completely useless as a medium." But, he added, "I do not doubt for an instant that, in my own way, I hold myself open to those often homeless powers, never ceasing to enjoy or to suffer their companionship."[27] Rilke's poetry everywhere bears witness to his mediumistic role as one of the twentieth century's preeminent poets of death. From his earliest volumes of poetry (such as *The Book of Hours*, which includes a section titled "The Book of Poverty and Death") to his later work (such as *Sonnets to Orpheus*, with its paean to dead Eurydice), Rilke dwells continually on the positive aspects of death, speaking of, for, and to the dead. At times, as in "Orpheus. Eurydice. Hermes" (1904) or "Alcestis" (1907), he seems half in love with death, portraying Eurydice and Alcestis as young women who achieve in death and passivity a completeness and fulfillment denied to their husbands, who remain wistfully behind in the world of the living. Later, in *Sonnets to Orpheus*, he redeems the death of Wera Oukama Knoop, the young family friend to whom the poems are dedicated, by portraying her as Eurydice, a beautiful dancer who turns her lover's "motion and gaze" toward death, "the perfect celebration." Orpheus, meanwhile, is exhorted in the *Sonnets* to enact Rilke's own privileged ability to pass back and forth between worlds, to dwell in a state of continual transformation:

> Be ahead of all parting, as though it were behind
>   you, like the winter that has just gone by.
> For among winters there is one so endlessly winter
>   that only by overwintering will your heart survive.
>
> Be forever dead in Eurydice—, more singing, ascend,
>   more praising, ascend back to the pure relation.
> Here, amidst vanishing ones, in the realm of decline,
>   be a ringing glass that shattered even as it rang.[28]

Anticipating death even before it occurs, praising life even after death, the Orphic poet is figured as a modernist hero, a "ringing glass that shattered even as it rang": fragmented yet still singing, materialized most memorably at the moment of his dissolution, dwelling forever in fruitful paradox.

Elsewhere in his poetry, to be sure, Rilke proves more ambivalent about the ability of the dead to communicate with the living. His moving 1909 "Requiem: For a Friend" addresses the ghost of Paula Modersohn-Becker, a close friend and talented painter who had died at the age of thirty-one from complications following childbirth:

> I have my dead, and I let them go
> and was amazed to see them so confident,
> so swiftly at home in being dead, so just,
> so unlike their reputation. Only you, you
> return; you brush past me, you haunt, you want
> to knock into something so it will sound of you
> and betray your presence.[29]

Although the poem claims to follow the actions of Paula Modersohn-Becker's errant spirit, these opening lines make clear that its real subject is Rilke's own desire to hear from her directly, to receive some material proof of spirit survival from this young woman who died before her time. "Tell me, should I travel?" he asks her: "Did you leave/some Thing behind that labors after you/and wants to find you?" Several years later, when the "Unknown Woman" of his Duino seances commanded him to go to Spain, Rilke would obey with alacrity, perhaps because his friend's death had resulted in no similar imperative, no opportunity to trace her ephemeral human existence.

Despite his professed yearning to communicate with her, Rilke ends "Requiem" by begging Modersohn-Becker not to return: "Stay dead with the dead. The dead have much to do." But then, practically in the same breath, he importunes her to remain forever alive inside him: "Help me . . . within me." Rilke's contradictory plea is typical of literary modernists' stance toward spirit communication and spirit survival. Real ghosts—the kinds who knock into furniture, who are clearly external and Other—are frequently urged, if their existence is acknowledged at all, to leave the living alone and proceed grandly toward Lawrence's "great goal of oblivion." Internalized or metaphorical ghosts, on the other hand—what Woolf calls "ghosts of the mind," what Lawrence dubs "the demon"—are embraced as necessary manifestations of the creative imagination. Even Rilke, who styles himself in *Sonnets to Orpheus* as a death-defying Orpheus figure, wanted to keep certain ghosts in their place: "Be forever dead in Eurydice"; "Stay dead with the dead."

In the case of Thomas Mann, real-life mediumistic experiences would be transposed into literary metaphor, taking on in their fictional setting a symbolic value that the author stopped short of granting them in real life. The two seance scenes that Mann describes in *The Magic Mountain* echo in numerous details the autobiographical essay about the Munich seance in which the author had recently taken part: the jovial yet jumpy comportment of the participants; the telekinetic displacement of various objects; the physical restraint of the medium's hands and legs (by Mann in real life, by Hans Castorp in the novel); the intense moaning and writhing of the medium, vividly depicted in both texts as a grotesque parody of parturition. Even the reactions of the two protagonists are nearly identical: Mann describes himself as feeling "queasy," seized by "nausea," like "a mild form of seasickness" ("Experience," 247, 249); Castorp experiences "a slightly qualmish feeling, a mild seasickness."[30] Later, when Castorp is warned by Settembrini—a character who serves as "a mouthpiece" for Mann himself (*Magic Mountain*, 724)—to "hold in abhorrence these luxations of the brain, these miasmas of the spirit" (667), his friend's words echo almost exactly Mann's own in the earlier essay: "I abhor luxations of the brain, I abhor morasses of the spirit" ("Experience," 256). Yet despite such apparent similarities, Mann made a number of significant changes when he fictionalized the real-life Munich seance, and in these changes we find some telling clues as to why he was drawn to spiritualism in the first place. Far from merely aestheticizing spiritualism—transforming a "preposterous" phenomenon into an acceptable literary subject—Mann uses the seance scenes in *The Magic Mountain* to address complex representational issues involving the borderline between rational and irrational thought, the nature and sources of poetic inspiration, and the relationship between sexual and artistic experience.

In his essay on the occult, Mann distances himself from popular spiritualism, which he dismisses as a credulous, irrational "Sunday afternoon diversion for the servants' hall":

For spiritualism—the belief in spirits, ghosts, *revenants*, spook intelligences with whom one gets into touch by interrogating a table and getting the most utter banalities by way of reply—spiritualism is in fact a kind of backstairs metaphysics, a blind credulity which is on the one hand not up to the conception of idealistic speculation, and on the other hand quite incapable of metaphysical orgies of emotion. ("Experience," 221)

In keeping with his stated antispiritualist bias, Mann goes on to describe his "occult" experience with Willy S. not as an attempt at spirit communication but as a "dream-performance," a bravura display of psychic and tenekinetic powers. In *The Magic Mountain*, in contrast, the seance scenes explicitly involve otherworldly communication: the "departed and etherealized spirit" of a young man named Holger speaks through the medium (*Magic Mountain*, 653), who later moves from trance speaking to materialization when an image of Castorp's dead cousin appears in the room. The "miasmas of the spirit" to which Settembrini refers in *The Magic Mountain* are therefore rather different from the "morasses of the spirit" that Mann invokes in his earlier essay. In this novel about people at a sanatorium dying of tuberculosis, the possibility of spirit survival becomes a crucially important issue, and the dangerous "luxations" of Castorp's brain specifically involve his questioning of the rationalist assumption that there can be no life after death. Thus spiritualist irrationality, which Mann glibly dismisses in his seance account, becomes in *The Magic Mountain* a central and paradigmatic theme.

Another key difference between the essay and the novel involves the latter's depiction of automatic writing as an explicitly literary act. Whereas Mann's real-life medium, Willy S., produced "a perfectly nonsensical jumble of large and small letters" on his typewriter ("presumably it would have been different if Willy himself knew how to type," Mann speculates ["Experience," 253]), *The Magic Mountain*'s Holger is an erudite spirit who poeticizes for hours via an upturned wine glass that points to letters on a Ouija board:

And what a surprising poem it was, this ventriloquistic effort, delivered to the admiration of the circle—stuff of magic, and shoreless as the sea of which it largely dealt. Sea-wrack in heaps and bands along the narrow strand of the broad-flung bay; an islanded coast, girt by steep, cliffy dunes. Ah, see the dim green distance faint and die into eternity, while beneath broad veils of mist in dull carmine and milky radiance the summer sun delays to sink! No word can utter how and when the watery mirror turned from silver into untold changeful color-play, to bright or pale, to spreading, opaline, and moonstone gleams—or how, mysteriously as it came, the voiceless magic died away. (*Magic Mountain*, 663)

The scene hovers exquisitely between satire and high seriousness, echoing as it does Hans Castorp's own hallucinatory vision several chapters earlier, as he wandered about lost in an alpine snowstorm, of an idyllic southern seascape inhabited by charming young maidens and toothsome lads (including a "lovely boy" [491] who bears an unmistakable resemblance to Tadzio, the Venetian youth ogled by Gustave Aschenbach throughout Mann's *Death in Venice*). By portraying Holger specifically as a poet, Mann points to the inherent kinship between mediumistic experience and literary production. At the same time, by drawing attention to his own tendency to lapse from time to time into Holger's mawkishly sentimental style, he uses the spiritualist setting to issue a bracing and hilarious self-parody.

Mann's fictional transposition of the seance scene's sexual undercurrents offers, by contrast, a more vexed and secretive self-critique. The real-life dentist of Mann's essay, who speaks with the voice of a spirit control named Minna, changes gender in the fictional realm of *The Magic Mountain*, where the medium is a blithe Danish girl named Ellen Brand who speaks with the voice of a male spirit, Holger. In his account of the Munich seance, Mann recalls being asked first to observe Willy making his toilet and then to restrain the medium's hands as Willy entered the thrashing trance state that Mann variously calls an "act of parturition," a "procreative labour," and a "masculine lying-in" ("Experience," 239). In the *Magic Mountain*, the scene is rendered even more explicitly sexual and procreative: Castorp enters the seance room with the same "peculiar and unforgettable mixture of feelings" that he had once felt upon visiting a brothel; as he holds the medium's hands and clasps her knees between his own, he is painfully conscious that she is wearing "a nightgownlike garment of white *crêpe*" and "little else"; and when she begins the writhing and groaning that signal the start of her "scandalous lying-in," he finds himself cast as the "husband" of the laboring "little mother," assisting in the "birth" of a materialized spirit who turns out, in a bizarre twist on this Freudian primal scene, to be his own cousin (*Magic Mountain*, 672–78).

Mann invokes here a series of familiar, even stereotypical, literary tropes: creativity springs from mysterious and sometimes frightening sources; intercourse with the unknown involves both titillation and shame; male and female elements must act together to produce a new life, a new work. In heterosexualizing an originally homoerotic scene, however, Mann effaces some of more intriguing sexual undertones of the actual seance that served as *The Magic Mountain*'s prototype. Mann's autobiographical essay betrays a scopophilic fascination not only with Willy's body but also with his mind, as Mann tries to fathom the young medium's emotions at the moment of entering into a trance:

> Wait. Let me think. Let me withdraw within myself and try to divine where may be the point, when the magical moment, in which a dream-picture objectivates itself and becomes a spatial reality, before the eyes of other people. Nausea. Clearly this point does not lie within the plane of our consciousness, or of the laws of knowledge as we know them. If anywhere, it is located in that state in which I see this lad now before me, and which is certainly a gate—whither? Behind the house, behind the world? ("Experience," 249)

The author's own thoughts mingle promiscuously here with the imagined thoughts of Willy, who seems to hold open a "gate" to a mysterious, forbidden, possibly naughty place, "behind the house, behind the world," where the laws of knowledge, and perhaps other kinds of laws as well, no longer hold sway. Willy's "masculine lying-in" thus points to a new, culturally subversive kind of procreative labor, as opposed to Ellen's merely conventional role as "little mother."

By the same token, Willy's co-identity with Minna proves to be more subversively gender-bending than is Ellen's relatively conventional channeling of Holger. Minna's materialized head, Mann reports wistfully, has been known to appear "above the shoulder of the sleeping Willy: the head of a charming girl, Slavic in type, with lively black eyes" (an uncanny precursor, at least in appearance, of *The Magic Mountain*'s seductive Madame Chauchat ["Experience," 260–61]). Lawrence Rainey notes that a materialized or "doubled" head can serve as "a somatic expression of all that has been repressed by patriarchal culture," even while it invokes "notions of seeing and surveillance . . . most typically linked with patriarchal ego or superego."[31] Such a paradox is certainly in operation here, but with several additional twists: the male Willy (was Mann aware of the English slang word meaning "penis"?), controlled by the female Minna (whose seemingly feminine name is in fact nearly an anagram of Mann's own, the German word for "man"), enters a feminized procreative state that is at the same time implicitly homoeroticized by Mann, whose attraction to Willy (an impulse heartily "repressed by patriarchal culture") bubbles just beneath the surface of his prose even as he takes on what Rainey calls the "typically . . . patriarchal" role of seer, surveyor, and interpreter.

In denouncing his own contradictory feelings about the Munich seance as "luxations of the brain" and "morasses of the spirit" ("Experience," 256), Mann apparently escapes, at least temporarily, from the "subterraneous region" of Willy's mediumship back to the high plane of reason. But his subsequent incorporation of so many crucial seance details into *The Magic Mountain* suggests an abiding attraction to, even an aesthetic affinity for, that slippery spiritualist realm where sexual identity and traditional modes of literary production are subverted, even inverted. In the paradoxes of real-life mediumship, Mann discovered compelling prototypes for his own imaginative productions. Indeed, the "low haunts" of popular spiritualism may well have provided him with more complex and troubling self-insights than he was willing, in the end, to admit.

DOING ELIOT IN DIFFERENT VOICES

Even more so than Mann, T. S. Eliot provides a prototype for the influential modernist writer whose work is infused with spiritualist elements that he himself repudiated. Biographer Peter Ackroyd reports (albeit without details or documentation) that Eliot attended seances in 1920 presided over by P. D. Ouspensky, and scholars such as Leon Surette and Timothy Materer have charted his occultist sympathies.[32] By and large, however, Eliot's published writings indicate that he found "convers[ing] with spirits" to be both silly and vulgar, just one among the many disreputable cultural practices—from astrology, palmistry, and haruspication to that most scurrilous speculative pastime of them all, psychoanalysis—that he excoriates in "The Dry Salvages" (1941) as the illusionary opiates of a desperate wartime populace. In that poem Eliot notes that mankind's fascination with "the womb, or tomb, or dreams" tends to become especially widespread whenever "there is distress of nations and perplexity": in periods, that is, of severe social upheaval, and especially in times of war.[33] His own apparent animus toward spiritualism followed a similar pattern, finding its most vivid expression in poems written just after the Great War ("Gerontion" and *The Waste Land*) and again during the Second World War (*Four Quartets*). These works, however, are products less of pure revulsion than of an ambivalent attraction, a recognition of the ways in which the tropes of popular spiritualism mirror and anticipate the central concerns of literary modernism.

In *After Strange Gods* (1934), Eliot assails the spiritualist cosmogony outlined by Yeats in *A Vision*:

> Mr. Yeats's "supernatural world" was the wrong supernatural world. It was not a world of real Good and Evil, of holiness and sin, but a highly sophisticated lower mythology summoned, like a physician, to supply the fading pulse of poetry with some transient stimulant so that the dying patient may utter his last words. In its extreme self-consciousness it approaches the mythology of D. H. Lawrence on its more decadent side.[34]

Yet although he rails here with High Church dudgeon against Yeats's "lower mythology," Eliot's own critical discourse is laced, like his poetry, with images drawn from popular spiritualism: otherworldly communication, mediumship, spirit survival. In his 1917 essay "Tradition and the Individual Talent," for instance, he confers upon the great authors of the past the status of remonstrative ghosts—"Not only the best, but the most individual parts of [a poet's] work may be those in which the dead poets, his ancestors, assert their immortality most vigorously"—and he urges the successful artist to undertake "a continual self-sacrifice, a continual extinction of personality" akin to that of a spirit medium: "The mind of the mature poet differs from that of the immature one not precisely in any valuation of 'personality,' . . . but rather by being a more finely perfected medium in which special, or very varied, feelings are at liberty to enter into new combinations." In *The Use of Poetry, and the Use of Criticism* (1933), he likens poetic production to "automatic writing," albeit of a kind distinct from the externally induced spiritualist variety: "In contrast to the claims sometimes made for the latter, the material has obviously been incubating within the poet, and cannot be suspected of being a present from a friendly or impertinent demon." And in *The Three Voices of Poetry* (1953), embracing the "friendly or impertinent demon" thesis that he had rejected two decades earlier, he describes poetic inspiration as a species of unwilled possession: "[The poet] is haunted by a demon, a demon against which he feels powerless, because in its first manifestation it has no face, no name, nothing; and the words, the poem he makes, are a kind of form of exorcism of that demon."[35] Eliot's vocabulary here recalls Lawrence's famous declaration that all great poetry is the work of an internal "demon" (or, in an earlier draft of the same 1928 essay, a "ghost" or "apparition").[36] Thus, despite his attack in *After Strange Gods* on the "decadent" spiritual heterodoxy of Yeats and Lawrence, Eliot resembles both rival poets in his formulation of poetic creativity as a haunting force at once internal and external to his own self, "a demon against which he feels powerless," a voice that speaks as though unwilled through the mediumistic poet's mouth.

Eliot's poetry, likewise, is steeped in a metaphorics of ghostly possession, even and sometimes especially when the poet seems most eager to disparage spiritualist pursuits. In "Gerontion" (1920), the aging narrator's refusal to conjure atavistic spirits—he claims to have "no ghosts" of his own and to practice no "concitation/Of the backward devils"—is implicitly contrasted with the mediumistic activities of "Madame de Tornquist," a woman whose professional disreputability is communicated, just in case we missed Eliot's other contextual clues, via her name, situation, and gestures: the twists and turns of "Tornquist," the "dark room" in which she plies her trade, her shifty action of "shifting the candles." Eliot's unflattering description of Madame de Tornquist anticipates his characterization of History, just one stanza later, as both a labyrinthine physical space and a devious woman: "History has many cunning passages, contrived corridors/And issues, deceives with whispering ambitions,/Guides us by vanities" (*Complete Poems*, 22). Not only do historical situations create the conditions in which fortune telling and mediumship thrive, Eliot suggests here, but history itself is like a spirit medium, whispering only the words that her gullible victims long to hear.

Even more so than "Gerontion," *The Waste Land* (1922) is filled with imagery that reflects Eliot's considerable ambivalence toward ghosts, mediumship, and spirit survival. When Ezra Pound complained that the poem's original epigraph, excerpted from Joseph Conrad's *Heart of Darkness*, was not "weighty enough to stand the citation,"[37] Eliot replaced Kurtz's dying words ("The horror! the horror!") with a passage about something even more horrifying than death itself: the anguished immortality of Petronius's caged Sibyl, granted eternal life but not eternal youth. The title of part 1, "The Burial of the Dead," evokes images of physical repose and emotional closure, yet the entire section turns out, like the epigraph, to challenge spiritualism's comforting promise of easy intercourse with the spirit world. The poem's opening lines—"April is the cruellest month, breeding/Lilacs out of the dead land, mixing/Memory and desire" (*Waste Land*, 135)—portray physical and spiritual resurrection as an excruciatingly painful process, one that reaches its logical conclusion not in cheerful images of springtime blossoms but rather in the emotional and epistemological crisis induced by the sight of a bouquet of hyacinths:

> Yet when we came back, late, from the Hyacinth garden,
> Your arms full, and your hair wet, I could not
> Speak, and my eyes failed, I was neither
> Living nor dead, and I knew nothing.
>
> (136)

The macabre ending of "The Burial of the Dead" puts a final stamp of irony on the section's title: far from resting in peace, we discover, the dead are germinating like malignant tumors in gardens all over London: "That corpse you planted last year in your garden,/Has it begun to sprout?" (136).

Like Baudelaire's "Fourmillante cité, cité pleine de rêves,/Où le spectre en plein jour raccroche le passant" (*Waste Land*, 147),[38] Eliot's "Unreal City" is haunted in the worst kind of way: by ghosts who do not confine their activities to nighttime graveyards, who are not even clearly dead. Instead, like the caged Sibyl or the hyacinth girl, they are suspended in a state of discomfiting betweenness, "neither/Living nor dead," impossible to classify and therefore impossible to exorcise. Even when, in part 5 ("What the Thunder Said"), Eliot shifts the setting of his poem from the teeming city to the open countryside—he mentions as intertexts both Paul's journey to Emmaus and Shackleton's Antarctic expeditions (147)—specters continue to accost the living "en plein jour," in full daylight, calling into question the perceptions and sanity of those to whom they appear. These are ghosts both verbal and visual, manifested sometimes as disembodied voices ("voices singing out of empty cisterns and exhausted wells" [145]) and sometimes, more eerily still, as voiceless bodies:

> Who is the third who walks always beside you?
> When I count, there are only you and I together
> But when I look ahead up the white road
> There is always another one walking beside you
> Gliding wrapt in a brown mantle, hooded
> I do not know whether a man or a woman.
>
> (144)

Like so many other figures in this poem where the dead often walk as though alive and the living often walk as though dead, the phantasm described here defies traditional oppositional hierarchies: is it male or female? alive or dead? a mirage or an authentic vision?

The hooded figure's ontological instability is signaled by the indeterminacy of its gender: "I do not know whether a man or a woman." Here and elsewhere throughout *The Waste Land*, Eliot uses tropes of gender ambiguity to explore the relationship between sexual and spiritual knowledge, between traditional gender roles and prophetic revelation, between the seemingly passive stance of the spirit medium and the transgressive, gender-bending qualities of her language. The poem's original title ("He Do the Police in Different Voices") bears witness to Eliot's own vexed and contradictory desire to become a kind of spirit medium himself, at once authoritative and absent, embodied and transcendent, ironic and invisible, speaking with the "different voices" of both men and women. Yet Eliot was clearly well aware of the pitfalls of possession, particularly for male mediums. A woman possessed by a male spirit has much to gain and little to lose from the gendered economy of mediumship, for she affirms normative ideals of femininity even while she dons a cloak of male cultural authority. A male medium who speaks for a female spirit, in contrast, risks a kind of double emasculation, a feminization both of posture and of voice. Thus, even while mediumistic discourse offered Eliot a liberatory model of language loosed from the strictures of literary and social convention, it was to remain for him a source of anxiety as well as emulation. Straining against the limits of the traditional lyric, holding his poem open to a range of voices and cultural registers, he proved loath in the end to renounce subjectivity entirely: to abandon, that is, his stable status as the author of his own text.

Eliot's ambivalence regarding his own mediumistic role plays itself out in *The Waste Land*'s many figures of failed or debased prophecy, who typically owe their dual gift and burden of inspired speech not to divine favor so much as to sexual violation. The caged Sibyl of the epigraph, according to classical tradition, derived her oracular powers from her physical possession by Apollo;[39] the fact that she is now old and withered, presumably too ancient for sexual congress, only drives home the point that successful prophecy demands a quasi-sexual openness to invasion. Philomela, the nightingale of part 2, was raped, brutalized, and silenced by her brother-in-law Tereus;[40] although the loss of her tongue enables, by Ovid's compensatory logic, her eventual metamorphosis into a bird, her "inviolable voice" (*Waste Land*, 137) has been purchased at a terrible sexual price. As for Lil the barfly—toothless and haggard at the age of thirty-one, saddled with five children, still recovering from a botched abortion—she earns no prophetic recompense whatsoever for her sexual servitude to a demanding yet absent husband; only the barman's background cry of "HURRY UP PLEASE IT'S TIME" invites us to associate her physical and spiritual decrepitude with the apocalyptic prophecy of the passage in part 2 in which she appears (138–39). All three women, then, exemplify Eliot's conflation of prophetic speech with physical infirmity, sexual violation, and a female subject position.

Two additional figures in the poem offer a more complex and nuanced commentary on the sexual shadings of visionary discourse. But they, too, ultimately confirm Eliot's apparent belief that otherworldly insight is linked to sexual deviancy. Both Tiresias and Madame Sosostris are female or feminized figures: Tiresias lived for seven years as a woman;[41] Madame Sosostris evokes such other mediumistic madames as H. P. Blavatsky and Eliot's own Madame de Tornquist, a connection that would have been made even more explicit had the poet followed his original intention of publishing "Gerontion" as a prelude to *The Waste Land* (127). Both characters suffer from physical infirmities that ironically undercut their claims to visionary power: Tiresias is blind, an "old man with wrinkled dugs" (141); Madame Sosostris has "a bad cold"

(136). All the same, both prove chillingly accurate in their visions of the future: Tiresias has "foretold" and "foresuffered" the sexual violation of the bored typist by the "young man carbuncular"(141); Madame Sosostris correctly predicts the "death by water" of Phoebus the Phoenician (148). Finally and most importantly, both characters apparently owe their visionary powers to their dual sexual identity, or at least to a kind of serial androgyny: "the two sexes meet" in Tiresias (148), whereas Madame Sosostris has, according to Grover Smith, "a masculine name" (Sesostris was an Egyptian king in the twelfth dynasty)[42] and may well have been named for a character in Aldous Huxley's 1921 novel *Crome Yellow*—"Sesotris, the Sorceress of Ecbatana"—who turns out to be a male fortune-teller disguised as a woman.[43] (An additional hint of Madame Sosostris's dual male/female identity can be found in Eliot's original typescript for *The Waste Land*, where s/he is initially described as a "famous clairvoyant" but later becomes, with the handwritten addition of the letter "e," a female "clairvoyante" instead [6–7]). In fact, although Eliot's endnotes name Tiresias as "the most important personage in the poem" (148), it is Madame Sosostris whose role in *The Waste Land* most closely resembles Eliot's own: both can be read, figuratively at least, as mediumistic men in drag, employing women's speech to communicate their most painful truths.

Eliot's appropriation of female voices in *The Waste Land* depended heavily on the inspiration and tutelage of the real women in his life, as when he modeled the exchange between Lil and her girlfriend in "The Fire Sermon"—originally titled "In the Cage," a designation that links Lil's debased prophecy to the more exalted pronouncements of the epigraph's ancient Sibyl—after a conversation recounted by his maid (*Waste Land*, 127). Eliot's friend Pound, however, was evidently uncomfortable with such convincing female ventriloquism. Although Pound's description of himself as *The Waste Land*'s "midwife" or "sage homme" implies that he played a feminine, nurturing role in performing the "caesarean Operation" that brought the poem into being, his main editorial principle (as the surgical metaphor hints) was one of excision, particularly where Eliot's most troubling female voices were concerned.[44] For instance, although Pound marked several passages spoken by male narrators with the enthusiastic adjective "ECHT," meaning "authentic" or "genuine" (41, 47), he scrawled next to two sections apparently spoken by a woman the pejorative comments "photo." and "photography," meaning, as he later explained, "too realistic a reproduction of an actual conversation" (126). Both passages, which occur shortly before the Lil dialogue in "The Fire Sermon," have been identified by critics with the real-life voice of Eliot's troubled wife Vivien,[45] who suffered from what Eliot described as "nerves, complicated by physical ailments, and induced largely by the most acute neuralgia" (xi) and was eventually committed by her husband to a mental institution: " 'What are you thinking of? What thinking? . . . What?/I never know what you are thinking. Think.' / . . . / 'Are you alive, or not? Is there nothing in your head?' " (11, 13). Significantly, although he acquiesced to the vast majority of Pound's editorial suggestions, Eliot opted to retain these two passages, which offer not the sustained meditative style favored by Pound but rather the fragmented, syntactically incoherent speech of the seance room and the asylum.

In addition to urging Eliot to delete some of his most "photographic" representations of real women, Pound also cut a number of passages that might have lent a more explicitly prophetic resonance to *The Waste Land* in general and to the poem's female voices in particular. In the Madame Sosostris section, he crossed out two parenthetical lines that underscore the poem's visionary subtext: "Those are pearls that were his eyes," from Ariel's song in Shakespeare's *Tempest*, and "I John saw these things, and heard them," from the New Testament book of Revelation (*Waste Land*, 9). Eliot reinstated the former passage, which lends an optimistic, transformative quality to Madame Sosostris's grim prediction of "death by water," but bowed to Pound's wishes in deleting the latter, which would have added further prophetic credence to the fortune-teller's pronouncements even while offering yet another hint of her secret male identity. Later, in a section of "The Fire Sermon" originally sandwiched between two fragmentary accounts by Philomela of her rape by Tereus, Pound crossed out another echo of Revelation, "I have seen and see," and deleted the second part of Philomela's song, thereby diluting Philomela's prophetic impact as well as the visionary power of the passage originally framed by her words (31, 43). Pound's expurgation of visionary certainties and revelatory statements when they occur in or around the speech of female characters—first Madame Sosostris, then Philomela—can be compared with his marginal comments about Tiresias, who earns an approving "Echt" when he speaks with prophetic confidence ("I Tiresias have foresuffered all") but whose more tentative diction elsewhere ("perhaps," "may") draws impatient outbursts from the irascible editor on two separate occasions: "Perhaps be *damned*"(45); "make up yr. mind you Tiresias if you know know damn well or else you dont" (47). Whereas Eliot worked hard to weave sexual ambiguity into the texture of *The Waste Land*, Pound sought to reestablish normative gender roles for the poem's characters and voices.

By persistently locating spiritual insights in bodies that are infirm, incomplete, violated, or sexually other, Eliot points out the explicitly sexual dangers of spirit mediumship. At the same time, however, *The Waste Land* validates the methods and forms, perhaps even the abject corporeality, of mediumistic discourse. Like any ghostwriting medium, Eliot seeks to enhance his own literary and cultural authority when he summons the great authors of the past (Dante, Baudelaire, Shakespeare) to speak through him. Their jumbled and fragmentary voices are frequently interrupted, to be sure, by other, less exalted forms of discourse: music hall ditties, pub conversations, the plaints of spirits without a name. But even the disruptions and static—like the relentless advertising jingles and other "white noise" so effectively satirized in Don DeLillo's eponymous paean to postmodern culture—confer rather than inhibit meaning. For Eliot in *The Waste Land,* just as for the spirit mediums he consciously or unconsciously imitates, the barriers to transmitting literary history are as crucial as the messages themselves; without them, the poet's own mediumistic work would be rendered unnecessary.

After his 1928 religious conversion, Eliot's appropriations of spiritualist tropes would become both less frequent and arguably less sympathetic. Images and metaphors drawn from popular spiritualism—specters, revenants—do find their way into his later poetry and plays; the garden scene in "Burnt Norton," for instance, has been said by critics to echo both Rudyard Kipling's 1902 short story "They" (about a garden haunted by the voices of ghostly children) and *An Adventure* by Charlotte Anne Moberly and Eleanor Jourdain, two Oxford scholars who claimed in 1911 to have seen the ghost of Marie Antoinette during a visit to Versailles.[46] But voices stridently different from his own—and especially female voices—are kept safely at bay throughout most of *Four Quartets.* Even the "familiar compound ghost/Both intimate and unidentifiable" whom the poet encounters in "Little Gidding" speaks in the cadences of high culture, grandly urging Eliot "to purify the dialect of the tribe" (*Complete Poems*, 140–42). Whether this enigmatic spirit represents

Dante, Swift, Yeats, Mallarmé (as various critics have suggested), or merely an earlier version of Eliot himself—the iconoclastic young poet whose "rhythmical grumbling" in *The Waste Land* no doubt haunted the staid Anglican for the rest of his life (*Waste Land*, 1)—he is clearly a figure of great literary repute, unambiguously male, who accosts the poet at night just as ghosts are supposed to do (rather than "en plein jour," like Baudelaire's disconcerting specter) and then courteously disappears at dawn.[47] Despite the ambiguities of his identity, then, this literary ghost ultimately confirms rather than troubles ontological certainties, validating Eliot's own status as an author worthy of being haunted by the great poets of the past.

CHAPTER FIVE

Modernist Hauntology

Now he is scattered among a hundred cities
And wholly given over to unfamiliar affections;
To find his happiness in another kind of wood
And be punished under a foreign code of conscience.
The words of a dead man
Are modified in the guts of the living.
                    W. H. Auden, "In Memory of W. B. Yeats"

[H. D.'s voice is a] voice from the past, a ghost in fact, still defining itself. She cut her name down to two letters a long time ago,
sixty years ago now; and her sense of herself became a few
glimpsed pictures, the quester on the shore, the supplicant, the
weaver of spells.
    Unlike most ghosts, she had the guts to keep coming back and
her hour may be here at last.
                    Hugh Kenner, reviewing H. D.'s *Hermetic Definition*

YEATS, MEDIUMS, AND THE DESOLATE PLACES

Modernist writers such as Lawrence, Woolf, Mann, and Eliot frequently employed spiritualist tropes in their writing but nonetheless
held themselves aloof from (or, in Mann's case, expressed deep reserva-
tions about) real-life spiritualist experience. Thus they were able to have
their proverbial cake and eat it too, drawing upon mediumistic
metaphors even while maintaining an ironic distance from spiritualism
itself. But what of those canonical modernists who—to borrow Auden's
and Kenner's shared alimentary metaphor in the epigraphs above—
were "gutsy" enough to give themselves over fully and unapologetically
to spiritualism's promise of otherworldly communication? In this chapter I argue that the spiritualist beliefs of W. B. Yeats and H. D.—two of literary modernism's most credulous spiritualist practitioners—not only

103

coexisted comfortably with but in many respects shaped their modernist poetics. Equally importantly, their modernist poetics shaped their spiritualism.

Yeats's lifelong fascination with spiritualism, mysticism, and the occult has, of course, long presented a particular challenge for his critics. Some have condemned his mystical involvement as atavistic, reactionary, and therefore politically dangerous. Others have praised his psychic experiments as good for his art if bad for his reputation.[1] But few if any commentators have noted the distinctly modernist tenor of Yeats's particular brand of spiritualism. Like Mann, Yeats sought in the netherworld of the seance room not easy enlightenment but a confirmation of his belief in the slipperiness of human consciousness, the precariousness of language, and the overwhelming complexity of modern life. Especially from 1911 onward, when he first began to experiment with spiritualism in earnest, he explored through his writings on spiritualism such prototypically modernist concerns as textual materialism, physical and psychic fragmentation, the ambiguities of gender identity, the generative nature of contradiction and paradox, the role of the unconscious in literary production, and the violent yet vital interchange between high art and popular culture.

Yeats's alliances and misalliances with organizations such as the Theosophical Society, the Brotherhood of the Rosy Cross, the Golden Dawn, and the Society for Psychical Research have been so thoroughly discussed by other scholars that I will not rehearse them here.[2] Instead, I focus specifically and exclusively on Yeats's engagements with popular spiritualism: his attempts to contact the "other world" via seances, automatic writing, and related means, and his writings on the subjects of mediumship, spirit communication, and spirit survival. Yeats's initial involvement with spiritualism during his student days in Dublin was as much a conscious act of filial rebellion as one of passive surrender: "It was only when I began to study psychical research and mystical philosophy that I broke away from my father's influence," he later confessed. (As William M. Murphy dryly notes, "It was fortunate that John Butler Yeats died three years before the publication of *A Vision*, for that book would certainly have killed him.")[3] Equally importantly, spiritualism offered Yeats apparently easy access to the unknown, a path to the creative inspiration he craved. At one memorable seance in the late 1880s, upon feeling himself seized by a power that seemingly came from outside himself, the young poet felt a thrill of great expectation: "Everybody began to say I was a medium, and that if I would not resist some wonderful thing would happen." But before long he was forced to acknowledge the dark side of mediumistic possession: "I was now struggling vainly with this force which compelled me to movements I had not willed, and my movements had become so violent that the table was broken."[4] His friend Katharine Tynan colorfully recalled the scene: "Willie Yeats was banging his head on the table as though he had a fit, muttering to himself. . . . He explained to me afterwards that the spirits were evil. To keep them off he had been saying the nearest approach to a prayer he could remember, which was the opening lines of *Paradise Lost*."[5]

Following this traumatic incident, Yeats stopped attending seances for a time, a decision reinforced by his affiliations with the Theosophical Society and the Order of the Golden Dawn, both of which discouraged spiritualism. ("Mediumship," wrote Helena Petrovna Blavatsky, "is the opposite of adeptship; the medium is the passive instrument of foreign influences, the adept actively controls himself and all inferior potencies.")[6] Years later, when he once again became involved in attempts to contact the spirit world, he did so only as an observer and conversant, preferring not to act as a medium himself. Nevertheless, spiritualist acquaintances such as Geraldine Cummins and Hester Dowden were fond of recounting the force of Yeats's psychic influence in helping or, more often, in hindering their own mediumship. Cummins recalls an afternoon when,

in a faltering manner, a communication was coming on the ouija-board. [Yeats] laid his hand lightly on Mrs. Dowden's shoulder in order, he believed, to reinforce her psychic power. It had a contrary effect. A few moments later her head went forward and she fell into an hypnotic sleep, much, as she told me afterwards, to her annoyance. It had spoiled the sitting, for it was a little while before she could be roused.[7]

On another occasion, Cummins reports, Yeats

used an exorcism for banishing a tiresome, lying spirit who was keeping out all other communicators. He paced to and fro drawing occult figures about the medium, muttering an incantation, banishing the spirit "for forty days." It was unfortunate that he named the number. Absent for forty days, the mischievous sprite turned up on the forty-first and continued for a time to plague Mrs. Dowden with irresponsible communications![8]

Although such anecdotes might well strike many scholars as silly, trivial, and even downright embarrassing, they echo several of the central themes of Yeats's own writings on spiritualism: the symbiotic relationship between spirit communication and imaginative literature (manifest in the *Paradise Lost* example); the role of language in mediating spiritual experience; and the inevitability of frustration and miscommunication in both spiritualist and literary practice. These themes are woven throughout Yeats's "Preliminary Examination of the Script of ER" (1913), his first and arguably most concerted attempt to articulate a theory (or, as he put it, a "philosophy") of otherworldly communication.[9] In 1909, probably at the urging of his friend W. T. Stead, Yeats had once again begun attending seances, after a hiatus of more than twenty years. A positive encounter with a medium during a 1911 visit to the United States encouraged him to immerse himself in the world of popular spiritualism, forming alliances both with the Society for Psychical Research (he became a member in 1913) and with non-SPR-approved mediums such as Etta Wriedt, an American somnambulist who had established herself in London under Stead's sponsorship.[10] In the spring of 1912, Yeats consulted Elizabeth Radcliffe, a young English medium with a gift for automatic writing, about a difficult personal dilemma; the advice of her spirit contacts saved him, he later wrote, from "a serious error in a crisis of life."[11] By 1913 he was so impressed by Radcliffe's automatic scripts that he decided to undertake a serious investigative report of the kind he was used to reading in the *Proceedings* of the SPR. To his skeptical father he wrote that he was "now elaborating a curious theory of spirit action which may I believe make philosophic study of mediums possible." And to Radcliffe herself he confessed his ambition to "lay the ghost of any possible form, however mystical, of the subconscious theory" of mediumistic communication.[12]

Yeats's "Preliminary Examination of the Script of ER" opens with a description of the automatic writings produced through Radcliffe's hand:

What I have contains script in English, Greek, Latin, Hebrew and of these—after English—Greek and Latin are most abundant, and besides these writings there are a few passages of German, Welsh, Italian and French, one passage in Provençal, one passage in Irish, a few words of Chinese, a Turko-Arabic word, and some Coptic letters, and some Egyptian hieroglyphics. The medium besides English knows only French, and enough Italian to ask her way. . . . It is noticeable that French is little used and Italian, I think, only twice. This suggests that these languages are left out deliberately as of less value as evidence than languages unknown to the medium.[13]

From the start, the essay's central concern is the spirits' use of language. What mattered to Yeats, as George Mills Harper and John S. Kelly note, "was not what was expressed but how it was expressed: the medium not the message" ("Preliminary Examination," 138). Yeats was clearly less intrigued by the linguistic prowess of Radcliffe's spirits than by their imperfections. For instance, he takes great pains to explain why, when they speak in foreign tongues, the spirits rely almost entirely on well-known quotations, occasionally committing orthographic or grammatical blunders of which no native speaker would be guilty. Having grown away from language during their long tenure in the spirit world, Yeats speculates, the communicating spirits must make use of whatever phrases they can find in the minds of those more recently arrived, "like robbers stealing the clothes of bathers" (169). That those "bathers" have in turn borrowed their mental clothing from sources such as Homeric epics, Provençal chansons, and grammar primers reinforces the power of literary language not only in the next world but in this one as well. Thus, much in the same way his spiritualist contemporaries claimed literary authority for themselves by populating heaven with libraries and dead poet societies, Yeats uses Radcliffe's accounts of literary borrowings in the other world to boost the stature of living poets like himself.

Whereas another investigator might well have attacked and ridiculed the "mass of fragments, of interrupted sentences, of unfinished thoughts" (161) that made up Radcliffe's scripts, Yeats apparently regarded their very incoherence as evidentiary. Fragmented language, he suggests, communicates more complex truths than ordinary human discourse. Under normal circumstances, "Our marginal thoughts are excluded because we communicate only by what we put into words." But when the "selective powers of the body" are removed—that is, when ideas are no longer subject to the strictures of speech and hearing—seemingly meaningless phrases and sometimes even the thoughts of nearby spirits get transmitted more or less unexpurgated through the medium's mind and hand (160). Yeats's description of the resulting linguistic mélange reads almost like a synopsis of Joyce's *Ulysses* or Eliot's *Waste Land*, foundational modernist texts as yet unwritten at that time:

> In the middle of one subject another will be interpolated; solemn sentences, in the midst of matter of fact statement, sometimes a meaningless sentence where all the rest is plain, such as "There are no lambs" and the allusion to radium on page—. The mood shifts, the surface seems to melt away and then another surface and another—a perpetual change of consciousness—allegory or vague religious sentences (as from some spirit who cannot come nearer to our life and thought than broken poetic reverie) interrupting some practical advice often so definite and simple that we seem talking merely to some particularly business-like and well-informed acquaintance. (161)

As early as 1901, Yeats had already begun to regard shifting consciousness and fragmented language as the ingredients of great poetry. In an essay on magic, which he defines as "the evocation of spirits," he lists three doctrines that form "the foundations of nearly all magical practices":

> (1) That the borders of our mind are ever shifting, and that many minds can flow into one another, as it were, and create or reveal a single mind, a single energy.
>
> (2) That the borders of our memories are as shifting, and that our memories are a part of one great memory, the memory of Nature herself.
>
> (3) That this great mind and great memory can be evoked by symbols.[14]

Although Yeats himself seldom wrote in the disjointed, parataxic modernist style he describes in his essay on Radcliffe, echoes of it surface in poems from the late 1910s and early 1920s, such as "Easter 1916," in which "polite meaningless words" uttered "among grey/Eighteenth-century houses" give way, suddenly and violently, to the "terrible beauty" of the Easter Rebellion.[15] Only political zealotry, the poem suggests, remains immune to the continual shifting of moods and melting of surfaces that characterize modern life. And only a poet, through the "evocation of symbols," can capture those shifting states in words.

Yeats never published the "Preliminary Examination of the Script of ER," although he did offer a detailed account of the Radcliffe experiments in a speech to the Dublin branch of the SPR on All Hallows' Eve, 1913. Harper and Kelly conjecture that, upon rereading the essay in 1914, he found it too tentative in its conclusions, too "thin in style and content," and too unsystematic in its methodology to stand up to scientific scrutiny ("Preliminary Examination," 138). Instead, the poet turned to writing "Swedenborg, Mediums, and the Desolate Places," a lyrical essay on spiritualist themes (written in 1914; published in 1920) that was meant to serve as the introduction to a collection of Irish folk tales assembled by Lady Gregory. Here, once again, although his ostensible subject is the universality of spirit communication and after-death experience, Yeats expounds a peculiarly modernist view of the spirit world, a realm marked by disconcerting physical metamorphoses, strange shifts of consciousness, and communicative frustrations that turn out to have enormous generative potential. He begins by noting the discrepancy between his exalted subject matter—dreams, death, the mysteries of eternal life—and the seemingly disreputable means by which he has achieved access to those mysteries: "I found much that was moving, when I had climbed to the top storey of some house in Soho or Holloway, and, having paid my shilling, awaited, among servant girls, the wisdom of some fat old medium."[16] Just as he would later defend his spiritualist pursuits by likening muses to "women who creep out at night and give themselves to unknown sailors and return to talk of Chinese porcelain," here he deliberately juxtaposes images of high and low culture, pointing out the interdependence of the two. Physical ascent ("when I had climbed to the top storey") parallels social descent ("among servant girls"); lofty emotional power ("much that was moving") emanates from insalubrious surroundings ("in Soho or Holloway"); visionary enlightenment ("wisdom") issues from deformed or decrepit bodies ("some fat old medium"). His sources, Yeats acknowledges, are lowly, but his intellectual aims are high: "Like Paracelsus who claimed to have collected his knowledge from midwife and hangman, I was discovering a philosophy" (22–23).

That philosophy, despite its pretensions to universality, turns out to have been based on a distinctively modernist belief that meaning resides not in a single unified principle but in discontinuity and fragmentation. With "Swedenborg, Mediums, and the Desolate Places," Yeats attempts to piece together seemingly disparate shards of knowledge—insights gleaned from sources as diverse as Paracelsus, Swedenborg, Irish folk tales, and Japanese Noh drama—to form a coherent understanding of the spirit world. That world, in turn, is marked by discontinuities and fragmentations of its own, slippages and splinterings of language and consciousness: the dead, Yeats writes, "have bodies as plastic as their minds that flow so readily into the mould of ours" ("Swedenborg," 35). Although such physical and mental fluidity might well seem a positive, even enviable, trait, it takes on freakish qualities elsewhere in the essay, when Yeats describes how the dead manifest themselves physically at seances:

> There will be few complete forms, for the dead are economical, and a head, or just enough of the body for recognition, may show itself above hanging folds of drapery that do not seem to cover solid limbs, or a hand or foot is lacking, or it may be that some *Revenant* has seized the half-made image of another, and a young girl's arm will be thrust from the withered body of an old man. . . . If an image speak it will seldom seem very able or alert, for they come for recognition only, and their minds are strained and fragmentary. (48–49)

Grotesquely truncated or even more grotesquely supplemented, like amputees or circus hermaphrodites, Yeats's materializing spirits serve as emblems of the fractured modern world they have left behind, a place where, within a year or two after this 1914 essay was written, soldiers with prosthetic limbs and "strained and fragmentary minds," often lacking "a hand or foot" or worse, would in fact become all too common a sight in the streets of London.[17]

Indeed, even as he was writing his Swedenborg essay during the early months of the Great War, Yeats was already well aware of the close connection between historical circumstance and spiritualist practice:

> Today while the great battle in Northern France is still undecided, should I climb to the top of that old house in Soho where a medium is sitting amongst servant girls, some one would, it may be, ask for news of Gordon Highlander or Munster Fusilier, and the fat old woman would tell in Cockny [*sic*] language how the dead do not yet know that they are dead, but stumble on amid visionary smoke and noise, and

how angelic spirits seek to awaken them but still in vain. ("Sweden-borg," 46)

Just as the newly dead, befogged and befuddled, cannot escape the hor-rors of the war still raging in the terrestrial sphere they have left behind, the living, too, in Yeats's vivid description, remain confined within the historical outlook of their own time whenever they try to imagine the spirit world:

> So heaven and hell are built always anew and in hell or heaven all do what they please and all are surrounded by scenes and circumstances which are the expression of their natures and the creation of their thought. Swedenborg because he belongs to an eighteenth century not yet touched by the romantic revival feels horror amid rocky unin-habited places, and so believes that the evil are in such places while the good are amid smooth grass and garden walks. (30)

Although he does not say so outright, Yeats hints here that the dead of the early twentieth century would feel more at home in Swedenborg's wild, windswept hell—a "rocky uninhabited place" not unlike, perhaps, Yeats's own beloved West of Ireland—than in a manicured garden heaven. By the same token, Yeats as modernist poet seems happiest con-templating a spirit world composed not of certainties but of questions, not of eternal physical forms but of constantly shifting images, not of straightforward, truthful spirits but of elusive, Protean ones:

> Here and there amongst them one discovers a wise and benevolent mind that knows a little of the future and can give good advice. . . . Yet we never long escape the phantasmagoria nor can long forget that we are among the shape-changers. Sometimes our own minds shape that mysterious substance, which may be life itself, according to desire or constrained by memory, and the dead no longer remembering their own names become the characters in the drama we ourselves have in-vented. (50)

The dead, according to Yeats, cannot help but share in the minds of the living: "All these shadows have drunk from the pool of blood and be-come delirious. Sometimes they will use the very word and say that we force delirium upon them because we do not still our minds" ("Sweden-borg," 51). Such interactivity is a hallmark of nearly all of Yeats's imaginative dealings with spirits. However much the poet credited the dead with inspiring him, he was clearly aware that he, conversely, often put words into their mouths. In May 1909, in a seance with Etta Wriedt at W. T. Stead's Cambridge House, Yeats had first encountered the spirit of Leo Africanus, a sixteenth-century Moorish scholar whom he initially assumed to be fictional but soon discovered to be a real historical figure. Although he heard from this spirit again a number of times over the next few years, it was not until Leo spoke to him at a "remarkable seance" with Mrs. Wriedt on July 20, 1915, and then again two days later through another medium, Miss Scatcherd, that Yeats began to recognize him as his own alter ego: "He asked me to write him a letter addressed to him as if to Africa giving all my doubts about spiritual things & then to write a reply as from him to me. He would control me in that reply so that it would be really from him."[18] The resulting essay was not in any real sense a work of automatic writing; Yeats made no claim to have relinquished authorial control when he wrote in Leo's voice, and he even confessed ruefully, "I am not convinced that in this letter there is one sentence that has come from beyond my own imagination."[19] Yet his "Leo Africanus" essay (which remained unpublished during Yeats's lifetime) articulates a number of ideas that would become central both to Yeats's spiritualist beliefs and to his poetics. Indeed, it serves as a kind of bridge between the psychological struggles Yeats would later outline in *Per Amica Silentae Lunae*—"We make out of the quarrel with others, rhetoric, but of the quarrel with ourselves, poetry"[20]—and what James Longenbach calls the poet's agonistic "theory of history":

> The dialogue between self and anti-self enacts the confluence of past and present. Because the voice of Leo Africanus forced Yeats to consider the possibility that the anti-self might be the spirit of someone who had once walked the earth, a psychological theory was transformed into a theory of history. This would have everything to do with Yeats's desire to map historical events in *A Vision*.[21]

Not surprisingly, much of what Leo has to say in the dialogue reinforces metaphysical ideas that Yeats had already long since been contemplating. In his Swedenborg essay, Yeats had described the spirit world as a realm exactly opposite to our own, like a photographic negative:

> In Lady Gregory's stories there is a man who heard the newly-dropped lambs of faery crying in November, and much evidence to show a topsy-turvydom of seasons, our spring being their autumn, our winter their summer. . . . Swedenborg saw some like opposition of the worlds, for what hides the spirits from our sight and touch as he explains, is that their light and heat are darkness and cold to us and our light and heat darkness and cold to them, but they can see the world through our eyes and so make our light their light. ("Swedenborg," 33)

And in "Ego Dominus Tuus," a poem completed just two weeks before he began writing the Leo essay, he had begun to develop a full-fledged doctrine of the anti-self: "I call to my own opposite, summon all/That I have handled least, least looked upon" (*Collected Poems*, 157). Leo, writing to and through Yeats, employs nearly identical oppositional terms: "I have shared in your joys & sorrows, & yet it is only because I am your opposite, your antithesis because I am in all things furthest from your intellect & your will, that I alone am your Interlocutor."[22] A similar idea reemerges in *A Vision*, in Yeats's description of "the Shiftings," a phase of afterlife existence during which the spirit "lives through a life which is said to be in all things opposite to that lived through in the world": "The victim must, in the *Shiftings*, live the act of cruelty, not as victim but as tyrant; whereas the tyrant must by a necessity of his or her nature become the victim."[23] With each evolution of the concept—oppositional world, oppositional anti-self, oppositional life—Yeats refines the "doctrine of 'the mask'" that he had been contemplating at least since the 1890s.[24] Thus, much as he describes Swedenborg to have done, Yeats expresses his own contemporary values and personal concerns via a spiritualist narrative, seeking otherworldly authority for his pet philosophies by ascribing them to communicating spirits.

In at least one important respect, to be sure, the Leo Africanus letter contradicts the view of the spirit world that Yeats had only recently set forth in his Radcliffe and Swedenborg essays. If, as he argues there, the spirits of the dead eventually evolve away from the terrestrial sphere, becoming ever more purified and remote, how could someone three hundred years dead possibly speak to the living with Leo's clarity and precision? In July 1913, in a journal that he kept for "stray notes on all kinds of things," Yeats had voiced one of the skeptic's most common objections to popular spiritualism: "Why has no sentence of literary or speculative profundity come through any medium in the last fifty years, or perhaps ever [?]" His answer at the time was that the material contingencies of spirit mediumship necessarily slow or sully communications from beyond:

> All messages that come through the senses as distinguished [from] those that come from the apparently free action of the mind—for surely there is poetic inspiration—are imperfect; that is to say, all objective messages, all that come through hearing or sight—automatic script, for instance—are without speculative power, or at any rate not equal to the mind's action at its best.[25]

Two years later, in the Leo Africanus essay, Yeats would skirt the problem of historical immediacy by admitting that Leo's words were quite likely a fabrication of his own mind. All the same, the Leo letter anticipates Yeats's eventual willingness to believe that otherworldly messages of great "speculative power" could indeed be communicated from the dead to the living, and even from the spirits of remote historical figures, if all the circumstances were favorable.

That Yeats's spiritualist "philosophy" was malleable enough to accept such a major shift in thinking became evident in 1917, when his bride of four days began to receive automatic messages from a host of otherworldly "communicators," some of whom claimed to be the spirits of ancestors long dead. In the summer of 1913, during the period when he was immersed in documenting the Elizabeth Radcliffe experiments, Yeats had spent two long weekends at the family home of Georgie Hyde-Lees, enlisting the enthusiastic young daughter of the house to undertake some research into the historical background of one of Radcliffe's spirit contacts.[26] Four years later, then, when Georgie "surprised" him a few days after their marriage "by attempting automatic writing,"[27] Yeats probably should not have been so astonished by his bride's spiritualist proclivities. With Radcliffe in mind as a model, and having experienced Yeats's credulity firsthand, Georgie knew all too well how to catch and hold the attention of her new husband, whose twenty-year obsession with Maud Gonne—and, more recently, with Maud's daughter Iseult—had not, by his own admission, entirely faded. Years later Georgie confessed to Richard Ellmann that her initial intention "was to fake a sentence or two that would allay [her husband's] anxieties over Iseult and herself, and after the session to own up to what she had done." But then, she recounted, "she suddenly felt her hand grasped and driven irresistibly. The pencil began to write sentences she had never intended or thought, which seemed to come from another world."[28]

In his introduction to the 1937 version of *A Vision*, Yeats would credit his wife's automatic writing with altering the whole course of his poetry:

> I put *The Tower* and *The Winding Stair* into evidence to show that my poetry has gained in self-possession and power. I owe this change to an incredible experience. . . . What came in disjointed sentences, in almost illegible writing, was so exciting, sometimes so profound, that I persuaded [my wife] to give an hour or two day after day to the unknown writer, and after some half-dozen such hours offered to spend what remained of life explaining and piecing together those scattered sentences. "No," was the answer, "we have come to give you metaphors for poetry."[29]

George Mills Harper and other scholars have traced a number of direct connections between the *Vision* seances—some 450 sittings, spread out over a period of thirty months and recorded in thirty-six hundred pages of notes—and Yeats's poems and plays of the same period. "Shepherd and Goatherd," for instance, written just after the January 1918 death of Major Robert Gregory, reflects a period of intense preoccupation with "the theory of Dreaming Back, which had recently been explained in the Script":[30] "He grows younger every second" (*Collected Poems*, 142). "Towards Break of Day," about a pair of lovers who dream complementary dreams, grew directly out of a January 1919 seance in which a spirit control named Thomas promised to give Yeats and his wife "a dream each": "In nervous states," Thomas told them, "you are more closely linked physically—the nightmare of one runs along this link creates a shock to the other & then reacts on the dreamer."[31] Yeats himself commented in April 1918 that he was writing some poems (probably "The Second Coming," "The Phases of the Moon," and "The Double Vision of Michael Robartes") that were based on his spirit instructors' metaphysical "system,"[32] and a number of additional poems—among them "The Phases of the Moon," "The Fool by the Roadside," "Leda and the Swan," and "All Soul's Night"—appear directly in the pages of *A Vision* to elucidate the volume's dense prose and intricate diagrams. Even long after his spiritualist experiments with Georgie had ended, Yeats would continue to meditate on themes of mediumship and otherworldly communication, as in his 1930 play *The Words upon the Window Pane* (see chapter 2) and his 1937 poem "The Spirit Medium," in which a medium, haunted by the voices and demands of the dead, turns from poetry and music to working the soil:

An old ghost's thoughts are lightning,
To follow is to die;
Poetry and music I have banished,
But the stupidity
Of root, shoot, blossom or clay
Makes no demand.

(*Collected Poems*, 315)

More subtle intertextual connections between Yeats's spiritualist pursuits and his poetry can be noted as well. Arnold Goldman lists numerous ways in which "the mediumistic scene or the objects of psychical research" find their way into Yeats's verse. In "The Second Coming," for instance, "the narrator's voice comes to resemble the voice of a control in a trance-vision," shifting between his own observations and those of a more authoritative speaker. In poems such as "The Tower," Yeats "often evinces an *activity* of spirit removed from the passivity of certain mediums, an activity which comes in part from his assumption of an active sitter-researcher's role in relation to his own mediumistic imagination."[33] And of course the theme of physical haunting permeates his work, from his 1913 "To a Shade" (in which he tells the ghost of Parnell, "You are safer in the tomb" [*Collected Poems*, 108]), to late poems such as "The Ghost of Roger Casement" and "The Apparitions": "*Fifteen apparitions have I seen;/The worst a coat upon a coat-hanger*" (332). But Yeats's involvement with popular spiritualism was not merely a one-way trajectory of influence: his spiritualist beliefs were shaped by his poetic practice just as much as vice versa. The interest in fragmented language and disrupted communication that marked his fascination with Elizabeth Radcliffe's mediumship remains a major concern of his poetry as well, which celebrates the necessity of discontinuity and rupture: "For nothing can be sole or whole/That has not been rent" (*Collected Poems*, 255). His attention to the material conditions of mediumship—the "selective powers of the body" that seemingly inhibit transmission of messages from the other world but in fact lend them their unique flavor—reflects his belief that physical imperfections can inspire artistic production, like the flawed stone of "Lapis Lazuli": "Every discoloration of the stone,/Every accidental crack or dent,/Seems a water-course or an avalanche" (293). And his embarrassed attraction to the disreputable, low cultural side of spiritualism—the fat woman and servant girls in the "old house in Soho" ("Swedenborg," 46)—anticipates his own eventual turn to writing poetry about Crazy Jane's filth and excrement, "the foul rag-and-bone shop of the heart" where all great art finds its source (*Collected Poems*, 336).

Just as Yeats's spiritualist involvement reflected and enabled his poetics, so too was his mediumistic collaboration with his wife symptomatic of his modernist sympathies. Nor was Georgie's mediumship as bizarre or aberrant a practice as some readers today might assume. A highly educated woman raised in a literary cultural milieu, Georgie Hyde-Lees first met her future husband through their mutual friend Dorothy Shakspear, who was the daughter of Yeats's former lover, Olivia Shakspear, and would later become the wife of Ezra Pound. An aspiring author in her own right, Georgie found an outlet for her frustrated literary talents in the seemingly passive but actively productive arena of spirit mediumship, providing the symbolic framework that enabled her husband's art. Brenda Maddox has convincingly argued that Georgie used her spirit communications not only to stoke her husband's (and her own) creativity but also to save her marriage: in addition to providing the "metaphors for poetry" that kept Yeats dependent on a diet of daily seances, "George's ghosts" issued strict instructions regarding the continuing physical, emotional, and sexual well-being of his young bride, even mandating the family planning that eventually resulted in the births of their two children.[34] Thus, like other literate mediums of her era such as Hester Dowden or Geraldine Cummins, Georgie discovered in spiritualism a path to cultural authority, literary productivity, and personal fulfillment.

Her husband's spiritualist pursuits, likewise, were more typical for his times than many of his commentators have cared to acknowledge. Like

Arthur Conan Doyle, Yeats sought escapist solace in Faeryland yet also turned to spirit communication to resolve real-world conflicts,[35] as when he tried repeatedly to ascertain his friend Hugh Lane's intentions regarding the disposition of his famous collection of paintings.[36] Like Rilke, he briefly played ghostwriter for a distinguished figure from the past (Rilke's "Count C.W.," Yeats's Leo Africanus) and continued, long after his spiritualist involvement had faded, to compose numerous poems that probe and destablilize the slippery boundary between life and death. And finally, like Thomas Mann, Yeats used spiritualism as a means of exploring his own fascination with the "subterraneous regions" of consciousness and the "low haunts" of the imagination: the places where a poet ends up when he gets down off his stilts and confronts not just the realm of the spirits but also the seedy underbelly of the modern world in which he lives.

H. D.'s Cryptopoetics

H. D., like Yeats, was a credulous, committed spiritualist whose experiences with mediumistic communication colored her modernist poetics and whose modernist aesthetics likewise influenced her spiritualism. Even long before she became involved with seances and spirit mediumship in the early 1940s, she was what might be termed a "cryptopoetic" writer, obsessed with concealment and revelation on the one hand and on the other hand with the poetics of death. Yet H. D. deployed cryptopoetic strategies not to reveal some timeless universal truth about death—the code broken, the hieroglyph interpreted—so much as to explore the slippery borderline between death and life and, by extension, the slipperiness also of the verbal signifiers we must use to describe whatever is unknown and unknowable. Her turn to popular spiritualism in the 1940s thus helped her to refine aesthetic and hermeneutic principles that she had already been exploring for decades.

In *The Cryptographic Imagination*, Shawn Rosenheim draws a useful distinction between the hieroglyph, which seeks to "reestablish the connection between the forms of nature and the forms [and meanings] of words," and the cryptogram or cryptograph, which "presumes the arbitrariness of signifying forms."[37] H. D., it seems, was interested in both: in her poetry, she strives to read not only the hieroglyphs inscribed in natural phenomena but also the cryptograms inscribed in cultural artifacts, including human speech. In "Birds in Snow," for instance, she describes how seemingly ordinary natural images such as birds' footprints in the snow can double as runes or hieroglyphs communicating ancient magic: "abracadabra/of a mystic's lore/or symbol/outlined/on a wizard's gate."[38] In *Trilogy*, conversely, she depicts language itself as a kind of secret code:

> I know, I feel
> the meaning that words hide;
>
> they are anagrams, cryptograms,
> little boxes, conditioned
>
> to hatch butterflies.
>
> (*Collected Poems*, 540)

Whether birds' footprints form words or words hatch butterflies—whether Nature speaks a language or language speaks Nature—the visionary poet's role, H.D. indicates, is to break the code, to "feel the meaning" behind the symbols.

Even death, H.D. suggests in a number of poems, can be pried open like a crypt to reveal secrets of spiritual resurrection. In "Epitaph," the penultimate poem of her 1931 volume *Red Roses for Bronze*, she proposes lyrics for a poet's gravestone, perhaps her own:

> so you may say,
> "Greek flower; Greek ecstasy
> reclaims for ever
> one who died
> following
> intricate songs' lost measure."
>
> (*Collected Poems*, 299–300)

In this instance, H.D. seems to acknowledge that cryptopoetics—the pursuit of "lost measure" and hidden meaning in the "intricate songs" of the past—can lead to the grave, the ultimate interpretive dead end. But the final poem in the volume, "The Mysteries," reverses this life-into-death trajectory, opening in a place very much like the inside of a crypt—"darkness on this side,/darkness over there"—but then moving quickly from darkness into light. The poem ends with a heterodox message of universal resurrection and renewal jointly mediated by Demeter (Greek goddess of agriculture), Bacchus (Roman god of wine), and Jesus Christ, who proclaims:

> "behold,
> behold
> the dead
> are no more dead.
> .　.　.　.　.　.　.
> I am red wine and bread"

> (304)

To be sure, H. D.'s poetics of mystical revelation is seldom so clear-cut and simplistic as in "The Mysteries." More often, particularly in her poetry of the 1910s through the 1930s, H. D. employs a cryptopoetic mode that obfuscates what it at first seems intended to illuminate. Her famous 1917 poem "Eurydice," for instance, opens, like "The Mysteries," in the realm of the dead—literally, as Eurydice addresses Orpheus from the underworld—and ends with a promise of resurrection:

> At least I have the flowers of myself,
> and my thoughts, no god
> can take that.
> .　.　.　.　.　.
> Though small against the black,
> small against the formless rocks,
> hell must break before I am lost;
>
> before I am lost,
> hell must open like a red rose
> for the dead to pass.

> (54–55)

In these final lines of the poem, flowers become a symbol first for the female poet—blooming even in the underworld, pushing up inexorably toward the light—and then for the underworld itself, which opens "like a red rose/for the dead to pass." H. D.'s meaning here, however, is cryptic: is the "red rose" of hell one of Eurydice's "flowers of herself"? Will the opening of hell spell Eurydice's doom ("hell must break before I am lost"), or will it bring new life to all the denizens of the underworld, including Eurydice herself? Although the poem ends, like "The Mysteries," with an image of new life emerging from death, H. D.'s demonic vision of hell breaking like a red rose is steeped in ambivalence, more disturbing than comforting, signaling apocalypse as much as renaissance.

As she rages against the dying of the light, H. D.'s Eurydice becomes, paradoxically, more vibrant and alive than Orpheus:

Against the black
I have more fervour
than you in all the splendour of that place,
against the blackness
and the stark grey
I have more light.

(54)

Such ontological reversals are common in H. D.'s poetry. Her dead seldom act dead: they feel, they reminisce, they talk, like the eponymous narrator of "A Dead Priestess Speaks," who spends eight pages doing just that. Conversely, the living often wish they were dead—"What can death mar in me/that you have not?" laments an anguished lover in "Fragment Sixty-Eight" (188)—or, like H. D.'s eternally vilified Helen of Troy, they appear deathly and ghostlike even while alive:

All Greece hates
the still eyes in the white face,
the lustre as of olives
where she stands,
and the white hands.

(154)

Despite their deathly thematics, then, these are not poems of decryption; no codes are broken, no secrets about the mystery and meaning of death are neatly revealed. Instead, H. D. persistently evokes crypts that fail to contain their dead: underworlds that, like Eurydice's hell-flower, rupture and spill their messy contents into the world of the living.

Although H. D. meditates frequently in her poetry of the 1910s through the 1930s on the permeability of the boundary that separates life from death, her poetry from that period contains little explicit mention of ghosts, hauntings, or spirit communication—a notable omission, given the frequency with which such images occur in works by her literary contemporaries. H. D. suffered several major personal losses during the Great War (including the deaths of her father and brother and the stillbirth of her child), but she evinced no interest at that time either in popular spiritualism or in spiritualism's pseudo-scientific cousin, psychical research. During a 1920 journey to Greece with her companion Bryher, however, she underwent three memorable visionary experiences that she later came to associate with the special receptivity characteristic of seance mediums and psychics. The first occurred on board ship when, standing with a man she called Peter Van Eck (actually Peter Rodeck), she sighted an island and a group of dolphins; later she realized that the dolphins, the island, and perhaps even Van Eck himself had been figments of her imagination. The second incident took place in Corfu later that spring; soon after having been informed that it would be too dangerous for two young women to travel alone to Delphi, a bitterly disappointed H. D. had her own Delphic vision of sorts, observing a series of simple images "write themselves" on the wall of her hotel room, all in the reassuring presence of Bryher, who ended the session with a vision of her own. Finally, the third incident occurred during one of their last evenings in Corfu, when H. D. found herself enacting for Bryher a series of hallucinated dance tableaux that seemed to originate, as she later wrote, in "the high regions of mystery and magic, of religious affinities, of hidden, secret storehouses of revelation and inspiration and healing."[39]

All three of these experiences made such a deep impression on H. D. that she would continue to write about them for decades to come. Surprisingly, however, virtually no reference to her Greek visions finds its way into her poetry or prose fiction written during the period in which they occurred. As she explained years later in "Majic Ring," "I did not know anyone in the psychic-research world [at the time] and anyhow, I think that I was afraid that my own experience or my own philosophy would not stand up to the proddings of the inexpert, of the unilluminated."[40] Throughout the 1930s, H. D. became increasingly interested in occultist lore, Moravian mysticism, astrology, and other esoteric doctrines, some of which she was already familiar with through her youthful friendship with Ezra Pound. In addition, her psychoanalytic sessions with Sigmund Freud in 1933–34 taught her to regard her visionary experiences as evidence of special poetic powers, despite the fact that Freud himself labeled the wall-writing episode a possibly dangerous "symptom" of psychic derangement.[41] Thus, by the time the Second World War began, H. D. was primed at last to traffic in both literal and literary ghosts. Caught up in the inevitable wartime resurgence of popular spiritualism, she joined the Society for Psychical Research, attended lectures on spiritualism, and took part in weekly group seances led by a Eurasian psychic named Arthur Bhaduri. Eventually, toward the end of the war, she began to undertake table-tapping sessions on her own, which culminated in a series of 1945 messages that she believed to have been communicated by dead R.A.F. pilots.

In contrast to her life-long interest in matters occult, H. D.'s involvement with popular spiritualism was to be relatively short lived, lasting only through the war. All the same, her seance experiments during the 1940s left an indelible mark on some of her most important literary productions. Virtually everything that H. D. wrote during and about the World War II years—her letters to friends, her short stories, her novels, her journal entries, her memoirs, her literary tributes, her poetry— bears witness to an abiding obsession with otherworldly communication, ghostly return, and the spectral phenomenology of memory. The cryptopoetic themes of her earlier poems are still present in her wartime writings. However, whereas her speculations about death and encoded meaning were once couched mostly in myth ("Eurydice"), classical imagery ("A Dead Priestess Speaks"), or theological symbolism ("The Mysteries"), now they occur in stories and poems that recount her own personal experiences with visionary consciousness. Her unpublished novel/memoir "Majic Ring," for instance, draws explicit connections between her previously repressed visions from the early 1920s and her seance experiments in the 1940s. Her autobiographical novel *The Gift* borrows imagery from the 1920 dance tableaux. And the "Writing on the Wall" section of *Tribute to Freud* traces the psychic and symbolic significance of the "hieroglyphs of the unconscious" that H. D. had seen on her hotel room wall in Corfu in 1920.[42]

In each of these works, memory proves a welcome and redemptive ghost. Events from the distant past, interpreted through the lens of H. D.'s spiritualist involvement, take on a new meaning in the war-torn present. In "Majic Ring," H. D.'s 1920 Corfu visions predict and validate her seance participation in the 1940s. And in *The Gift*, a new temporal layer is added when H. D. employs imagery from the "Indian dance scenes" she enacted for Bryher in Greece to describe a much earlier event from her distant childhood: "I used the psychic experience [from 1920]," she recalls in "Majic Ring," "but I worked it into a sequence of reconstructed memories that I made my grandmother tell me, as if in reverie or half-dream or even trance."[43] These "reconstructed memories" in turn involve the grandmother's youthful experience of being mystically imbued with the spiritual knowledge of a group of Moravian ancestors who had lived a hundred years before her: "She herself became one with the *Wunden Eiland* initiates and herself spoke with tongues, hymns of the spirits in the air, of spirits at sun-rise and sun-setting, of the deer and the wild squirrel, the beaver, the otter, the kingfisher and the hawk and eagle."[44] Thus, in *The Gift*, H. D. telescopes together five separate events, spread out over several hundred years but linked in their spiritual significance: the heterodox religious rapture experienced jointly by the Moravian settlers and a group of sympathetic Native Americans; the grandmother's experience a century later of "becoming one" with the dead settlers and the Indians in their moment of mystical revelation; the child Hilda's reception of her grandmother's story and its accompanying "gift" of spiritual enlightenment; the dance tableaux that H. D. performed for Bryher in Corfu in 1920, which find their way into the grandmother's memories of how it felt to be possessed by ancestral spirits; and, last but not least, H. D.'s struggle for emotional survival in blitz-torn London, the setting of *The Gift*'s framing narrative.

H. D.'s wartime seances are not explicitly mentioned in *The Gift*, which she wrote during a period of increasing involvement in spiritualist experiments. However, spiritualist themes—communication after death, mediumistic possession, spirit survival—permeate the novel.[45] The voices of H. D.'s Moravian ancestors speak from beyond the grave to reveal, elliptically, the long-buried secret that only heterodox religious practice, as exemplified by the early American settlers' act of spiritual bonding with the Indians, can bring about an end to war. The message of *The Gift* is essentially identical to the one expressed at the end of

H. D.'s earlier poem "The Mysteries," which celebrated the alliance of Christian and pagan myth. But now the secret, although more urgent than ever in a world torn by war, has become more difficult to excavate (buried in time, secreted among the winding passages of *The Gift*'s non-linear prose) and more complex in form and expression.

In the "Writing on the Wall" section of *Tribute to Freud*, similarly, H. D. perceives multiple layers of meaning—"We can read my writing, the fact that there was writing, in two ways or more than two ways"[46]—in events buried under accumulated layers of time. Sitting at her desk in 1940s London, she recalls how she reclined on a sofa in 1930s Vienna and told Freud about occurrences that took place in 1920s Greece. Her recollection of her thoughts during the "writing on the wall" experience is couched, significantly, in the language of death and resurrection:

> I may be breathing naturally but I have the feeling of holding my breath under water. . . . I know that I must drown, as it were, completely in order to come out on the other side of things (like Alice with her looking-glass or Perseus with his mirror). I must drown completely and come out on the other side, or rise to the surface after the third time down, not dead to this life but with a new set of values, my treasure dredged from the depth. (*Tribute to Freud*, 53–54)

H. D. recounts her visionary experience, as Alec Marsh points out, "in classically occult terms as labor of katabasis leading to palingenesis."[47] Yet popular spiritualism, at least as much as occultism, proves to be one of the "buried treasures" or hidden subtexts of "Writing on the Wall." H. D.'s meditations on virtually every subject she addresses—psychology, theology, poetry, politics, Freud himself—become intertwined, at one point or another, with the theme of life's continuation after death. ("It was all a séance and a fortune-telling bee," H. D. even wrote at one point of her psychoanalytic sessions—in French, *séances*—with Freud.)[48]

Early on in "Writing on the Wall," H. D. declares her certainty that Freud himself would never really die: "It worried me to feel that he had no idea—it seemed impossible—really no idea that he would 'wake up' when he shed the frail locust-husk of his years, and find himself alive" (*Tribute to Freud*, 43). Later, despite Freud's own lifelong repudiation of the idea of life after death, she portrays him as a kind of spiritualist of the psyche who cured his patients by resurrecting their past selves: "He did not pretend to bring back the dead who had already crossed the threshold. But he raised from dead hearts and stricken minds and maladjusted bodies a host of living children" (101). (In a 1933 letter, she went so far as to call him "Jesus-Christ after the resurrection, he has that wistful ghost look of someone who has been right past the door of the tomb.")[49] H. D. even finds a way of acknowledging and deftly redeeming Freud's stubborn resistance to her own spiritualist beliefs. "Writing on the Wall" was composed between September 19 and November 2, 1944 (111). On October 19 of that same year, H. D. received (via Bhaduri) the seance message in which Freud's spirit told her, "you are the instrument—you will prove the work of this Master (Freud) did not represent a finality but a THRESHOLD. Not science, only lever that opened door."[50] Borrowing the doorway metaphor invoked by Freud's spirit, H. D. manages in her "tribute" both to celebrate the famous psychoanalyst's memory and to skewer his most deeply held beliefs, portraying him as a "beloved light-house keeper" who "shut the door on transcendental speculations" but whose denial of the afterlife would in time be proven wrong:

> It was well for a Prophet, in the old tradition of Israel, to arise, to slam the door on visions of the future, of the after-life, to stand himself like the Roman Centurion before the gate at Pompeii who did not move from his station before the gateway since he received no orders to do so, and who stood for later generations to wonder at him, embalmed in hardened lava, preserved in the very fire and ashes that had destroyed him. (*Tribute to Freud*, 102)

She concludes her memoir by associating herself with Goethe's Mignon, leading her symbolic father and protector ("o Vater," "o mein Beschützer") over terrifying "chasms or gulfs" to the promised land far beyond the grave, "the land where the orange-tree blossoms" (109–11).

Whether she pictures herself diving underwater (as in her description of the wall-writing scene) or crossing airy chasms (as in her reading of Mignon's song), H. D.'s revelatory vocabulary depends heavily on spatial metaphors. A list of her wartime titles—"Dark Room," "Majic Ring," "Writing on the Wall," *Within the Walls*, "The Walls Do Not Fall"[51]—reads like a veritable architectural tour through different kinds of visionary spaces: the darkened room of the stereotypical spirit medium; the "majic ring" of her seance circle; the wall upon which her Greek visions were projected. "We are all haunted houses," H.D. remarks in the "Advent" section of *Tribute to Freud*, describing the "intermediate ghosts" who frequently appeared in her dreams during the period of her analytic sessions with Freud: hotel page-boys, for instance, symbolically "ghosting for" dead relatives (146). Such ghosts prove to be intimate, even comforting presences, spatialized emblems of a salutary atemporality. In a wartime poem titled "May 1943," H.D. describes a carpenter who repairs an orangery window destroyed by incendiary bombs: "he has his chisel,/I have my pencil: // he mends the broken window-frame of the orangery,/I mend a break in time" (*Collected Poems*, 493). Paradoxically, in her wartime writings, she "mend[s] a break in time" not by reinstating but rather by shattering conventional notions of linear temporality, confounding history by collapsing past, present, and future into a single "spectral moment": a temporal unit, in Jacques Derrida's definition, "that no longer belongs to time, . . . that is not docile to time."[52]

In a short story written early in the war, H.D. conflates the destruction of physical spaces in London with the kind of psychological rupture that makes possible spiritual discovery: "A wall of our house is down," she writes; "The wall of our psychic house is down, to let in unknown, uncharted sensation."[53] A similar image occurs two years later in the "Walls Do Not Fall" section of *Trilogy*, where the bombed ruins of London become a "shrine open to the sky," admitting the poetic inspiration that could not have entered an intact edifice or a closed mind:

ruin everywhere, yet as the fallen roof
leaves the sealed room
open to the air,

so, through our desolation,
thoughts stir, inspiration stalks us
through gloom:

unaware, Spirit announces the Presence;
shivering overtakes us,
as of old, Samuel:

trembling at a known street-corner,
we know not nor are known;
the Pythian pronounces—we pass on

to another cellar, another sliced wall.

(*Collected Poems*, 510)

Here, spatial disruption—the fallen roof, the sliced wall—not only parallels but in fact makes possible the poem's disruption of temporality:
the inspired poet, stalked by untimely apparitions, herself becomes a
ghostly figure from the past, a seer compared, in a slick syncretist move,
both to the Old Testament prophet Samuel and to the Greek Pythia,
priestess of the god Apollo. H. D. ends her poem by repeating the comforting message of its title: "still the walls do not fall." Her reassertion of
spatial boundaries, however, like her transcendence of temporal ones,
has been accomplished through an act of rupture. In contrast to T. S.
Eliot, who two decades earlier shored fragments of history against the
ruins of a war-torn waste land, H. D. uses imagery drawn from her spiritualist interests to redefine the modernist trope of fragmentation, which
she posits not as a symptom of psychic derangement but as a precondi-
tion for physical and emotional survival. Spatial disclosures are enabled
by temporal layerings; "breaks in time" open new spaces for writing.

Only by affirming and admitting the past, H. D. suggests in *Trilogy*—
only by exposing the crypts of our minds to the open air, by inviting
ghosts to inhabit the haunted houses of our psyches—can we withstand
the assaults of the present. Later, however, as the war drew to a close,
H. D.'s spiritualist beliefs took a more negative turn. In August 1945, experimenting on her own with a tapping table, H. D. received a series of
spirit messages from dead R.A.F. pilots warning her—or so she interpreted their communications—about the environmental disasters that
would result from the dropping of the atomic bomb on Hiroshima.[54]
Until that time, H. D. had not attempted to speak to the dead either directly or alone; instead, she and Bryher had always participated in small
group seances led by Bhaduri, whose spiritualist mode conformed remarkably closely to H. D.'s own poetic principles. The messages communicated via Bhaduri—involving Viking ships, Egyptian lilies, and mysterious Indian guides—were densely symbolic stream-of-consciousness
affairs which H. D. in turn delighted in recording and meditating upon

at sometimes extraordinary length.[55] Almost without exception, H. D. interpreted these and other visionary experiences from the early war years as positive symbols of hope and salvation. *Trilogy*, for instance, contains images of an alabaster-skinned "Master" who came to H. D. in a 1941 dream and a mysterious lady in white who appeared to her spiritualist circle during a 1943 seance: both are complex but clearly redemptive figures. Her 1941 poem "R.A.F.," similarly, recounts a ghostly visitation from a dead pilot on the first anniversary of the Battle of Britain. ("This was an actual experience," she later insisted.)[56] The poet laments the pilot's death—"for I am stricken . . . by the thought/of ineptitude, sloth, evil/that prosper,/while such as he fall"—but overcomes her sorrow and anger by envisioning him as Hermes, an "emissary" from the world of the dead, "the coming-one/from a far star," "my particular winged messenger" (*Collected Poems*, 486–91).

When H. D. began to receive communications from the "R.A.F. boys," however, her writing and emotions took a different course. This troubling encounter with the voices of the dead, coming just weeks after the dropping of the atomic bomb, re-opened rather than healed the wounds of war. Far from requiring complex symbolic interpretation, their messages were direct, curt, almost telegraphic in their brevity: "We couldn't spell very well but we could write awkwardly, all helping one another, g-a-l-e, o-a-r. . . . Together we painfully printed out our letter."[57] Mediated neither by Bhaduri nor through a protective buffer of arcane personal symbolism, the R.A.F. communications introduced a starkly apocalyptic note to H. D.'s previously redemptive modernist pattern of cyclical destruction and resurrection. Indeed, they edged her toward precisely the kind of psychic breakdown from which she had once hoped her spiritualist experiments would protect her. Faced with the prospect of a "break in time" that she would not be able to mend with her poet's pencil, H. D. eventually retreated, at least for a time, into the fog of mental collapse. After her recovery, she never again attempted to contact the spirit world, and the notion of an irreparably shattered future—a time in which time itself, human history as we know it, might no longer exist at all—remained for her an unspeakable and unredeemable specter.

Yet despite her apparent disavowal of spiritualist practice, H. D. continued to pursue cryptopoetic themes even long after her 1945 breakdown. In her 1961 epic *Helen in Egypt*, in particular, she marshals ghosts from the past into symbols of spiritual survival who are also the bearers of hidden meaning. Helen's ability to decode secrets seemingly enables her privileged understanding of the mystery of death, which culminates in her revelation, in the final verse of *Helen in Egypt*, that death itself is nothing more than an encrypted message of spiritual redemption and resurrection, a secret so obvious that it "is no secret":

> so the dart of Love
> is the dart of Death,
> and the secret is no secret;
>
> the simple path
> refutes at last
> the threat of the Labyrinth,
>
> the Sphinx is seen,
> the Beast is slain
> and the Phoenix-nest
>
> reveals the innermost
> key or the clue to the rest
> of the mystery.[58]

Elsewhere in *Helen in Egypt*, however, H. D. hints at the inadequacy or in-efficacy of the very strategies of decoding that the poem's ending appears to celebrate. Thus, although Helen proves adept at interpreting not only Egyptian hieroglyphs but also the "natural or human symbols" found everywhere around her, the poem itself is full of questions that go unanswered, identificatory issues that remain unresolved, and prose fragments that contradict or complicate the lyric passages they seem positioned to elucidate (*Helen in Egypt*, 22–23). "It is not necessary to 'read' the riddle," one of those prose fragments even assures us, for "the pattern itself is sufficient and it is beautiful" (32).

This Saussurean pronouncement, which urges the reader to privilege signifier over signified, words over meaning, is dramatized imagistically throughout *Helen in Egypt*. H. D.'s spectral Helen is intent on self-discovery, yet the opaque objects that persistently float about her—the "veil of Cytheraea" that cloaks her displacement to Egypt (46), the scarf through whose "transparent folds" Achilles catches tantalizing glimpses of her hands and wrists and throat (56)—seem to symbolize not revelation and discovery but rather visionary experience deflected and obscured. Even the ontological status of Helen herself—is she real? an illusion? alive? dead?—eludes any final resolution. The poem pays extensive lip service to Helen's power as a reader of secret texts, yet what it enacts, paradoxically, is interpretive indeterminacy instead. Emily Dickinson reminds us, in what is either a critique of or an important hint about her own penchant for riddling, that "The Riddle we can guess/We speedily despise": unsolved mysteries, not comprehensible ones, are the ones that hold our interest.[59] Similarly, H. D. warns toward the end of *Helen in Egypt*, just as the reader approaches what seems to be the moment of final illumination, that "you may penetrate every shrine, an initiate, and remain unenlightened at last" (262).

From her precarious position at the margins of literary respectability, H. D. wrote poetry, prose, and criticism that explores physical and psychological borderlines of various kinds: the liminal spaces where sea and shore become indistinguishable (as in her early poem "Oread"), where traditional genre definitions blur (as in her lyrical, nonlinear novels), where people from diverse racial and cultural backgrounds enact their misunderstandings (as in *Borderline*, the 1930 art film she starred in opposite Paul Robeson). It was this emphasis on hermeneutic uncertainties, rather than any desire to erect rigid boundaries or maintain stable meanings, that fueled her enduring fascination with secrecy and discovery, writing and mystery, riddles and hieroglyphs, communication and silence, death and resurrection. H. D.'s crypts are borderline spaces, her codes receptacles of borderline meaning; even her seance message from Freud celebrates the opening rather than the closing of doors. Like Yeats, H. D. turned to popular spiritualism not to escape the ambiguities of modern existence but to affirm them. Only when their messages became starkly unambiguous, requiring action rather than interpretation, did H. D. reject her wartime spirits and replace them with the metaphorical, purely literary ghosts who haunt the beaches and pages of *Helen in Egypt*.

CHAPTER SIX

Ghostwriting Postmodernism

I sit with my cup
to catch the crazy falling alphabet.

Ruth Stone, "Poetry"

The glacier knocks in the cupboard,
    The desert sighs in the bed,
And the crack in the teacup opens
    A lane to the land of the dead.

W. H. Auden, "As I Walked Out One Evening"

PLATH, MERRILL, AND THE POETICS OF OUIJA

In the second half of the twentieth century, a number of writers sought to provide a fresh twist on the ancient prophetic paradigm by foregrounding more explicitly than ever before the relationship between spirit mediumship and literary production. Poets Sylvia Plath and James Merrill, for instance, would move beyond the low cultural qualms of their high modernist forebears to explore the affinities and alliances between automatic writing—a mode of mediumship that affirms the special selection of its practitioners even while conveniently displacing the very act of authorship—and their own poetic creativity. Other recent writers, such as Vladimir Nabokov, A. S. Byatt, and Ted Hughes, deploy popular spiritualism thematically to highlight tropes of textual indeterminacy and critical agency. Postmodern in sensibility if not necessarily in form, these writers exhibit a playful, self-consciously literary approach to spiritualism that distinguishes them from such influential modernist predecessors as Yeats, Rilke, and H. D., all of whom were tempted by spiritualism's vatic promise but proved conspicuously hesitant to invoke their mediumistic experimentation directly in their poetry.[1]

Both Plath and Merrill composed major works—Plath's "Dialogue over a Ouija Board" (written in 1957 but first published in 1981) and

Merrill's *The Changing Light at Sandover* (published in four installments from 1976 to 1982)—that recount and reenact their respective experiments, undertaken roughly contemporaneously beginning in the 1950s, with the form of automatic writing known as the Ouija board. Plath's eleven-page "Dialogue" documents a single session with the board, whereas Merrill's monumental *Sandover* trilogy spans 560 pages and nearly three decades. But despite these essential differences of structure and scope, their Ouija works are notable above all for their similarities, all the more so because they were written by two poets of very different temperaments who were almost certainly unaware of one another's spiritualist efforts. Both poems, by alternately attributing the Ouija board's pronouncements to otherworldly spirits and to the equally chaotic unconscious minds of the board's manipulators, place an intriguing Freudian slant on age-old questions of internal versus external inspiration. Both poems depict Ouija sessions that depend on the collaboration of two lovers—indeed, of two writers—whose personal bonds imperil as much as they impel the board's communications. Both poems, rejecting modernist poetry's somewhat embarrassed stance toward popular culture, confront head-on the spiritualist proclivities of their authors—scrutinizing, interrogating, and even mocking the very visionary experiences that they enact. And finally, both poems exploit the Ouija board's almost boundless metaphorical potential in order to explore (albeit in different ways and to very different ends) the nature, the sources, and ultimately the limitations of poetic language.

The Ouija board itself provides both the method and the metaphor for Plath's and Merrill's visionary poetics. A deceptively simple device, a Ouija board consists of a flat piece of cardboard or paper inscribed with the letters of the alphabet (usually arranged in a circle or arc), the numbers from 0 to 9, and a few other common words and symbols such as YES, NO, and "&."[2] Although it can, in theory, be employed by a solitary sitter, the board is usually operated by two or more persons who place their hands lightly on a small three-legged pointer or any other fairly mobile object (Merrill used an overturned teacup, Plath a wineglass). As the pointer glides from letter to letter without the conscious will or direction of its manipulators, one of the sitters uses a free hand to write down the board's messages, which are spelled out without punctuation marks or word breaks and can arrive, especially for experienced sitters, with breathtaking speed. (Merrill counted five to six hundred words an hour.)³ Although similar devices have been in use for more than two thousand years, the Ouija board was first manufactured commercially in 1892. Its name (which is now a registered trademark of Parker Brothers and hence is capitalized throughout this book) derives from *oui* and *ja,* the French and German words for "yes."⁴ In a celebrated 1920 tax court case, the Baltimore Talking Board Company, then owner of the patent, claimed that the Ouija board was a "medium of communication between this world and the next" and hence should not be subject to games taxes. The company lost the case, and the court declared that the board, while "seriously used by some persons in the belief that it affords mysterious spirit communications," was nonetheless legally a game, because it is "sold with the expectation that it is to be used merely as a means of social amusement or play."⁵

Plath's and Merrill's accounts of their spiritualist experiences indicate that they relied mostly on homemade Ouija boards for their own experiments, although Merrill initially used a store-bought one.⁶ However, their very knowledge of the device no doubt depended heavily on the board's commodification and enviable brand-name recognition. "Ouija" has been practically a household word, and the board itself has enjoyed steady commercial popularity, for more than a century. Its very status as a commercial object, and moreover as a board game that can be found on toy store shelves between Monopoly and Parcheesi, could well explain some of its tremendous symbolic appeal for two poets earnestly (and independently) attempting to fashion a visionary poetics appropriate to a literary generation caught between modernist mythopoesis and postmodernism's self-conscious romance with commodity culture. For both Merrill and Plath, the Ouija board functions as a sort of psychic leveler, a fulcrum balancing the prophetic pretensions and iconoclastic impulses of high and low culture. As a tool for otherworldly inspiration that is also a best-selling parlor game, it imbues the ancient vatic impulse with a sense of self-reflexive irony and even of play.

At the same time, the Ouija board provides a spirited, provocative means for both poets to explore the paradoxes of poetic authority and the vicissitudes of poetic language. Several critics have noted that the Ouija board, "a symbol system that offers potentially unlimited combinations of letters and numbers, affirmations and denials," can be read as a "metaphor for language itself":⁷ like language, it is an instrument of communication, a clumsy but effective mediatory apparatus, a site of ambivalence, creativity, deception. With its simple ring of letters and its slow, cumbersome pointer, the Ouija board forces the poet, "spelling" in senses both magical and scriptorial, to rethink and reexperience the very act of writing—to "relearn the alphabet," in Denise Levertov's evocative phrase. Yet even while it bears out the commonplace that all poetry is finally about poetry, the board itself is no mere stooge to aphorism; its dubious cultural status and unabashed commerciality encourage, even compel, both Merrill and Plath to explore the limits of poetic authority and to interrogate their own motives in seeking outside inspiration.

In the end, Merrill and Plath come to very different conclusions about the efficacy of the Ouija board as a poetic and revelatory device. Whereas Merrill increasingly embraced the board's revelations and used them, over a period of thirty years, to construct a sweepingly complex visionary poetics, Plath soon abandoned the board and turned instead to other sources of spiritual authority. Two brief verses chronicling their initial experiments and frustrations with the board—Merrill's 1955 "Voices from the Other World" and Plath's 1957 "Ouija"—foreshadow these respective creative trajectories. While Plath's poem sounds an almost relentless note of visionary failure (a note that will be tempered but never entirely abandoned in "Dialogue over a Ouija Board"), Merrill, anticipating the circumspect optimism of *The Changing Light at Sandover*, hints at the ways in which the Ouija board might open the door to new forms of creative experience.

Merrill wrote "Voices from the Other World" in 1955, some two years after he had received a Ouija board as a birthday gift but within just a week after David Jackson, who would soon thereafter become his lover and longtime companion, first joined him in his attempts to contact "the other world."[8] Based on the two men's actual experiences at the board, the poem conveys the author's disappointment at receiving "no real Sign" from beyond—although he does communicate with a series of rather undistinguished doomsayers—and his growing conviction that the board's most important function is, ultimately, to put him back in touch with the world of the living:

Because, once looked at lit
By the cold reflections of the dead
Risen extinct but irresistible,
Our lives have never seemed more full, more real,
Nor the full moon more quick to chill.[9]

Above all the poem emphasizes the personal, even intimate, nature of visionary experience. Merrill portrays the Ouija board, whose other-worldly revelations are most effectively attained through the physical and psychic collaboration of two people, not only as a potential tool for cosmic outreach but also as a covert metaphor for sexual union. On the night after they received a particularly ominous yet typically banal spirit message, the narrator recalls, "we . . . tossed/Till sunrise striped the rumpled sheets with gold"—a locution hinting both at a shared bed and at a disturbance of sheets not due to insomnia alone.[10] In the following stanzas, the poet notes that the board's once frightening "voices" have already begun to have an opposite, paradoxically calming effect—"Some warn of lives misspent, and all of doom/In ways that so exhilarate/We are sleeping sound of late"—and goes on to describe long, tranquil evenings of relaxed togetherness: "In the gloom here,/our elbows on the cleared/Table, we talk and smoke." The progression of events and emotions resembles nothing so much as the early stages of a love affair: physical passion and "rumpled sheets" give way to exhilarated content-ment, contentment to conversational intimacy (and even to the stereo-typical postcoital cigarette), and intimacy, in turn, to a sense of utter fulfillment—tempered, to be sure, by intimations of mortality, as repre-sented by the moon, "so quick to chill."

By outlining the erotic contours of spiritualist practice, Merrill sug-gests here that love and sex, at their best, are visionary experiences in their own right. Yet "Voices" also hints that inspiration, at its worst, re-sembles not sexual ecstasy but a rape-like violation: "Last night the teacup shattered in a rage," the narrator recalls at one point of the wil-lowware cup that has been serving as a Ouija board pointer, reminding us that otherworldly revelation can overwhelm its fragile human ves-sels. The teacup's destruction points to sexual union as well as to nar-rative and psychic rupture, for it recalls the shattered glass that, in Jew-ish tradition, symbolizes marriage. Merrill will allude to that tradition in his epigraph to the third book of *Sandover*, where a broken crystal becomes "le symbole de l'indestructible union," foreshadowing the cli-mactic moment at the end of the book when, in what is explicitly de-scribed as a wedding scene, DJ and JM (Jackson and Merrill) together shatter a mirror and afterward celebrate with champagne.[11] But the fracturing of teacup and mirror, even while marking a marriage of true minds, tenders a warning as well: the dark side of otherworldly inspiration—not to mention of human sexuality—is tension, surrender, and even violence.[12]

Plath's "Ouija" lacks the vital erotic undercurrent of Merrill's "Voices from the Other World," as the poem's only apparent sexual attraction concerns not two human participants but rather the Ouija board's "doddering," vampiric, god—"The glass mouth sucks blood-heat from my forefinger./The old god dribbles, in return, his words"—and a "rotten . . . bawdry queen of death."[13] But this absence of human sexuality is significant in its own right: where romance is shriveled, sordid, and debased, Plath indicates, so too is prophetic vision. To be sure, the speaker of "Ouija" succeeds in communicating with an underworld deity of considerable symbolic potency. Much like Merrill's "Voices," however, the poem is mostly about the poet's disappointment that she can spell "no succinct Gabriel from the letters here," no useful otherworldly message. In "On the Decline of Oracles," another poem from the same period, Plath—who, according to Ted Hughes, often experienced "flashes of prescience" but "always about something unimportant"[14]—complains about the triviality of her own psychic insights compared with those of the great classical prophets: "Worthless such vision to eyes gone dull/That once descried Troy's towers fall,/Saw evil break out of the north" (*Collected Poems*, 78). "Ouija" expresses a similar frustration. Indeed, with its stilted vocabulary and strained form, the poem enacts the very lack of prophetic authority it bemoans. Plath wrote "Ouija" at a time when she herself was, in a sense, still acting as a medium for the voices of various poetic precursors: as several critics have noted, the "eerie splendor" of the poem's opening lines quickly degenerates into a rather poor imitation of Wallace Stevens, while other verses from the same period echo Ransom, Roethke, Thomas, and of course Hughes.[15] Above all, as Plath herself no doubt recognized, the poem's florid vocabulary—"ruddle," "aureate," "maundering," "hauteur"—points to the inspiration not of theophany but thesaurus; the poet is still less God's trumpet than, in Plath's own rueful self-description, "Roget's strumpet."[16]

As Timothy Materer has noted, Plath's "Dialogue over a Ouija Board," although probably composed in the same year as "Ouija" and articulating many of the same doubts, represents a significant shift in Plath's visionary poetics, a breakthrough both "to the subjects that truly inspired her imagination" and to a more forceful, less derivative poetic style. In fact, although the poem has been accorded little attention by critics,

Materer argues that "the quality of its verse and its dramatic form make it one of her most important works."[17] Some of the poem's vitality no doubt arises, like that of Plath's later, explosively intimate *Ariel* poems, from its personal, close-to-home subject matter and its theme of creative conflict. In contrast to "Ouija," Plath's "Dialogue" focuses not on an abstract, "doddering god" and a frustrated poet but on the problematic partnership—sexual, connubial, literary—of a man and a woman who work the board together. The poem is based on what Ted Hughes, in his note to the poem, calls "the actual 'spirit' text of one of the ouija sessions" in which he and Plath participated between 1956 and 1958 (Plath, *Collected Poems*, 276). Plath wrote it in the summer of 1957 but apparently never showed it to her husband (who consequently banished it to the footnote section of Plath's *Collected Poems*), perhaps, as Materer speculates, because it was too "photographic": "the husband and wife . . . are transparently Ted and Sylvia revealing not only their occult interests but their desire for a child and the competitiveness of their lives together as poets."[18] Ultimately, the poem, expressing both erotic turmoil and artistic self-doubt, questions rather than affirms the Ouija board's usefulness as an aid to poetic inspiration. Yet although it is both slighter in scope and less optimistic in visionary outcome than Merrill's monumental *Sandover* trilogy, "Dialogue" addresses to equally great effect many of the same issues—death, desire, sexuality, knowledge, doubt—and examines with similar intensity the nature and sources of poetic inspiration.

Although the Ouija board serves throughout "Dialogue," much as in Merrill's "Voices," as a complex symbol of sexual union, it is above all a site of doubt and disquietude, reflecting the poet's own uncertainty as to the origins and authenticity of her visionary experiences. The poem's two protagonists are poets, but the essential contrast between them is made evident in the names that Plath bestows on each: the husband, Leroy, is kingly and self-assured, while the wife, Sibyl, fears yet also desires a more passive role as divine mouthpiece. Leroy, the voice of reason and Freudian self-knowledge, sees the board's communicative spirit, Pan, as a spokesman—conveying, like Yeats's spirit voices, new "metaphors for poetry"—for his and Sibyl's own unconscious minds: "He'll spell a line/Of poetry from these letters, but the beat/Will be our beat, just as the gift is ours" (*Collected Poems*, 283). Sibyl admits that Leroy is probably right—that "Pan's a mere puppet/Of our two intuitions" (279)—but wants desperately to believe otherwise, to discern "some

other party speaking through/Our separate veins and this glass mouth."
Whereas Leroy, in other words, sees the Ouija board as a mirror—Pan
"still bores/You to taunts though," notes Sibyl, "when he reflects a
face/Other than your own" (283)—Sibyl sees it as a pond or pool (pun-
ning on the football pools that Pan has failed to help the couple win),[19] a
symbol of frightening otherworldly depths rather than psychic surfaces:

> By some mishap,
> Instead of fat fish on the line, you've plumbed
> Deeper than your own ocean floor, and got
> A barnacle-pated, moss-wigged, lobster-limbed
> Chimera on the hook.
>
> (283)

Soon thereafter, Pan claims that he dwells "IN CORE OF NERVE" (and not,
as he had previously asserted, "IN GODHEAD," which would imply that his
messages have divine origins), and a disappointed Sibyl must admit to
Leroy that "My will has evidently/Curtseyed to yours," since the Ouija
board's mysterious otherworldly "chimera" has revealed itself to be a
mere "fat fish" of the mind after all (282–84). When Sibyl finally breaks
the wineglass that has been serving as a Ouija board pointer and thereby
puts an end to the evening's messages, her act, like the shattering of
teacup and mirror in Merrill's Ouija poems, is meant to symbolize a
nuptial union achieved, paradoxically, through rupture: "we grew
one/As the glass flew to its fragments" (285). Yet her argument with
Leroy is never really resolved, and the poem's deceptively harmonious
ending—"When lights go out/May two real people breathe in a real
room" (286)—belies the passion and intensity of the debate that has
preceded it.

Sibyl/Sylvia and Leroy/Leo (the latter was Ted Hughes's astrological
sign) personify, despite some crossover emotions, wishful spiritualism
counterposed against skepticism, desire pitted against doubt: Plath's
own internal conflicts, that is, dialogically polarized. In *The Changing
Light at Sandover*, similarly, Merrill enacts a crisis of belief on the level of
form, with the Ouija board itself serving as an emblem of antithetical
struggle. But where "Dialogue" confines itself to two human voices communicating with a single otherworldly contact, *Sandover*—loosely modeled on Dante's *Divine Comedy*—eventually expands to offer a whole

panoply of speaking characters, including "God Biology," Nature, the Muses, and historical and literary figures ranging from Plato and Jesus to Wallace Stevens and W. H. Auden (the latter being Merrill's answer to Dante's Virgil). Each book of Merrill's trilogy represents a different segment of the board: the twenty-six sections of "The Book of Ephraim" (unofficially subtitled "The Book of a Thousand and One Evenings Spent/With David Jackson at the Ouija Board/In Touch with Ephraim Our Familiar Spirit" [*Sandover*, 4]) begin with consecutive letters of the alphabet, from A to Z; the ten divisions of *Mirabell's Books of Number* are labeled 0 through 9; and the three lengthy texts that comprise *Scripts for the Pageant* take as their respective rubrics YES & NO. Thus the poem recounts, by means of its very structure, its own myth of origins. The Ouija board is not only the subject of the poem, not only the conduit for its spiritualist Ur-text (Merrill admits that he reworked and reworded most of the board's messages to make them fit into his polished metrical scheme),[20] but also the model for its overall structure and indeed for Merrill's own poetics, which revolves around the board's built-in dialectic of "YES & NO."

In an interview with Fred Bornhauser, Merrill explains why the final section of his final book ends with negation even though the word "Ouija" is itself a double affirmative:

> I think what you have on the board are the raw materials of language—of thought itself. The YES and NO came to be especially telling, the more I realized how important it was—not only for the poem but for my own mental balance—to remain of two minds about everything that was happening. One didn't want to be merely skeptical or merely credulous. Either way would have left us in reduced circumstances.[21]

Like Plath with the opposition of Sibyl and Leroy, Merrill employs the contraries YES and NO to symbolize his own mixed feelings about poetic inspiration, and particularly about the problematic cultural status of the board itself, which he recognizes as an unlikely and even inappropriate vehicle for vatic utterance. To be sure, much as Plath's "Dialogue" brings about a final, optimistic union between Sibyl and Leroy, Merrill cannot resist ending *Sandover* on a note of adamant closure, concluding "The Higher Keys"—a coda that follows the NO section of *Scripts for the Pageant*—with the poem's very first word and thereby bringing his whole lengthy epic full circle, tail in mouth. Throughout most of the poem, however, his focus is on ambivalence and ambiguity, a poetics of fruitful opposition.

In response to a rather anguished query by J. D. McClatchy as to whether he ever finds "the idea of the Ouija board" embarrassing, Merrill noted that his poem's YES/NO two-mindedness—whereby he constantly juxtaposes the grandiose and the giddy, subsuming within his poem frank admissions both of credulity and doubt—depends above all on his own willingness, even eagerness, to undercut high cultural pretensions with pop culture pastiche:

> The mechanics of the board—this absurd, flimsy contraption, creaking along—serves wonderfully as a hedge against inflation. I think it does embarrass the sort of reader who can't bear to face the random or trivial elements that coalesce, among others, to produce an "elevated" thought. That doesn't bother me *at all*.[22]

Although Merrill's justification for his Ouija experimentation is less fraught with class and gender contradictions than is Yeats's metaphor about his wayward muse, the message remains the same: "elevated" literary expression often finds its roots in the random, the trivial, the absurd. But whereas Yeats avoided writing explicitly spiritualist poetry, Merrill deploys the Ouija board not just as a mediumistic tool but also as a built-in inoculatory device, protecting himself from potential ridicule by foregrounding his own acts of stylistic sabotage.

Plath's "Dialogue," although generally more high-minded in tone and diction, is similarly self-conscious and even self-mocking in regard to its spiritualist subject matter: "Oh, he'll go clever/Like all the others and swear that he's a puma/In Tibet, or a llama in Zanzibar," sighs Sibyl at one point of the irrepressible Pan (*Collected Poems*, 281). Embracing low as well as high cultural modes of revelation, skepticism as well as belief, external as well as internal otherness, both Merrill and Plath use the Ouija board to accommodate and focus many oppositional pairings. But ultimately the board's most important function is not so much mediatory as transformative: it offers a compelling if unlikely symbol for the metaphoric and metamorphic capacities—delineated, appropriately enough, almost entirely through metaphor—of visionary experience and poetic language. At one point in *Sandover*, DJ worries that the Ouija board may be "a door/Shutting us off from living" (217). For the most part, however, it is represented, like Alice's looking glass, as an open threshold between the "other world" and this one: Merrill calls it a "Revolving door into a lobby" (300), while Plath's Sibyl, in response to Leroy's taunt that "Gods grow too proud to practice doorman duties/At the whim of a wine-glass," notes wryly that "Saints' door apart, backdoor's a door" (*Collected Poems*, 280). The board is a bridge (its letters form the shape of an arc) spanning the chasm between the living and the dead, a diving board into the psychic ether, a radio set picking up signals from the unknown (*Sandover*, 555). Merrill's instructive spirits call it in quick succession an altar ("LANGUAGE IS THE POET'S CHURCH," declares his mentor Auden [252]), a theater stage with twenty-six footlights (147, 253), and even a cosmic version of Noah's Ark (253). But although it serves as the point of contact between disparate worlds—life and death, here and beyond, old and new—the Ouija board is also a field, in senses both agricultural and martial, of human endeavor and conflict. In *Sandover* it provides "A FIELD OF WORK . . . EARTH-RICH IN TRUST & EAGERNESS/& OBEDIENCE TO A HAND AT THE TILLER" (*Sandover*, 253), while in "Dialogue" it becomes, for Sibyl and Leroy, simply "our battlefield" (Plath, *Collected Poems*, 284).

In fact, both Merrill's and Plath's fascination with the Ouija board as a poetic and revelatory device has as much to do with the interpersonal dynamics of the human partners who receive its missives as with the nature and sources of the "voices" that dictate them. In *Sandover*, the roles of those partners are complementary rather than antagonistic: DJ is the "Hand," the physical and psychical conduit of the messages from the other world, while JM is the "Scribe" who transcribes those communications and eventually shapes them into verse. (Any similarity to W. B. and Georgie Yeats is not lost on Merrill; toward the end of *Sandover*, Yeats's ghost even arrives to praise David Jackson's receptive role: "YOU WERE NEARLY AS GOOD AS A WIFE" [481].) In "Dialogue," in contrast, competition threatens to sabotage cooperation; Sibyl and Leroy, both "scribes" in their own right, need each other in order to work the board, yet each suspects the other of "cheating" by guiding, consciously or unconsciously, the movements of the glass. During the early days of their marriage, in late 1956 and early 1957, Plath had enthusiastically described her relationship with Hughes in terms of its spiritualist potential—"we shall become a team better than Mr. and Mrs. Yeats"—as well as its artistic fruitfulness: "we have become mystically one. [O]ur writing is found in the inspiration of the other and grows by the inimitable criticism of the other."[23] And in 1958, a year after she wrote "Dialogue," she and Hughes would ask Pan when their next books would be published and, practically in the next breath, how many children they would have, as though the writing of books and the conception of children were equivalent, even identical, operations.[24] Yet "Dialogue" itself, written during a creatively frustrating summer holiday in 1957, voices far more anxiety of influence than collaborative self-confidence. Composed at a time when Plath was figuring the writing process both as a terrifying labor—"like giving birth to some endless and primeval baby"—and as a "painful, botched rape" of the page, a time when she herself was plagued, paradoxically, by fears of both pregnancy and artistic sterility,[25] the poem, despite moments of dualistic optimism, reflects above all Plath's own unhappy belief that creativity breeds and is bred by conflict.

In "Dialogue," that conflict is explicitly sexual as well as literary; leonine Leroy and sibylline Sibyl, the king and the mediatrix, microcosmically enact the war between the sexes in their struggle for poetic knowledge and power. The Ouija board is not only their battlefield but also their troubled nuptial bed, the place where the connubial wineglass shatters and where Pan, the disquieting Pandora of their minds, has been conceived and delivered: "our first-breached brat/Fusing two talents, a sort of psychic bastard/Sprung to being on our wedding night" (Plath, *Collected Poems*, 280). In *Sandover*, likewise, the conjugal relationship between DJ and JM is a central theme. But, whether because the poem's homosexual paradigm precludes gender conflict (H.D., similarly, ascribed her visionary powers in part to her harmonious relationship with her lesbian companion Bryher),[26] or simply because Merrill and Jackson enjoyed a more tranquil and less competitive personal and literary relationship than did Plath and Hughes, sex is not among the many dualistic tensions foregrounded within Merrill's epic. Instead, Merrill deliberately links sexuality, and specifically homosexuality, to artistic creativity: "LOVE OF ONE MAN FOR ANOTHER OR LOVE BETWEEN WOMEN/IS A NEW DEVELOPMENT OF THE PAST 4000 YEARS/ENCOURAGING SUCH MIND VALUES AS PRODUCE THE BLOSSOMS/OF POETRY & MUSIC," reports one of his spirit contacts (*Sandover*, 156). In particular, Merrill highlights his and Jackson's spiritualist proclivities when DJ asks, "Are we more usable than Yeats or Hugo,/Doters on women, who then went ahead/To doctor everything their voices said?" to which JM humorously replies, "We're more the docile takers-in of seed./No matter what tall tale our friends emit/Lately—you've noticed?—we just swallow it" (154). In his 1957 novel *The Seraglio*, Merrill describes a Ouija board that displays as its reigning spirit the likeness of a female face; here, similarly, he could be said to feminize visionary experience, equating his own role as a "docile taker-in of seed" with stereotypically female traits of passive receptivity. But whereas Plath, who calls Pan the "precocious child" of "rival parents" (*Collected Poems*, 284), invokes familiar procreative metaphors in affirming her own role as female poet, at least some of Merrill's spirit contacts suggest that both artistic fertility and the poet's role as priest—for, according to God Biology, "THE SCRIBE SHALL/SUPPLANT RELIGION" (*Sandover*, 180)—are best served by sodomistic sterility: "KEEP IN MIND THE CHILDLESSNESS WE SHARE THIS TURNS US/OUTWARD TO THE LESSONS AND THE MYSTERIES" (216). All the same, many of Merrill's spirit guides through *Sandover* seem, in the end, as much JM's and DJ's imaginative offspring as Pan is the "psychic bastard" of Sibyl and Leroy.

In keeping with the relentlessly dialogical quality of both poets' Ouija poetics, DJ/JM and Sibyl/Leroy are portrayed not only as the psychic progenitors but also as the students, or at the very least as the fellow pupils, of such playful Ouija creatures as Plath's Pan and Merrill's Mirabell. The Ouija board is a classroom, a blackboard, a scene of otherworldly instruction where each participant must trace out his or her own alphabet sampler. Plath's Sibyl and Leroy cannot begin their lessons in otherworldly existence until Pan has taken them for a "slow ramble" around the board, as though he too, childlike, must each time "learn the letters new" (*Collected Poems*, 277). And Merrill, in *Sandover*, constantly employs schoolroom imagery to describe the workings of the Ouija board. Early in *Mirabell's Books of Number*, for instance, DJ and JM acquire from "our school's/New kindergarten teacher," one of their helpful spirit guides, a "kit of tiny tools": punctuation marks to augment the Ouija board's clumsy capitals (*Sandover*, 129). Soon Merrill is regularly referring to his seances as "seminars": "INDEED IT IS OUR SMALL PRIVATE SCHOOL," comments Auden, who later likens the Ouija sessions to "OXFORD UNDER NEWMAN" (154, 197). When, in *Scripts for the Pageant*, Merrill's guiding spirits sponsor an otherworldly "FORUM . . . TO/STUDY THE

MIND OF MAN" (407), a bemused DJ remarks that "I felt like a fresh-man/In a graduate seminar" (324).

In both poems, the effect of so much educational imagery is, para-doxically, to assure us of Plath's and Merrill's visionary authority by re-minding us of the even higher authority of their teachers. At the end of *Sandover*, however, Merrill takes the pedagogical process one step farther when he turns the schoolroom tables on his ghostly instructors and stages a reading of his own lengthy epic for a gathering of literary lumi-naries that includes Austen, Dante, Eliot, Goethe, Mallarmé, Nabokov, Rilke, Stevens, and, inevitably, Yeats: "26 CHAIRS IN ALL," representing the twenty-six letters of the alphabet (*Sandover*, 547). Thus Merrill in-structs his most powerful precursors (particularly those, such as Dante, Rilke, and Yeats, with vatic pretensions of their own) that visionary po-etry is alive and well, but that it can survive into the twenty-first century only if, like Merrill's epic, it is packaged in self-conscious camp and de-flective candor.

As readers, of course, we too are Merrill's pupils, guided through the grand schema of *Sandover* letter by letter and number by number, with the poem itself serving as our alphabet primer, our cosmic encyclopedia. Nonetheless, Merrill never allows us to forget that the Ouija board is fi-nally not a textbook but a parlor game, its poetic and spiritual lessons taught, appropriately, mostly through wordplay. Merrill's spirit guide Mirabell (whose name, not coincidentally, echoes Merrill's own) uses metaphor so frequently to explain the ineffable workings of the universe that he flashes the code letter M to signal such moments: "M IS AT ONCE OUR/METHOD & THE MIDPOINT OF OUR ALPHABET THE SUMMIT/OF OUR RAINBOW ROOF" (*Sandover*, 222). Merrill's own similar tendency to de-scribe the Ouija board and its half-circle of letters in playful yet sugges-tive metaphorical terms—as a pond (6), a mirror (517), a door (300), an ark (253), a field (253), a stage (147), an altar (252), a schoolroom (154), a radio (555), "a devil's darning needle" (6), and even a "cosmic carpool" (262)—exposes his complicity in Mirabell's instructive game. Yet metaphor and wordplay, Merrill reminds us elsewhere, are not just tools for edification or education. They "ground the lightning of ideas," shielding poet and reader alike from the potentially blinding impact of unmediated vision.[27]

Plath is far more wary than Merrill of such playful deflective tactics. Indeed, it is in large part this wariness that marks the departure of her Ouija poetics from Merrill's. Plath's Pan, "prone to compose queer poetry/In apt iambics" (*Collected Poems*, 280), speaks, like Mirabell, mostly in metaphor, yet Plath ends "Dialogue over a Ouija Board" with a wholesale rejection of figurative language and thought. Early on, Leroy affirms the redemptive capabilities of the poetic imagination: "we face/Obliteration hourly unless our eye/Can whipcrack the tables into tigers and foist/Castles upon the smug-shaped chairs" (279). But by the end of the poem, Plath's two shaken protagonists want only to "resign our stand/At the unreal frontier" (285) of creative fancy; "The table looks as if it would stay a table/All night long," says Sibyl hopefully, and Leroy agrees: "The chairs won't vanish or become/Castles when we glance aside" (286). Elsewhere, in a poem titled "The Ghost's Leavetaking," Plath describes the disorienting realm of Sibyl and Leroy's fears—the "chilly no-man's land of about/Five o'clock in the morning"—in almost utopian terms, as a "cloud-cuckoo land of color wheels/and pristine alphabets."[28] In "Dialogue," however, the world of dreams, visions, and metaphorical inversions is not cheerfully "pristine" but thorny and twisted: the Ouija board, a seemingly simple apparatus—"a circle of letters: twenty-six/In all. Plus Yes. Plus No. And this bare board" (276)—becomes under Pan's influence a locus of "jabberwocky" and "balderdash" (279), an "unequivocal/Thicket of words" (286), and finally a "labyrinth" inhabited by a dangerous "beast" (286). (Even in renouncing metaphor, it seems, Sibyl and Leroy, with their overdetermined names and poetic habits of mind, cannot help using it.)

Ultimately, Plath shies away completely from all that the Ouija board represents, both psychically and linguistically: otherworldly authority, the maze of the mind, the prison house of language. As a poet, of course, Plath could not herself maintain the rejection of metaphor so vehemently mouthed by Sibyl and Leroy in their desperation to escape the board's "welter of contending words" (*Collected Poems*, 286). But she would increasingly spurn external devices like the Ouija board and its spirit voices, searching in her later work for meaning, metaphor, poetic authority, and even "pristine alphabets" in the equally mysterious reaches of the human body instead: "From her lips ampersands and percent signs/Exit like kisses. / . . . / ABC, her eyelids say" ("An Appearance," in *Collected Poems*, 189).

The Ouija board is a compelling poetic instrument—but, for Plath, ultimately a suspect one—precisely because it displaces the creative process, shifting language, action, and expressive responsibility away from the poet's mind and body and onto its own metaphor-ridden surface. Less given to epic sweep and ironical introspection than Merrill, less intrigued by the unruly vitality of pop culture (her own poetry would for the most part remain safely lodged in the realm of the "high"), desiring in the end to be "seized up/Without a part left over" ("Mystic," in *Collected Poems*, 268) by visionary experience rather than to suffer the awkward mediation of material commodities, Plath would eventually reject the Ouija board's collaborative framework—"Dangerous to be so close to Ted," she later remarked[29]—and evolve a poetics dependent on other, more private sources of inspiration: memory, myth, self-absorption, desire, rage. For Merrill, in contrast, the Ouija board would become an increasingly important poetic tool: a liberating principle, an epic framework, a metaphor for metaphor. *The Changing Light at Sandover*, with its extraordinary mixture of cosmic high-seriousness and comic impudence, both affirms the artistic fruitfulness of Merrill's relationship with David Jackson and plays for all it is worth the Ouija board's capacity to bring into fertile conjunction the conflicting tropes of high prophecy and popular culture, of myth and modernity, of otherworldly authority and authorial self-fashioning, of spiritualist revelation and material mediation.

Both Plath and Merrill initially took up the Ouija board not only as a way of probing their own unconscious minds, not only as a method of trawling the unknown for new "metaphors for poetry," but also as a potential means of communicating with—or, in Merrill's case, of assuaging his guilt regarding—the dead fathers who haunt their work.[30] More to the point, perhaps, both writers saw the board as a way of making contact with their poetic fathers: the modernist poets whose works and examples most deeply influenced their own at the time. For Merrill, one of those spiritual forebears was Rilke, who was first introduced to the spiritualist practice of planchette pushing by the Princess Marie von Thurn und Taxis; it seems "no accident," then (to use Merrill's own favorite phrase), that one of the first Ouija voices to speak in Merrill's "Voices from the Other World" belongs to an imperious aristocrat who identifies himself as "OTTO VON THURN UND TAXIS." For Plath (who had translated Rilke's poem "The Prophet" while she was a student at Cambridge),[31] a comparably important father figure was Yeats, whose spiritualist collabo-

ration with his wife she had hoped to emulate through her own relationship with Hughes, whose tower in Ireland would later arouse in her
"the uncanny feeling I had got in touch with Yeats' spirit," and whose
former house in London, where she would eventually rent a flat, would
serve as "a real inspiration to my writing."[32] Yet if, when they first began
experimenting with automatic writing, Plath and Merrill intended to follow in the psychic footsteps of Rilke and Yeats, they soon strayed from
their precursors' path of psychic circumspection by composing poems
that unabashedly detail their own spiritualist experiences. Moreover,
their specific choice of the Ouija board as a communicative tool further
undercuts their modernist forebears' high seriousness by reminding
their readers—in ways that spiritualist props such as Rilke's planchette,
H. D.'s turning table, and Yeats's receptive wife do not—that poetry, and
perhaps life itself, is finally "only a game." Moving beyond modernism's
rigid antipathy toward popular culture, Merrill and Plath use the Ouija
board—"this absurd, flimsy contraption, creaking along"[33]—to transport
the age-old prophetic mode toward the cynical, subversive, ludic realm
of the postmodern.

THE HAUNTING OF TED HUGHES

Whereas Plath and Merrill forthrightly explore the literary im-
plications of real-life mediumship, other late-twentieth-century authors
probe the relationship between literature and popular spiritualism in a
more loosely metaphorical, if often equally irreverent, mode. Writers as
otherwise diverse as Vladimir Nabokov, A. S. Byatt, and Ted Hughes, for
instance, employ spiritualist tropes to unsettle traditional definitions of
authorship, mock academic institutions, challenge scholarly interpretive
paradigms, and examine the role of commodity culture in literary production and reception. Their self-reflexive, arguably postmodern spin
on popular spiritualism goes far to explain contemporary literary criticism's obsession with mediumship, ghosts, and haunting, which I discuss
in the epilogue to this book. Ghostwriting, for these writers, is not
merely a literary act but a metacritical one as well.

In Nabokov's 1962 *Pale Fire*, allusions to ghosts and spirit survival form
the backbone of the author's satirical commentary on American academic criticism. Ostensibly penned by an Appalachian poet named John
Shade, the novel's eponymous centerpiece poem, "Pale Fire," is accom-

panied by a lengthy introduction and even lengthier line-by-line commentary signed by Charles Kinbote, a quirky visiting professor from the land of Zembla who believes himself to be that country's exiled king but could just as well be a delusional madman. Shade's poem, like his name, contains both ghosts and ambiguity about ghosts, as it grapples with what Shade calls "the grand potato," or "le grand Peut-être": the question of whether the spirit survives the body after death.[34] Ironically and with considerable humor, Shade narrates his daughter Hazel's attempts, as a teenager, to communicate with a rapping spirit in a haunted barn; his own hilarious semester-long stint as a visiting lecturer at IPH, the Institute of Preparation for the Hereafter; Hazel's tragic suicide and its emotional aftermath; Shade's hopeful visit to a woman who, according to a magazine article, had seen a "tall white fountain" during a near-death experience, replicating exactly a vision that Shade too had once had; and finally, the poet's crushing disappointment upon learning that the woman had in fact seen a mountain, not a fountain:

> Life Everlasting—based on a misprint!
> I mused as I drove homeward: take the hint,
> And stop investigating my abyss?
> But all at once it dawned on me that *this*
> Was the real point, the contrapuntal theme;
> Just this: not text, but texture; not the dream
> But topsy-turvy coincidence,
> Not flimsy nonsense, but a web of sense.[35]

Shade's conclusion—that the answer to the question of spirit survival lies not in a single, unifying symbol but in "the contrapuntal theme; . . . not text but texture"—offers a key to reading *Pale Fire* itself, a novel whose meaning, insofar as it offers any stable meaning at all, resides in the intricate intertextual interplay of Shade's poem and Kinbote's commentary: the "web of sense" woven not within them but between them.

Many of the novel's most enthusiastic critics, to be sure, seem to miss this cardinal point. Not only has Nabokov's own professed interest in spiritualism led, inevitably, to a certain amount of simplistic spook-hunting in his works,[36] but considerable scholarly debate has focused on the ways in which the novel's spiritualist subtext might reveal the "true" authorship of both "Pale Fire" and its accompanying commentary. Some scholars believe that, according to internal hints planted by Nabokov, Shade wrote the commentary himself, in effect inventing Kinbote; others insist that Kinbote had a role, if not in actually writing Shade's poem, then at least in "stitch[ing] the poem and commentary together with gossamer verbal threads."[37] More recently, in a controversial essay, Brian Boyd has tried to resolve the internal authorship conundrum by attributing the "uncanny coincidences" between poem and commentary to the posthumous influence of Shade's ghost, who appears, Boyd argues, in the form of a shadowy character named Jakob Gradus, aka Jack Gray: "I suggest that we are invited to see here that Shade's shade, his ghost, influences Kinbote's paranoia. [As Kinbote] writes his commentary under Shade's influence, . . . the poem now explodes with 'richly rhymed life' to a degree the mortal Shade could never have imagined."[38]

Boyd's ingenious solution betrays a desire for the kind of single, unifying meaning that Shade himself rejects and Nabokov repeatedly deflects. In this novel about critical misappropriation, the many allusions to spiritualism teach us not that ghosts can solve all our interpretive problems but that literary interpretation is a haunting, haunted undertaking. In a 1966 interview, Nabokov himself obligingly decoded the seemingly nonsensical spirit message received by Hazel in the haunted barn—"pada ata lane pad not ogo old wart alan ther tale feur far rant lant tal told"—as a covert warning that Shade ("pada" or papa) should not go across the lane to his neighbor's house after he finishes writing his poem.[39] But far from authorizing us to read the novel as an elaborate puzzle with a pat solution, Nabokov's cryptopoetic gloss smacks of self-parody, exposing the slipperiness of the interpretive process itself. John Shade is dead, but his poem still exercises a posthumous influence upon the anguished Kinbote. Kinbote's commentary, in turn, haunts the poem, which can no longer be read without reference to his own regicidal fantasy. Nabokov refuses, in fact, to grant us the kind of simple inspirational allegory that we find in early-twentieth-century representations of literary ghostwriting such as Kipling's 1902 story "Wireless," in which a young chemist speaks with the voice of Keats, or Yeats's 1930 play *The Words upon the Window Pane*, in which a spirit medium channels the words of Swift and his two literate lovers. Here, instead, literary meaning resides in the complex interactions of text, reader, and posthumous author upon one another. Indeed, as the commentaries of Boyd and other critics make clear, even the new "web of sense" woven between and among competing discourses eventually takes on an independent, ghostly life of its own.

A. S. Byatt draws similar parallels between spirit communication and literary interpretation in her 1990 novel *Possession*, which adumbrates upon the theme of posthumous authorial influence already explored in her earlier novella, *The Conjugial Angel*. Frequently described as a Victorian postmodernist,[40] Byatt skips back and forth throughout *Possession* between the mid-nineteenth and late twentieth centuries, weaving together two separate romantic plots: one involving a pair of Victorian poets, Randolph Henry Ash and Christabel LaMotte, the other a pair of literary scholars who set out a century and a half later to uncover the sexual/textual relationship that motivated the poets' lives and informed their poetry. A spiritualist subplot—at one point Ash attends a seance to seek the truth about his and LaMotte's illegitimate child—adds to the novel's authentically Victorian aura, replaying elements of Robert and Elizabeth Barrett Browning's famous squabble over their respective spiritualist beliefs.[41] But Byatt's allusions to popular spiritualism subvert as well as historicize, for they lend structure and shape to her postmodern reflections on authorship, ownership, and the limitations of literary interpretation.

Spiritualism, we learn in *Possession*, is largely a matter of personal interpretation based on private knowledge—something like reader-response criticism—as when Ash and LaMotte attend the same seance but come away with wildly different impressions. (Ash, although a skeptic, assumes that the medium's messages concern his lost child, whom he unjustly suspects LaMotte to have killed; LaMotte interprets those same messages as coming from her erstwhile lover, Blanche Glover, for whose suicide she feels responsible.) Literary interpretation, conversely, begins to look a lot like popular spiritualism: speculative, deceptive, sometimes comforting, always involving jockeyings for authoritative stature. Mortimer Cropper, an American academic who has made a career of tracking down and possessing artifacts associated with Ash, hails from Robert Dale Owen University, a fictional institution named for the famous spiritualist author of *The Debatable Land between This World and the Next*. Many of Cropper's literary purchases, moreover, are funded by an endowment left by his own great-grandmother, a devoted spiritualist who corresponded with both Ash and LaMotte about their otherworldly beliefs.

Each of these details reminds us to recognize "possession"—whether of the mediumistic or materialist variety—as a multivalent and ultimately ironic term for any kind of interpretive power play.

Byatt takes her novel's epigraph from Robert Browning's spiritualist satire, "Mr. Sludge, 'The Medium,' " in which Browning, despite his obvious antipathy toward spiritualism, likens professional mediums to poets. In "Mummy Possess'd," a Browningesque interior monolog supposedly penned by Ash, Byatt adds a materialist twist to Browning's commentary on the close kinship of spiritualism and art, both of which, she notes, express supposedly eternal truths by means of a compromising medium:

> Consider this. Arts have their Medium—
> Coloratura, tempera, or stone.
> Through medium of paint the Ideal Form
> Of the Eternal Mother shows herself
> (Though modelled maybe on some worthless wench
> No better than she should be, we may guess).
> Through medium of language the great Poets
> Keep constant the Ideal, as Beatrice
> Speaks still to us, though Dante's flesh is dust.
> So through the Medium of this poor flesh
> With sweats and groanings, nauseas and cries
> Of animal anguish, the sublimest Souls
> Make themselves known to those who sit and wait.[42]

The novel's title links spiritualist possession to tropes of intellectual possession (the two twentieth-century protagonists are possessed by their quest to possess the truth about Ash and LaMotte) and sexual possession (both LaMotte and her descendent, poststructuralist literary critic Maud Bailey, fear losing their self-possession if they succumb to the temptations of love and desire). But it is material possession, above all, that drives the novel's plot, as various scholars vie for physical custody of Ash and LaMotte's unpublished correspondence. All human knowledge, these scholars soon discover, is contingent and embodied. As "Mummy Possess'd" makes clear, ideal form (or transcendent knowledge, or historical accuracy) cannot exist independently of mediatory physical artifacts, any more than "the sublimest Souls" can make themselves heard except via the fleshly "sweats and groanings, nauseas and cries" of the human bodies through which they communicate.

Both *Pale Fire* and *Possession* represent popular spiritualism as a pliant, playful metaphor for the hermeneutic process. Ted Hughes's *Birthday Letters* might seem an unlikely text to place in their company; indeed, Hughes's stylistically conservative and thematically conventional collection of eighty-eight poems—some movingly elegiac, some mawkishly sentimental, some so clearly self-serving as to negate all sympathy for their anguished author—appears at first glance no better a candidate for the label "postmodern" than does the confessional poetry of Sylvia Plath, Hughes's erstwhile partner at the Ouija board. Most of the *Birthday Letters* are addressed directly to Plath, who committed suicide in 1963, by a speaker who is transparently Hughes himself: a lyric poet in the most traditional sense of the word, singing his emotions directly from the heart, transforming personal tragedy into myth. In their treatment of ghostwriting and haunting, however, Hughes's Plath poems have less in common with the metaphorical mediumship of modernist writers such as Lawrence, Woolf, Eliot, or Mann than with the explicitly metacritical spiritualism of Nabokov, Byatt, or, as I have intimated, Plath herself.

Hughes's lifelong interest in the occult is well known,[43] and his experiments with Plath at the Ouija board are documented not only in her poetry ("Ouija," "Dialogue over a Ouija Board") but in his as well ("Ouija").[44] Casual spiritualist references abound throughout *Birthday Letters*: visible ghosts flit through poems such as "Wuthering Heights," "The Chipmunk," and "Portraits" (61, 63, 104); Hughes describes Plath's face as "a spirit mask transfigured every moment/In its own séance" (23); a number of poems, such as "Ouija" and "Life after Death," bear explicitly spiritualist titles (53, 182). Hughes writes incessantly of haunted objects: tables and scissors and pens and vessels that communicate, like ghosts, traces of an earlier, happier existence. Like the moving elegies that Thomas Hardy wrote about his dead wife in 1912–13, these poems employ visual, tactile, often sartorial imagery— Plath's "blue flannel suit" and "pink wool knitted dress," reminiscent of Emma Hardy's "original air-blue gown"—to convey a palpable, echoing anguish that belies the poet's real-life rejection of the woman he now claims so desperately to miss. Yet the real work of haunting in these poems is not imagistic but intertextual, a matter of literary inheritance.

Hughes's poems are haunted by Plath's language, which echoes everywhere in his own; by her extraordinary fame ("Sylvia Plath haunts our culture," writes Jacqueline Rose);[45] by her literary representations of Hughes, who depicts himself in his own poems as a helpless victim caught in the clutches of her myth.

Hughes does not seek to document in *Birthday Letters* any actual spirit communications from Plath. Instead, he delineates her literary afterlife, the haunting influence of her writing upon his. In "Black Coat," for instance, he describes how her father, Otto, whose premature death haunted her imagination, now inhabits his own identity via poems such as Plath's "Man in Black" and "Daddy," enduring literary works in which Ted and Otto are forever superimposed:

> I had no idea I had stepped
> Into the telescopic sights
> Of the paparazzo sniper
> Nested in your brown iris.
>
> .   .   .   .
>
> How that double image,
> The eye's inbuilt double exposure
> Which was the projection
> Of your two-way heart's diplopic error,
> The body of the ghost and me the blurred see-through
> Came into single focus.
>
> .   .   .   .
>
> I did not feel
> How, as your lenses tightened,
> He slid into me.
>
> (*Birthday Letters*, 102–3)

In a number of other poems throughout *Birthday Letters*, Hughes similarly employs allusions to photographs (Plath as a young Fulbright scholar; Plath sitting with her children among daffodils; Otto Plath standing at a blackboard) as springboards for meditations on the dramatic irony of memory. In "Black Coat," however, photographic imagery functions not so much to fix and record a real-life event—Hughes's dim recollection of wearing the black coat that Plath would later use to associate him with her father—so much as to convey literature's power to shape and distort reality. For Roland Barthes, photography is at once a death-defying act and a harbinger of death: "The Photograph . . . represents that very subtle moment when, to tell the truth, I am neither subject nor object but a subject who feels he is becoming an object: I then experience a micro-version of death (of parenthesis): I am truly becoming a specter."[46] Hughes, similarly, depicts himself as having been "shot" in senses both photographic and funereal. Simultaneously immortalized and murdered by Plath's deadly, death-defying gaze, he has been rendered not merely a specter but, worse yet, a specter of the father's specter, a "blurred see-through" with no haunting power of his own. "Picture of Otto," another photography-laced poem, relays this point even more bluntly: "Your ghost inseparable from my shadow" (*Birthday Letters*, 193).

In a 1976 essay titled "Myth and Education," Hughes relates the story of a magazine photographer who, for reasons Hughes declares himself unable to fathom, continued to snap pictures of a woman and her pet tiger even after the tiger began to attack its mistress:

> This photographer—we can easily understand him because we all belong to this modern world—had become his camera. . . . Whatever his thoughts were he went on taking photographs of the whole procedure while the tiger killed the woman, because the pictures were there in the magazine. And the story was told as if the photographer had indeed been absent. As if the camera had simply gone on doing what any camera would be expected to do, being a mere mechanical device for registering outer appearances.[47]

In "Black Coat," it is clearly Plath who has "become the camera," losing all sense of human proportion as a result of her "heart's two-way diplopic error"—a mechanical rather than purely emotional failure. Yet Hughes, too, bears a striking resemblance to the hapless photographer of his own anecdote, as he offers up for publication one snapshot after another of a woman being slowly and painfully destroyed before his seemingly helpless, but in fact deeply complicit, gaze.

Hughes, after all, not Plath, is the author of *Birthday Letters*, the creator of his own vivid photographic imagery. For, as his tiger anecdote memorably illustrates, it is the living who regulate representations of the dead, however much lip service authors like him may pay to the haunting power of ghosts. As longtime executor of Plath's literary estate, Hughes was infamous among scholars for his attempts to control her image by stifling certain kinds of critical discourse about her work even while he profited handsomely (and, some say, very cannily) from the posthumous publication of her poems, letters, and journals.[48] In *Birthday Letters*, he depicts literary critics as bloodthirsty hyenas who "batten/On the cornucopia" of Plath's body, who "Jerk their tail-stumps, bristle and vomit/Over their symposia" (195–96). Yet he also freely offers up a new cornucopia—his own confessional poems, his own figurative body—to those same carnivorous critics.

In breaking nearly thirty-five years of literary reticence about Plath at a time when he knew he was dying, Hughes actively and self-consciously positioned himself as her partner in death as well as in life, marrying himself forever to her myth. A man who knew from personal experience the extraordinary power of dead authors—in "Costly Speech," for instance, he describes how Plath's "dead fingers so deftly unpicked" U.S. copyright law to allow the publication of works he had tried to ban (170–71)—Hughes sets himself up, with *Birthday Letters*, to become Plath's fellow specter. Yet he does so with the full and ironic knowledge that neither he nor she will have the last word in their interminable marital squabble. Just as spirits need living mediums, however dull their intellects or tawdry their surroundings, in order to speak or write, so Hughes must now and forever after depend on the very critics, reviewers, and literature professors he so despised to keep his voice alive.

Birthday Letters focuses neither on actual mediumship (as in Plath's and Merrill's Ouija poems) nor on metaphorical mediumship (as in the novels of Nabokov and Byatt, which draw lively parallels between popular spiritualism and literary interpretation). Instead, Hughes takes ghostwriting to a new and arguably more complex level, suggesting that poets and readers alike are caught up in a network of haunting that, because it takes place in and through published texts, is ultimately more real, more closely grounded in systems of material exchange and commodification, than other modes of spirit communication. And yet, like Nabokov in *Pale Fire* (where Kinbote boasts constantly about his supposed friendship with John Shade) and Byatt in *Possession* (where Maud Bailey, the literary critic, turns out to be a literal descendent both of Randolph Ash and Christabel LaMotte), Hughes also reminds us with *Birthday Letters* that the haunting power of the famous dead is at its most potent and inescapable when some kind of close personal connection exists between a dead writer and the readers, critics, editors, executors, translators, and interpreters who serve as his or her literary heirs. Thus postmodern ghostwriting turns out to be at least as firmly implicated as Victorian or modernist-era spiritualism in Oedipal anxieties about authority, individuality, and personal inheritance.

Needless to say, contemporary invocations of spirit communication can reflect many other cultural anxieties as well, including some not touched upon at all in Hughes's poems. In the era of the Internet, for instance, as texts themselves become increasingly ghostlike and ephemeral—present on the World Wide Web one day, gone the next, unless preserved in what is tellingly called a hard copy—Victorian analogies between spirit mediumship and new communication technologies become more relevant than ever, offering fruitful parables about the promises and frustrations of materialized meaning. Jean Baudrillard defines postmodernism as an "implosion *of the medium and of the real*, in a sort of nebulous hyperreality, in which even the definition and the distinct action of the medium are no longer locatable."[49] Spirit mediumship, which similarly blurs the dividing line between "the medium" (that is, the material reality of the medium's body and text) and "the real" (the spiritual reality of the medium's messages), produces its own version of "hyperreality" and thus can serve, perhaps, as an instructive prototype for the paradoxical functionings of other mediumistic modes still relatively new to twenty-first-century culture: for example, the cellular phone, the instantaneous satellite image, the hypertext website, and the various simulations and simulacra that parade under the label "virtual reality."

Not surprisingly, the proverbial "ghost in the machine" invoked by Arthur Koestler in 1967 has by now become a well-established trope in contemporary cyberpunk and science fiction. In William Gibson's 1988 *Mona Lisa Overdrive*, for instance, a global computer network turns out to be inhabited by ancient voodoo gods; in Neal Stephenson's 1993 *Snow Crash*, a virus that affects both humans and computers is discovered to have been responsible for destroying ancient Sumerian culture by randomizing its language and bringing about Babel; and in Philip Pullman's 1997 *The Subtle Knife*, disembodied angels communicate with an Oxford physicist via her computer's word processing program. Spiritualists, conversely, have eagerly leapt aboard the digital bandwagon, as evidenced by publications such as Patricia Kubis and Mark Macy's 1995 book, *Conversations beyond the Light,* which bears the subtitle *Communication with Departed Friends and Colleagues by Electronic Means.* Indeed—speaking of virtual reality—one no longer even needs a physical Ouija board these days to talk with the dead. Instead, a "WWW Talking Board" website invites computer users, eyes closed, to "ask yourself a question and use your mouse as an electronic planchette."[50] Whether or not electronic spirits will ever mediate the creation of literary works as ambitious and effective as Plath's "Dialogue over a Ouija Board" or Merrill's *Sandover* trilogy remains, of course, to be seen. "Don't take this seriously!" the Ouija site's webmaster warns. "After all, it is just a web page." That might be the only prompt a seriously postmodern ghostwriter needs.

Ghostreading

Now fills the air so many a haunting shape
That no one knows how best he may escape.

                          Goethe, *Faust* 2, act 5, scene 5

"But then I'm inclined to think that we are all ghosts, Pastor Man-
ders, every one of us. It's not just what we inherit from our moth-
ers and fathers that haunts us. It's all kinds of old defunct theories, all sorts of old defunct beliefs, and things like that. It's not
that they actually *live* on in us; they are simply lodged there, and
we cannot get rid of them."

                                   Henrik Ibsen, *Ghosts*

When I first decided to write a book about modernist literature and popular spiritualism, it seemed I was venturing into unclaimed
critical territory. Historians, especially feminists, had become intrigued
by the spiritualist movement a decade or two previously, and so I was fortunate enough to have access to a number of excellent studies of nineteenth-century spiritualism, mostly published in the late 1970s and
1980s, as well as a handful of books on spiritualism in nineteenth-century literature.[1] Two books—Marjorie Garber's *Shakespeare's Ghost Writers*
(1987) and Avital Ronell's *Dictations: On Haunted Writing* (1986)—addressed the haunting effects of Shakespeare and Goethe, respectively,
on modern culture. But I found very little published work either on
modernist-era spiritualism or on connections between spiritualism and
literary modernism (George Mills Harper's writings on Yeats's *Vision* papers being a notable exception). I felt like a pioneer in wide-open field.

   I did not, however, remain isolated for long. Throughout the 1990s,
virtually every new book catalog I opened, every journal I read, every
conference I attended, bore witness to the distressing fact that numerous other literary scholars were encroaching upon the academic turf I
had marked out for myself—and, worse yet, they had arrived there be-

fore I did. While I completed other projects and embarked upon this one, I witnessed the publication of at least a book a year on topics pertaining to spiritualism and literature: Daniel Cottom's *Abyss of Reason* in 1991; Diana Basham's *The Trial of Woman* in 1992; Leon Surette's *The Birth of Modernism* in 1993; Jacques Derrida's *Specters of Marx* in 1994; Timothy Materer's *Modernist Alchemy* in 1995; Jean-Michel Rabaté's *The Ghosts of Modernity* in 1996; a special issue of *Paradoxa* devoted to the uncanny in 1997; Kathleen Brogan's *Cultural Haunting* in 1998; Brenda Maddox's *Yeats's Ghosts* in 1999. (Terry Castle published not just one but two "hauntological" books in the 1990s: *The Apparitional Lesbian* in 1993 and *The Female Thermometer: Eighteenth-Century Culture and the Invention of the Uncanny* in 1995.) Even new scholarly works that did not discuss spiritualism as a cultural phenomenon often invoked ghosts, haunting, and spirit mediumship in their titles.[2] In 1996, Warwick University in England hosted an entire conference on the theme of "homospectrality." Meanwhile, articles on spiritualism and literary production, modernism and the occult, and tropes of haunting in modern literature and culture sprouted like mushrooms in journals and edited collections.[3]

None of the studies listed above duplicates, or in most cases even overlaps much with, the subject matter of this book. Cottom and Basham deal only with nineteenth-century spiritualism; Surette and Materer focus exclusively on the occult; Rabaté's *Ghosts of Modernity* discusses ghosts and haunting almost entirely in metaphorical terms, with little if any reference to the historical particularities of the spiritualist movement. All the same, it was disconcerting to find that what I had initially considered a highly original, even unconventional, project had become, inadvertently, a trendy one instead. Far from being a pioneer, it seemed, I was just another passenger on an already crowded bandwagon.

Spiritualism has not always been so fashionable. Scholars of literary modernism's occult influences (S. Friedman, Harper, Materer, Surette, Tryphonopoulos) document in sometimes bitter detail what Surette, in a 1993 polemic, called "the blinkers that continue to protect the scholarly community from any exposure to the occult components of literary modernism."[4] Similar blinkers have long screened popular spiritualism, especially its twentieth-century forms, from academic scrutiny. As an undergraduate studying canonical High Modernism in the early 1980s, I learned all about modernist writers' irony, angst, and ennui but nothing of their occult or spiritualist pursuits. And even when, as a graduate student writing a dissertation on prophetic poetry, I finally became aware of Yeats's seances, H. D.'s table tilting, and Rilke's planchette experiments, I was often made to feel that I was treading on forbidden, or at least on dangerously boggy, ground. H. D.'s daughter, Perdita Schaffner, replied graciously and candidly, if not as helpfully as I had hoped, when I sent a letter asking whether she had been aware of her mother's spiritualist involvement in the early 1940s:

> She was "into" those things. At the time I didn't have much patience with any of it. If it amused and comforted her, as it seems to have, well and fine by me. She went off to her seances in World War II, I daresay, but I was so busy with my job, friends, life, and she didn't disclose her experiences to me.[5]

A venerable German H. D. scholar to whom I posed a similar query, however, expressed considerably less sympathy for the direction my research was taking me. Speaking both for himself and for his wife, who sometimes assisted him with his scholarly work, he wrote:

> We have no interest at all in the gender sides of your thesis. Even about the prophetic stance we have our doubts and we rather hope that MSS like her *Magic Ring* [*sic*] or *The Sword Went Out to Sea* with the descriptions of her crazy spiritistic table wrapping [*sic*] during the war years in London will remain unpublished.[6]

Yet H. D.'s "crazy spiritistic table wrapping" continued to intrigue me, so much so that I eventually turned my critical gaze from modernist prophecy to modernist ghost-mongering. My academic route into popular spiritualism—a journey from high culture to low, by way of feminist criticism, cultural studies, textual materialism, and the New Historicism—can be recognized, in retrospect, as a fairly typical one for a literary scholar of the 1990s. Yet tracing my own path does relatively little to explain why intellectuals as diverse as Jacques Derrida and Stephen Greenblatt, Jacqueline Rose and Leon Surette, even archrivals Lawrence Rainey and Susan Stanford Friedman, should find common ground in their invocations of ghosts, spiritualism, and the occult. I opened this book by asking how we can account for the striking persistence of popular spiritualism in the age of literary modernism. I wish to close with a somewhat different question: How can we explain the extraordinary proliferation of spiritualist tropes—ghosts, haunting, mediumship, automatic writing—in recent criticism and theory? What is it about our own cultural moment, in other words—the end of the twentieth century, the dawn of a new millennium—that inspires literary critics to see ghosts everywhere?

In the second half of the nineteenth century, as I have noted, popular spiritualism appealed to an astonishingly wide range of people across national, ethnic, class, and gender lines. (The educated classes did, to be sure, tend to write about it more.)[7] More than a century later, spiritualism's surprising resilience—at least as a literary and critical trope, if not necessarily as a respectable intellectual pursuit—can be attributed, similarly, to its elastic ability to satisfy diverse, even opposing, critical sensibilities: for instance, by affirming the kind of philosophical complexity that it seems at first glance to abnegate. Needless to say, haunting can always be historicized; its forms and meaning change with the times. In the nineteenth century, popular spiritualism brought together anti-orthodox religious faith and scientific progressivism, offering Victorian intellectuals and non-intellectuals alike a means of coming to grips with contemporary developments in communication technology, social theory, even evolutionary biology. Modernist writers discovered in mediumistic discourse fruitful ways of conceptualizing and representing literary production, gender transformations, and the stubborn materiality of language. And postmodernists—ironically, given spiritualism's origins as a religious movement intended to allay ontological uncertainties—have found themselves drawn to the slipperiness and subversiveness of ghosts, their apparent affirmation of the radical indeterminacy of the postmodern condition.

Indeed, for poststructuralist literary critics such as Avital Ronell (*Dictations; The Telephone Book*), Nicholas Royle (*Telepathy and Literature*), and Jean-Michel Rabaté (*The Ghosts of Modernity*), ghosts enact a whole deconstructive vocabulary. They endlessly evade and defer meaning (Derrida's *différance*); they are simultaneously present and absent (leaving behind "traces of traces"); they exist through a chain of substitutions and mediations (the "logic of the supplement"); they point, by dint of their own materialized insubstantiality, to the arbitrary nature of the sign (mediating between *langue* and *parole*).[8] Derrida himself, meanwhile, employs a sustained metaphorics of haunting to reconcile his own "deconstructive thinking of the trace, of iterability, of prosthetic synthesis, of supplementarity" with explicitly Marxist concerns about history, economics, and political power. In *Specters of Marx*, he argues for the fundamental "spectrality" of many different aspects of human existence: ethics (ghosts importune justice); mourning (ghosts "ontologize remains"); the past ("haunting is historical"); the future ("the specter is the future"); inheritance ("One never inherits without coming to terms with some specter"); religion ("Christ is the most spectral of specters"); translation ("the words of translation . . . disorganize themselves . . . through the very effect of the specter"); imagination ("The specter is also . . . what one thinks one sees and which one projects"); phenomenology ("the phenomenological form of the world itself is spectral"); capitalism (money is "a production of ghosts, illusions, simulacra, appearances, or apparitions"); dialectical materialism ("the logic of the ghost . . . exceeds a binary or dialectical logic"); political repression ("Haunting belongs to the structure of every hegemony"); academic culture ("There has never been a scholar who really, and as scholar, deals with ghosts"), and postmodern communication technologies: "[the power of the media] cannot be analyzed . . . without taking into account so many *spectral* effects, the new speed of *apparition* (we understand this word in its ghostly sense) of the simulacrum, the synthetic or prosthetic image, and the virtual event."[9] In fact, as these examples make evident, Derrida deploys the words "specter" and "spectral" so often, in so many different permutations and contexts, that they threaten to become verbal specters themselves: suggestive, thought-provoking, ethereal entities drained of all stable referential meaning.

Nonetheless, Derrida's breezy interweaving of Marxist, historical, deconstructive, psychoanalytical, and philological discourses provides some insight into the appeal of spirits and spiritualism for literary critics of many different—even radically opposing—methodological persuasions. For feminist literary critics such as Diana Basham and Bette London, spirit mediumship offers a useful paradigm for exploring relationships between authorial empowerment and the politics of gender. For postcolonial critics such as Patrick Brantlinger, Marjorie Howes, and Gauri Viswanathan, likewise, spiritualism and the occult provide frames of reference for understanding the paradoxes implicit in imperialist doctrines of cultural conquest and hegemony. For Marxist critics such as Jeff Nunokawa and Andrew H. Miller, ghosts stand in for any of the various cultural agents that exceed and outlast their own origins, acting upon society yet refusing embodiment: capital, imagination, fame. For queer theorists such as Terry Castle, Hugh Stevens, and Patricia White, ghostliness represents not only a symptom of repression—"Once the lesbian has been defined as ghostly . . . she can then be exorcized," writes Castle—but also, more ominously, a return of the repressed, as when Henry James finds himself haunted by the specter of Oscar Wilde's homosexuality, or when the protagonist of Shirley Jackson's 1959 novel *The Haunting of Hill House* channels her repressed lesbianism into the nighttime hauntings of an ominous poltergeist. Similarly, for psychoanalytic critics such as Marjorie Garber and Jacqueline Rose, haunting signals a repetition compulsion, defined by Freud not only as a return of the repressed but also as a constituent element of the uncanny: "this 'perpetual recurrence of the same thing' that strikes us as uncanniness in life and as structure in art," writes Garber, "is one of the functions performed in Shakespeare's plays by the figure of the ghost." For sociologists such as Avery F. Gordon and ethnologists such as Christine Bergé, the conjuration of spirits is a compensatory gesture, a reaction against various social pressures; Bergé argues, for instance, that spirit mediums "escape the mortuary grip" of industrialism by turning themselves into "spiritual machines" who can therefore better control their own fate. And finally, for cryptographic critics such as Nicolas Abraham, Maria Torok, and Shawn Rosenheim, ghosts affirm the interpretive imperative of all modern existence, communicating in code (raps, knocks, anagrams, opaque metaphors) from beyond or within the mysterious crypts they inhabit.[10]

For proponents of the New Historicism, ghosts possess a doubled appeal. The study of popular spiritualism offers a wealth of opportunities for historically minded scholars to mine hitherto unexplored cultural archives and emerge with new literary insights, as when Gillian Beer reads George Eliot through spiritualists' beliefs about the afterlife, or when Cathy Davidson reads Hawthorne through Mesmer and Daguerre, or when Lawrence Rainey reads Marinetti and Mussolini through contemporary spirit photography.[11] Moreover, in addition to being a fascinating historical phenomenon in its own right, popular spiritualism parallels the workings of history itself, thereby validating the work of historians. All haunting is historical, as Derrida notes,[12] and all history is haunted: at least since classical antiquity, writers have invoked ghosts and spirits to symbolize the discomfiting resurgence of the past into the present. And if literary texts, human beings, culture itself, are ineluctably haunted by the past, then historians, literary critics, biographers, even psychoanalysts, function as spirit mediums of a sort: their task is to make the dead speak.[13] Indeed, like the literate mediums of the modernist era, contemporary critics have a strong professional interest in proving themselves indispensable as the messengers and interpreters of voices from a remote "other world": of literature, the unconscious, the past.

Ghosts, after all, are hermeneutic entities, both etymologically—like Hermes, the Greek messenger god, they possess a privileged ability to pass between the worlds of the living and the dead—and practically: all ghosts demand interpretation. Their indeterminacy appeals mightily, as we have seen, to a postmodern sensibility. Yet their very insubstantiality also offers a kind of interpretive cloud cover, an exhilarating opportunity for those who invoke them to escape semantic precision. Thus terms such as "possession," "dictation," "spectral," "apparitional," and "medium" pepper the writings even of contemporary critics who show little interest in spiritualism as a historical phenomenon. And how many words in our language can match the extraordinary flexibility of "haunt"? Virtually no literary or interpretive act, it seems, is exempted from this modest verb's metaphorical reach. Critics, we learn, haunt texts; texts haunt critics; authors haunt texts; texts haunt authors; authors haunt readers; readers haunt authors; texts haunt readers; readers haunt texts; early authors haunt later authors; later authors, according to Harold Bloom, can even haunt their precursors. Every one of us, meanwhile, is haunted by history, by time, by texts, by dead ancestors, even by ourselves. Haunting can be used as shorthand, in fact, for just about any kind of troubled or troubling relationship—physical, spiritual, emotional, literary, temporal—between one entity and another. For many literary critics, it serves as a synonym for "intertextuality."

Ironically, in this age of ecstatic, ubiquitous haunting, the literate mediums who were such a real and visible presence throughout the modernist era have come close to disappearing from our cultural radar screen. True, we can dial Psychic-Line or tune to Fox Television's *Crossing Over* for electronically transmitted demonstrations of mediumship in action. We can watch popular feature films such as *Ghost*, *The Sixth Sense*, or *The Gift*, which play upon Americans' continuing fascination with spirit survival and otherworldly communication. We can read books by New Age "channelers" such as Shirley MacLaine, who, speaking with the voices of long-dead past selves, offer a version of mediumship particularly well suited to a self-absorbed, channel-surfing video generation. But it would be difficult today to find a well-known spirit medium with the literary lineage of Rosamond Dale Oliphant, or the literary contacts of Hester Dowden, or the literary sensibilities of Geraldine Cummins, or the literary influence of Catherine Dawson Scott. Perhaps well-educated, articulate writing mediums like these are no longer necessary in a high-speed, globalized society in which, as Marshall McLuhan famously put it, the medium is the message.[14] Perhaps literary and cultural critics, in recognizing their own kinship to spirit mediums, have inherited something of the modernist medium's interpretive, consolatory, paradox-affirming role. Or perhaps ghostwriting will take on, as the twenty-first century progresses, some new and different form that we cannot yet discern or anticipate. For as long as human beings are subject to bodily death, we will undoubtedly continue to seek ways of communicating with our dead, of assuaging our terror of the unknown, and of expressing our uncertainties, fears, and hopes by means of the written word.

Notes

Preface

1. See Freud, "Thoughts for the Times on War and Death"; idem, *Future of an Illusion;* Jung, "Psychological Foundations of Belief in Spirits" (read before a general meeting of the London Society for Psychical Research [SPR], 4 July 1919); Bergson, "'Phantasms of the Living' and 'Psychical Research'" (presidential address to the London SPR, 28 May 1913). Jung's interest in spiritualism dates back as early as 1902, when he devoted most of his doctoral thesis to a case study involving a family friend who claimed mediumistic capabilities. See Jung, "On the Psychology and Pathology of So-Called Occult Phenomena."

2. Pound: Longenbach, *Stone Cottage,* 184. Eliot: Ackroyd, *T. S. Eliot,* 113. Loy: Burke, *Becoming Modern,* 277–78.

3. Yeats, "Gratitude to the Unknown Instructors," in *Collected Poems,* 249; idem, *A Vision,* 8.

4. Several recent literary studies discuss metaphors of haunting in modernist texts; others trace the significance of occult and theosophical doctrines in the works of major modernist writers. However, none of these works focuses exclusively or extensively on popular spiritualism as a historical phenomenon. See Friedman, *Psyche Reborn;* Harper, *Yeats and the Occult;* idem, *The Making of Yeats's "A Vision";* Howes, *Yeats's Nations;* Longenbach, *Stone Cottage;* Materer, *Modernist Alchemy;* Rabaté, *Ghosts of Modernity;* Surette, *Birth of Modernism;* Tryphonopoulos, *Celestial Tradition.* Bette London's brilliant study of women's literary partnerships, *Writing Double,* appeared just as I was completing this book; London's independently conceived conclusions about the literate mediumship of modernist-era spiritualists such as Geraldine Cummins, Hester Dowden, and Georgie Yeats anticipate and confirm many of my own findings.

5. Yeats, *A Vision,* 24.

6. Todorov, *The Fantastic;* Freud, "The 'Uncanny,'" 220.

7. Derrida, *Specters of Marx,* 10.

Introduction. Ghostwriting

1. *American Heritage Dictionary,* 3d ed. Spiritualism is also sometimes referred to, especially in nineteenth-century texts, as spiritism.

2. Davenport, *Death-Blow to Spiritualism,* 89, 90.

3. Gaudon, *Ce que disent les tables parlantes,* 9: "Il lui faut longtemps pour dire de choses, car il y a plus de z qu'on ne croit dans la langue française." (Throughout this book, all translations from the French and German, unless otherwise noted, are mine.) At Hugo's seances, sitters called out letters of the alphabet until the table on which they had placed their hands *stopped* tapping.

167

4. See, for instance, Baer, *Black Spiritual Movement;* Barrow, *Independent Spirits;* Basham, *Trial of Woman;* Brantlinger, *Rule of Darkness;* Braude, *Radical Spirits;* Cottom, *Abyss of Reason;* Douglas, *Feminization of American Culture;* Oppenheim, *Other World;* Owen, *Darkened Room;* Winter, *Mesmerized.*

5. Cottom, *Abyss of Reason,* 108.

6. Philosophers (Henry Sidgwick, William James, Henry Bergson) and psychologists (Sigmund Freud, Carl Jung, F. W. H. Myers, Edmund Gurney): Oppenheim, *Other World.* Jurists: on William Cullen Bryant, see Braude, *Radical Spirits,* 16. On New York State Supreme Court Justice John W. Edmonds see Brandon, *Spiritualists,* 19. Physical scientists (Sir John Tyndall, Sir William Crookes, Sir William Barrett, Sir Oliver Lodge): Oppenheim, *Other World,* 326–90. Mathematicians (Eleanor Mildred Balfour): Oppenheim, *Other World,* 121. Astronomers (Camille Flammarion): Flammarion, *Spirit Communications.* Evolutionary biologists (Charles Darwin, Alfred Russel Wallace): Oppenheim, *Other World,* 291, 296–325. Social reformers (Robert Owen): Goldfarb and Goldfarb, *Spiritualism and Nineteenth-Century Letters,* 123–24. Abolitionists (Sojourner Truth): Braude, *Radical Spirits,* 29. Journalists: on Horace Greeley, see Brandon, *Spiritualists,* 19, and Goldfarb and Goldfarb, *Spiritualism and Nineteenth-Century Letters,* 41. On Thomas Wentworth Higginson, see Kerr, *Mediums, and Spirit Rappers, and Roaring Radicals.* On W. T. Stead, see Stead, *After Death.* On Hannen Swaffer, see Swaffer, *Northcliffe's Return* and *My Talks with the Dead.* Religious leaders: on William Stainton Moses, see Oppenheim, *Other World,* 82. On Mary Baker Eddy, see Eddy, "Christian Science versus Spiritualism," in *Science and Health,* chap. 4. Theosophists (Allen Kardec, A. P. Sinnett, and, for a short time, Helena Petrovna Blavatsky): Oppenheim, *Other World,* 159–97. (Also, on Blavatsky's contradictory stance in regard to spiritualism—"We assert that the spirits of the dead cannot return to earth . . . save in rare and exceptional cases"—see Friedman, *Fictional Death and the Modernist Enterprise,* 142–43.) Inventors: on Thomas Edison, see Ebon, *They Knew the Unknown,* 130. On Thomas A. Watson (Alexander Graham Bell's assistant in the invention of the telephone), see Ronell, *Telephone Book,* 237–76. Financiers (Cornelius Vanderbilt): Chamberlain, *Enterprising Americans,* 144. Educators (Rudolf Steiner): Steiner, *Dead Are with Us* and *Presence of the Dead on the Spiritual Path.* Politicians: on Abraham Lincoln, see Maynard, *Was Abraham Lincoln a Spiritualist?* On Arthur Balfour and W. E. Gladstone, see Oppenheim, *Other World.* On Mackenzie King, see Ortzen, *When Dead Kings Speak,* 63, 97, 123–33. Royalty: on Emperor Napoleon and Empress Eugénie, see Cottom, *Abyss of Reason,* 30. On Czar Alexander II, see Cottom, *Abyss of Reason,* 30, and Goldfarb and Goldfarb, *Spiritualism and Nineteenth-Century Letters,* 79. On Queen Victoria, see Tisdall, *Queen Victoria's Private Life.* On other members of the royal family, see Ortzen, *When Dead Kings Speak*—the work, admittedly, of an unreliable popular journalist who claims, among other things, that Queen Victoria received messages from Prince Albert (26), that Princess Louise received messages from Queen Victoria (30), and that Prince Charles tried to make contact with the spirit of Lord Mountbatten (37). Frontier hero (Wild Bill Hickok): Gauld, *Founders of Psychical Research,* 30.

7. Tyndall, "Science and the 'Spirits,' " 475; Huxley, *Life and Letters of Thomas Henry Huxley,* 1:452.

8. Marx quoted in Cottom, *Abyss of Reason,* 43.

9. Details about the spiritualist involvement of these and other authors can be found in numerous sources, including but not limited to those listed below. Whittier: Goldfarb and Goldfarb, *Spiritualism and Nineteenth-Century Letters,* 61. Cooper: Braude, *Radical Spirits,* 16. Owen, Irving, and Longfellow: Brandon, *Spiritualists,* 41. Bulwer-Lytton, the Brownings, Thackeray, and Ruskin: Oppenheim, *Other World,* 12; Porter, *Through a Glass Darkly.* Tolstoy: Goldfarb, "From Hydesville to Yasnaya Polyana." Tennyson, Carroll, and Ruskin: Op-

penheim, *Other World,* 36. Stowe: Beecher, *Spiritual Manifestations.* The Rossettis: Goldfarb and Goldfarb, *Spiritualism and Nineteenth-Century Letters,* 116–18. Oliphant: Margaret Oliphant, *Memoir of the Life of Laurence Oliphant.* Haggard and Kipling: Brantlinger, *Rule of Darkness,* 243. Lang: Brantlinger, *Rule of Darkness,* 231–45; Oppenheim, *Other World,* 39. Maeterlinck: Maeterlinck, *Unknown Guest* and *Our Eternity.* Huysmans: Boucher, *Séance de spiritisme,* 14–15. Whitman: Goldfarb and Goldfarb, *Spiritualism and Nineteenth-Century Letters,* 60.

10. Emerson: quoted in Brandon, *Spiritualists,* 48; Cottom, *Abyss of Reason,* 24. Hawthorne: quoted in Goldfarb and Goldfarb, *Spiritualism and Nineteenth-Century Letters,* 57. George Eliot: letter to Sara Sophia Hennell, 18 October 1856, in Eliot, *Letters,* 2:267. Shaw: quoted in Oppenheim, *Other World,* 28.

11. Braude, *Radical Spirits,* 26–27.

12. Dickens: Goldfarb and Goldfarb, *Spiritualism and Nineteenth-Century Letters,* 93–94; Ebon, *They Knew the Unknown,* 73–96. Barrett Browning: letter to Miss E.F. Haworth, 16 June 1860, in Barrett Browning, *Letters,* 2:395.

13. Browning, "Mr. Sludge, 'The Medium'"; Hawthorne, *Blithedale Romance;* Howells, *Undiscovered Country;* James, *The Bostonians;* Melville, "Apple-Tree Table"; Tolstoy, *Anna Karenina;* Twain, "Schoolhouse Hill"; Benson, *All about Lucia;* Coward, *Blithe Spirit;* Menotti, *The Medium;* Singer, "The Séance"; Smith, "Mrs Simpkins."

14. "Spirit Rapping," *National Miscellany,* 5 May 1853, 129 (quoted in Goldfarb and Goldfarb, *Spiritualism and Nineteenth-Century Letters,* 75); Gillson, *Table-Talking.* Special thanks to Carol Engelhardt for bringing the latter citation to my attention.

15. Kerr, *Mediums, and Spirit Rappers, and Roaring Radicals,* 82. Kerr dedicates an entire chapter of his book to "Satiric Attacks on Spiritualism and Reform" (82–107).

16. Goldfarb and Goldfarb, *Spiritualism and Nineteenth-Century Letters,* 165.

17. Douglas, *Feminization of American Culture,* 318.

18. Brandon, *Spiritualists,* 48; see also Owen, *Darkened Room,* 10.

19. Barrett Browning: Porter, *Through a Glass Darkly.* Phelps: Braude, *Radical Spirits.* Stowe: Beecher, *Spiritual Manifestations.* Corelli: Corelli, *Romance of Two Worlds* and *The Life Everlasting.* Somerville: Cummins, *Dr. E. Œ. Somerville;* Collis, *Somerville and Ross.* Wilcox: Wilcox, *The Worlds and I.* Dawson Scott: Dawson Scott, *From Four Who Are Dead* and *Is This Wilson?* Lehmann: Lehmann, *Swan of the Evening.* Caldwell: Stearn, *Search for a Soul.*

20. W.B. Yeats, letter to Dorothy Wellesley, 28 November 1936, in Yeats, *Letters of W.B. Yeats,* 868; idem, *Autobiography,* 125.

21. Braude, *Radical Spirits,* 26.

22. Cottom, *Abyss of Reason,* 57, 55.

Chapter 1. Necrobibliography

1. Freud, "Thoughts for the Times on War and Death," 289.

2. Fine houses and priceless furnishings: Harris, *Talks with Spirit Friends,* 152, 204. Travel opportunities: Sherwood, *Post-Mortem Journal,* 50; Owen and Dallas, *Nurseries of Heaven,* 31; Stead (Spirit), *Life Eternal,* 96. Household help: Boyd, *What Are They Doing Now,* 25 ("There are people who serve us. It is not a question of class, but of development; the less developed serve those who are more advanced.").

3. Douglas, *Feminization of American Culture,* 226.

4. Fruits without peel: Agnes, *Voice of Marie Corelli,* 49. Pets without fleas: Boyd, *What Are They Doing Now,* 40–41. Sports without sweat: Boyd, *Next World,* 20. For a more recent reit-

eration of this idea, see Thompson, *Life in the Hereafter,* 14. Sex without contraception: Sherwood, *Post-Mortem Journal,* 32.

5. John Lennon in the afterlife: Keen, *John Lennon in Heaven.* Typing on a celestial computer: Kubis and Macy, *Conversations beyond the Light,* plate 1.

6. High-tech millennialism: on March 26, 1997, thirty-nine members of the cult calling itself Heaven's Gate committed mass suicide in southern California. The cult members believed that by leaving their earthly bodies behind, they would "graduate" to a higher sphere of existence, to which they would be transported by a UFO traveling in the shadow of the comet Hale-Bopp.

7. Foucault, "What Is an Author?" 159.

8. Podmore quoted in Rouse, *Through Séance to Satan,* 31; Freud, *Future of an Illusion,* 48; Adorno, "Theses against Occultism," 241–42.

9. Bodies drying instantly ("Don't think of us as waterproof, but rather as glass, which dries of its own accord"): Boyd, *Next World,* 44. Heavenly Muzak: Harris, *Talks with Spirit Friends,* 26. Fish that don't die: Boyd, *Next World,* 20. Defecation is unnecessary ("This food comes off as a vapour from our bodies"): Stead (Spirit), *Life Eternal,* 87.

10. Douglas, *Feminization of American Culture,* 202.

11. See Cummins, *Unseen Adventures;* Bentley, *Far Horizon;* Garrett, *Many Voices;* Dawson Scott, *From Four Who Are Dead;* Barker, *War Letters from the Living Dead Man;* Cory, *My Letters from Heaven;* Oliphant, *Mediators.*

12. Cory, *My Letters from Heaven,* iv.

13. Oliphant, *Mediators,* 63.

14. Stead (Spirit), *Blue Island,* 48; Sherwood, *Post-Mortem Journal,* 79.

15. The entire film, in fact, introduces a spiritualist subtext largely missing from Sagan's novel. An early scene, for example, shows Ellie trying to contact her recently deceased father via ham radio. Later, Ellie's fantasy of extraterrestrial contact is represented through stereotypically spiritualist imagery: on a tropical beach, complete with the sparkling water, swaying palm trees, and palpably thick and pliant air described in so many otherworldly narratives, she meets not the "little green men" she claims to have been searching for but rather her dead father.

16. Death as matriculation: Sherwood, *Post-Mortem Journal,* 91; Stead (Spirit), *Life Eternal,* 136–37; idem, *Blue Island,* 148. Descriptions of otherworldly schools: Owen and Dallas, *Nurseries of Heaven,* 31, 154; Stead (Spirit), *Life Eternal,* 121–22. Otherworldly universities: Brandon (Spirit), *Open the Door!* xix; Owen, *Life beyond the Veil;* Pole, *Private Dowding.* (Owen and Pole are quoted in Dowding, *Many Mansions,* 44–47, 57.) Libraries: Coblentz, *For All Who Seek* (these communications, although not published until 1973, were received by Coblentz beginning in the 1930s); Stead (Spirit), *Blue Island,* 55; idem, *Life Eternal,* 91; *One Step Higher,* 67–68. (Although their title pages give no indication of the fact, the latter two books were both written via the mediumship of Hester Dowden.) Research projects by the dead: Roberts and Woolcock, *Elizabethan Episode,* 176; Allen, *Talks with Elizabethans,* 35.

17. Visitors from Neptune: Harrison, *Wireless Messages from Other Worlds,* 49. Cosmic field trips: Owen and Dallas, *Nurseries of Heaven,* 31. Replica of Oxford: the spirit of T. E. Lawrence in Sherwood, *Post-Mortem Journal,* 66. World War I pilot: Harris, *Talks with Spirit Friends,* 187. Psychoanalysis: Stead (Spirit), *Blue Island,* 133. For an explicitly Freudian account of otherworldly existence as a sloughing off of past lives, see also Sherwood, *Country Beyond,* 107.

18. Dowding, *Many Mansions,* 47.

19. Thompson, *Life in the Hereafter,* 13.

20. Sherwood, *Post-Mortem Journal,* 67; Mallarmé, "The Book: A Spiritual Instrument," 692; Woolf, "How Should One Read a Book?" 245.

21. Cummins, *Beyond Human Personality*, 28. Rosamond Dale Oliphant and W. T. Stead, too, are among the many spiritualists who use literary (in these two cases, Shakespearean) metaphors to justify their belief in spirit communication. "What is more delightful, the pleasure of an ox gazing stupidly at the binding of a volume of Shakespeare, or the pleasure of a book-lover reading the same pages?" (Oliphant, *Mediators*, 73). "The intrinsic value of three-fourths of the 'Letters from Julia' is no more dependent upon theories as to their origin than the merits of Shakespeare's plays depend upon theories of their authorship" (Stead, *After Death*, xxxvii).

22. Cottom, *Abyss of Reason*, 56–57. For a slightly different perspective on the social function of spirit communication, see Basham, *Trial of Woman*, 118: "If the communicating spirits produced a version of the after-life that simulated the conditions of human existence but with all the pressures and anxieties removed, automatic writing could perform the same function in relation to the anxieties of authorship. Writing, painfully instilled as a task and acquired as a civic duty, became under those conditions an irresponsible pleasure."

23. Dawson Scott, *From Four Who Are Dead*, 116.

24. *One Step Higher*, 68, 71.

25. Barrett, *Personality Survives Death*, 198. The book consists of communications received by Florence Barrett from her late husband, Sir William Barrett, through the mediumship of Mrs. Osborne Leonard. This quotation is from the epilogue, which appears to have been written by Florence Barrett. For another metaphor drawn from Britain's imperialist legacy, see W. T. Stead's spirit's description (via medium Pardoe Woodman) in *Blue Island*: "[Dying] was like walking from your own English winter gloom into the radiance of an Indian sky" (38).

26. Steiner, *Presence of the Dead on the Spiritual Path*, 54–55.

27. Cottom, *Abyss of Reason*, 63.

28. Evans, "Spiritualism and Language," 11.

29. Wilde (Spirit), *Psychic Messages from Oscar Wilde*, 37; Cooke, *"Thy Kingdom Come,"* 105; Shakespeare (Spirit), *Shakespeare's Revelations*, 116–17.

30. Spirits reading books written since their own deaths: Dodd, *Immortal Master*, 97. Lawrence on reading via his medium: Sherwood, *Post-Mortem Journal*, 48. Reading through the "spectacles of some human mind": Roberts and Woolcock, *Elizabethan Episode*, 41. Wilde on seeing through the eyes of the living: Wilde (Spirit), *Psychic Messages from Oscar Wilde*, 37.

31. Wilde (Spirit), *Psychic Messages from Oscar Wilde*, 30.

32. Conan Doyle, preface to Payne, *Soul of Jack London*, 13. W. R. Bradbrook, "The Recorder's Impressions," in Cooke, *"Thy Kingdom Come,"* xvi.

33. Shelley (Spirit), *Fortune of Eternity*, 14.

34. Twain (Spirit), *Jap Herron*, 5, 20, 6.

35. Foucault, "What Is an Author?" 147.

36. Baker, *Our Three Selves*, 105, 123. Hall's communications from Batten were received via Gladys Osborne Leonard, a well-known London medium.

37. Cummins, *Unseen Adventures*, 112.

38. *London Times*, 22 July 1926.

39. Cummins, *Unseen Adventures*, 112.

40. Dowden as secretary: introduction to Stead (Spirit), *Life Eternal*, 13. See also Stead's spirit's comment that "A good automatic writer can be as serviceable as a good typewriter" (207). Dawson Scott as stenographer: Dawson Scott, *Is This Wilson?* 32. Wallace's messages through his secretary: Barbanell, *Some Discern Spirits*, 181.

41. Cummins, *Unseen Adventures*, 112.

42. The title page of the original Rider edition reads as follows: "*The Blue Island. Experiences of a New Arrival Beyond the Veil.* Communicated by W.T. Stead. Recorded by Pardoe Woodman and Estelle Stead. With a Letter from Sir Arthur Conan Doyle."

43. Joint author entries: *Catalog Rules: Author and Title Entries,* compiled by the Committees of the American Library Association and the British Library Association (Chicago: American Library Association, 1908), rule 2. Pseudonymous and supposititious books: *Rules for Compiling the Catalogs in the Department of Printed Books in the British Museum* (London: British Museum, 1906), rule 30. Neither code contains specific guidelines for cataloging mediumistic communications.

44. *American Library Association Catalog Rules: Author and Titles Entries,* prepared by the Catalog Code Revision Committee of the American Library Association with the collaboration of a Committee of the (British) Library Association (Chicago: American Library Association, 1941), rule 9.

45. Tait, *Authors and Titles,* 81, 82. The 1941 version of the ALA code was republished, in significantly expanded form, in 1949; the entry on mediumistic writing remains exactly the same as in the 1941 code but was renumbered as rule 11. Tait's comments refer to the 1949 code.

46. *Anglo-American Cataloging Rules,* rules 22.14 and 21.26. Like its previous incarnation, the *American Library Association Catalog Rules,* this new code was jointly issued by the American and British Library Associations. In its most recent edition (1988), it continues to set the standard for cataloging new books on both sides of the Atlantic.

47. For reasons of consistency and comprehensiveness I have used the 1988 ALA cataloging rules throughout these notes, even when I have had to change author designations and titles from the way they appear in most print catalogs.

48. Jolley, *Thoughts after Paris,* 1963, as quoted in Tait, *Authors and Titles,* as an epigraph (flyleaf).

49. Sir Frank Francis, preface to *The British Museum Catalog of Printed Books. Photolithographic Edition to 1955* (London: Trustees of the British Museum, 1965).

50. Payne, *Soul of Jack London;* Cooke, *"Thy Kingdom Come."*

51. Stead published only one book of spirit communications during his lifetime: *Letters from Julia* (1898), later republished in expanded form as *After Death* (1914). Books containing spirit messages from Stead or supposedly authored by him posthumously include the following, in chronological order by date of publication, with the communicating medium listed first. Various mediums: Coates, *Has W. T. Stead Returned?* (1913). Ellen A. Pennau-Cook: Stead (Spirit), *Message from William T. Stead* (1917). Hester Dowden: Travers Smith (née Dowden), *Voices from the Void* (1919). Madame Hyver: E. Stead, *Communication with the Next World* (1921). Pardoe Woodman: Stead (Spirit), *Blue Island* (1922). Pardoe Woodman, Hester Dowden, and others, sponsored by Stead's daughter Estelle: E. Stead, *Faces of the Living Dead* (1925). E.M. Moore: Moore, *Spirit-Messages* (1928). Catherine Dawson Scott: Dawson Scott, *From Four Who Are Dead* (1926). Hester Dowden: Stead (Spirit), *Life Eternal* (1933). Charles L. Tweedale: Tweedale, *News from the Next World* (1940). Various mediums: E. Stead, *Spirit Return of W. T. Stead* (1947).

52. The only book that lists Dowden (aka Hester Travers Smith) as its author is her earliest publication, *Voices from the Void* (1919). (Dowden used her married name, Travers Smith, during the 1910s and early 1920s, but by the early 1930s she had reverted to her maiden name.) Other books containing messages received via her mediumship include, in chronological order by date of publication: Wilde (Spirit), *Psychic Messages from Oscar Wilde* (1924); Bradley, *Towards the Stars* (1924); E. Stead, *Faces of the Living Dead* (1925); Bond, *Gospel of Philip the Deacon* (1932); Stead (Spirit), *Life Eternal* (1933); *One Step Higher* (1937);

Gillespie (Spirit), *Knowledge of Thy Truth* (1939); Boyd, *What Are They Doing Now* (1941); idem, *Next World* (1942); Dodd, *Immortal Master* (1943); Fripp, *Book of Johannes* (1945); Allen, *Talks with Elizabethans* (1947); Vivian (Spirit), *Curtain Drawn* (1949); idem, *Christmas Dinner* (1950). Joyce Vivian, whose pen name was Heather, was a young author who died in a riding accident at the age of eighteen after publishing a successful children's book.

53. See, for example, Gillespie (Spirit), *Knowledge of Thy Truth;* Boyd, *Next World;* idem, *What Are They Doing Now; One Step Higher.* Dowden served as the medium for each.

Chapter 2. The Undeath of the Author

1. Miller, "Limits of Pluralism," 446, as quoted in Gilbert and Gubar, *Madwoman in the Attic,* 1.

2. Bloom, *Anxiety of Influence,* 15.

3. Twain, "Schoolhouse Hill," 206.

4. Chatterton, who committed suicide in 1770 at the age of eighteen, left behind a collection of poems that he claimed had been written by a fifteenth-century priest. Disputation as to their true authorship continued for many years after his death. William Wordsworth remembered him as "the marvellous boy . . . that perished in his pride," and John Keats dedicated *Endymion* to his memory. See the entry under "Chatterton" in *The Cambridge Guide to Literature in English,* ed. Ian Ousby (1993).

5. "The Jabberwock Traced to Its True Source," *Macmillan's Magazine* (February 1872), as quoted by Martin Gardner in Carroll, *Annotated Alice,* 193–94. The brilliant German version of "Jabberwocky" included in the article was in fact written by Scott himself.

6. Browning, "Mr. Sludge, 'The Medium,' " 403, 411.

7. Kipling, "Wireless," 36. The page numbers of all subsequent quotations are given in the text.

8. See, for instance, Basham, *Trial of Woman;* Brandon, *Spiritualists;* Cottom, *Abyss of Reason;* Rainey, "Taking Dictation."

9. Oppenheim, *Other World,* 396.

10. See, for instance, such book titles from the 1910s and 1920s as Harrison, *Wireless Messages from Other Worlds,* and Saunders, *First Successful Attempt to Broadcast Spirit Voices.* See also Upton Sinclair's account of his experiments with mental telepathy, *Mental Radio* (1930).

11. H.D., "H.D. by Delia Alton," 199.

12. Oppenheim, *Other World,* 133. The spirit communicators included Henry Sidgwick, F.W.H. Myers, and Edmund Gurney (three of the SPR's most respected founding members) as well as Mary Catherine Lyttelton, a young woman who decades earlier had been involved in a romance with Arthur Balfour, later prime minister of Great Britain.

13. Yeats, *Words upon the Window Pane,* 239. The page numbers of all subsequent quotations are given in the text.

14. Maddox, *Yeats's Ghosts,* 216. Maddox attributes her information about the alleged affair to "a long interview with Dolly Travers-Smith Robinson" (427 n. 3).

15. See Yeats, *Yeats's Vision Papers.* The role of frustration in Yeats's spiritualist experiments is discussed in further detail in chapter 5.

16. Tennyson, *In Memoriam A. H. H.,* 130.1–2.

17. Eliot, *Complete Poems and Plays,* 140–42; Heaney, "Station Island," 212.

18. Cottom, *Abyss of Reason,* 69.

19. Gilbert and Gubar, *Madwoman in the Attic,* 47, 48.

20. Shelley (Spirit), *Fortune of Eternity*, 11; Drouét, *Station Astral*, 71; Osborne Leonard, *My Life in Two Worlds*, 74; Cory, *My Letters from Heaven*, 123, 116; Bentley, *Far Horizon*, 87.

21. Cultural heritage: Dowding, *Beauty—Not the Beast*, 12; Garrett, *Many Voices*, 15. Directly from parents: Cummins, *Unseen Adventures*, 34; Maddox, *Yeats's Ghosts*, 216, 249.

22. For instance, Geraldine Cummins, Helen Dallas, and Edith Harper ghostwrote for F. W. H. Myers; Daisy Oke Roberts for Myers and Sir Oliver Lodge; Gladys Osborne Leonard for Sir William Barrett; Rosamond Dale Oliphant for Robert Dale Owen (her real father); Jane Revere Burke for William James; Eileen Garrett, Elizabeth Thompson, Estelle Roberts, and Grace Cooke for Arthur Conan Doyle; Hester Dowden, Catherine Dawson Scott, and E. M. Moore (among others) for W. T. Stead; and so on. Cummins/Myers: Cummins, *Beyond Human Personality*. Dallas/Myers: Dallas, *Mors Janua Vitae?* Harper/Myers: G. M. Harper, introduction to Yeats, *Yeats's Vision Papers*, 1:2. Roberts/Myers and Lodge: Roberts, *How Do We Live?* Osborne Leonard/Barrett: Barrett, *Personality Survives Death*. Oliphant/Dale Owen: Oliphant, *Mediators*. Burke/James: Burke, *One Way*. Garrett/Conan Doyle: Garrett, *Many Voices*, 8; Fuller, *Airmen Who Would Not Die*. Thompson/Conan Doyle: Thompson, *Life in the Hereafter*. Roberts/Conan Doyle: Barbanell, *Some Discern Spirits*. Cooke/Conan Doyle: Cooke, *"Thy Kingdom Come."* Bibliographical citations for mediums claiming to have communicated with Stead: see chapter 1, n. 51.

23. Stead (Spirit), *Life Eternal*, 9–10, 13.

24. Leichtman, *Eileen Garrett Returns;* Allen, "Was It Hester Dowden?" 160.

25. Browning: Staff, "Communication with Robert Browning." Conan Doyle: see n. 22 above. Conrad and Crane: Conrad, *Did Joseph Conrad Return as a Spirit?* Eliot: Doucé, *Incredible Alliance.* Lawrence: Sherwood, *Country Beyond* and *Post-Mortem Journal.* London: Payne, *Soul of Jack London.* Poe: Doten, *Poems from the Inner Life.* Shakespeare (Spirit), *Shakespeare's Revelations.* Shelley (Spirit), *Fortune of Eternity.* Turgenev (Spirit), *Beyond Earth's Fears.* Twain (Spirit), *Jap Herron.* Wells: Hawley and Rossi, *Bertie: The Life after Death of H. G. Wells.* Wilde: Wilde (Spirit), *Psychic Messages from Oscar Wilde.*

26. Charlotte Brontë: Beecher, *Spiritual Manifestations.* (See also, for an even earlier account, Horn, *Strange Visitors.*) Elizabeth Barrett Browning: Staff, "Communication with Robert Browning." Marie Corelli: Agnes, *Voice of Marie Corelli;* Wild, *No Matter.* Male ghostwriting mediums: Sinnett, *Tennyson an Occultist as His Writings Prove;* Tweedale, *News from the Next World;* Wild, *No Matter.*

27. Modernist-era mediums have also conveyed messages from a wide range of famous spirits whose reputations were not primarily literary, including Mary Baker Eddy (via Ursula Roberts); Havelock Ellis (via Ellis's former lover, Françoise Delisle); Harry Houdini (via Arthur Ford); Lord Kitchener (via Mary Nixon Robertson); and Woodrow Wilson (via Catherine Dawson Scott). See Horwood, *Mary Baker Eddy;* Delisle, *Return of Havelock Ellis;* Emery, *Houdini Unmasked;* Robertson, *"The Other Side God's Door";* Dawson Scott, *Is This Wilson?* Significantly, at least three of these figures—Eddy, Houdini, and Ellis—are known to have actively eschewed spiritualism during their lifetimes.

28. Shelley (Spirit), *Fortune of Eternity*, 12; Payne, *Soul of Jack London*, 139; Wilde (Spirit), *Psychic Messages from Oscar Wilde*, 150.

29. London: Payne, *Soul of Jack London*, 98. Eliot on "that odious trickery": letter to Sara Sophia Hennell, 18 October 1856, in Eliot, *Letters*, 3:359. Eliot's spirit messages: Horn, *Next World*, 155. Browning: Staff, "Communication with Robert Browning," 99.

30. Twain's otherworldly novel: Twain (Spirit), *Jap Herron.* Twain on spiritualism: Goldfarb and Goldfarb, *Spiritualism and Nineteenth-Century Letters*, 131. Wells's spirit messages: Hawley and Rossi, *Bertie: The Life after Death of H. G. Wells.* Wells's dismissal of spiritualism: Goldfarb and Goldfarb, *Spiritualism and Nineteenth-Century Letters*, 136. Eliot's spirit mes-

sages: Doucé, *Incredible Alliance*, 9. Dickens's ghostwritten novel: Dickens (Spirit), *Part Second of the Mystery of Edwin Drood*. Dickens on spiritualism: Goldfarb and Goldfarb, *Spiritualism and Nineteenth-Century Letters*, 152. Conan Doyle on Dickens: Conan Doyle, "Alleged Posthumous Writings of Great Authors," 727.

31. Hugo: Simon, *Chez Victor Hugo;* Gaudon, *Ce que disent les tables parlantes*, 11. Stowe: Beecher, *Spiritual Manifestations*, 33. Conan Doyle: Conrad, *Did Joseph Conrad Return as a Spirit?* 7. Gide: Sherard, *The Real Oscar Wilde*, 214–15. Caldwell: Stearn, *Search for a Soul*, 102. Plath and Hughes: Stevenson, *Bitter Fame*, 351.

32. H. D., *Tribute to Freud*, 51.

33. "Notes" to "Majic Ring" (unpublished manuscript located among H. D.'s papers at the Yale Collection of American Literature, Beinecke Library, Yale University), as quoted in Sword, *Engendering Inspiration*, 168.

34. Merrill, *Changing Light at Sandover*, 128.

35. Bloom, *Anxiety of Influence*, 141.

36. Freud, "Thoughts for the Times on War and Death," 297; Freud, *Future of an Illusion*, 76.

37. Jung, "Psychological Foundations of Belief in Spirits," 78–79; Abraham, "Notes on the Phantom," 287, 289; Castle, *Apparitional Lesbian*, 117, 119; Lay, *Man's Unconscious Spirit*, 198–99.

38. See, for instance, *War Letters from the Living Dead Man* (by Elsa Barker, 1915); *Six Million Men Killed in the Great War: Messages from the Dead to the Living* (by F. T. A. Davies, 1921); *Gone West: Being the Experiences of Our Soldiers and Others after Death as Seen and Told by the Author* (by J. S. M. Ward, 1917); *Gone West: By a Soldier Doctor* (edited by Harriet McCrory Grove and Mattie Mitchell Hunt, 1919); *Private Dowding: A Plain Record of the After-Death Experiences of a Soldier Killed in Battle, and Some Questions on World Issues Answered by the Messenger Who Taught Him Wider Truths* (by Wellesley Tudor Pole, 1918).

39. Conan Doyle's eldest son, Kingsley, was wounded at the Somme and died of pneumonia in 1918 (Jones, *Conan Doyle and the Spirits*, 129.) A detailed account of the seance messages from Kingsley is given in Conan Doyle, *Pheneas Speaks*.

40. See Dowding, *Many Mansions* (1943) and *Lychgate* (1945). The spirit testimonies that Dowding discusses in *Many Mansions* include, significantly, Wellesley Pole's 1918 book of messages from a young First World War soldier named Private Dowding (cited above). Although Hugh Dowding claimed no actual relationship to this former schoolmaster who supposedly "went West" in 1916 at the age of thirty-seven, the air chief marshal's interest in this particular book was no doubt piqued by the family resemblance. Given his birth date, Private Dowding could have been Hugh Dowding's brother, as they were born just three years apart. Given his age and rank at death, however, Private Dowding resembles instead Hugh Dowding's symbolic children, those young R.A.F. airmen who died under the air chief marshal's command and with whose spirits he later claimed to have communicated.

41. Wilcox, *Worlds and I;* Lehmann, *Swan of the Evening*.

42. Derrida, *Specters of Marx*, 9.

43. Freud, "Thoughts for the Times on War and Death," 291; Shakespeare, sonnet 107.

Chapter 3. Necrobardolatry

1. Borges, "Everything and Nothing," 116–17. Although the poem was first published in Spanish, its original title was in English.

2. On the reception and appropriation of Shakespeare's plays from the Restoration

through most of the eighteenth century, see Dobson, *Making of the National Poet*, 4–5. On Shakespeare scholarship in Victorian England, see Schoenbaum, *Shakespeare's Lives*, 273–444. On Shakespeare's "commodity identity" in postmodern American literary criticism and popular culture, see Charnes, *Notorious Identity*, 154–55.

3. Anon., *The Visitation;* Woodward, *Familiar Verses*, 8.

4. Shakespeare (Spirit), *Shakespeare's Revelations;* idem, *My Proof of Immortality;* Drouét, *Station Astral*, 93; Dodd, *Immortal Master;* Allen, *Talks with Elizabethans;* Roberts and Woolcock, *Elizabethan Episode;* Leichtman, *Eileen Garrett Returns*, 5–6; Merrill, *Changing Light at Sandover*, 164.

5. Bentley, *Far Horizon;* Cummins, *Unseen Adventures*, 16; Swaffer, *Adventures with Inspiration*, 12; Roberts and Woolcock, *Elizabethan Episode*, 35.

6. Asimov, "Immortal Bard," 97–99.

7. Kingsmill, *Return of William Shakespeare*, 215, 342.

8. Freud, "The 'Uncanny,'" 250.

9. Garber, *Shakespeare's Ghost Writers*, xiv.

10. Derrida, *Specters of Marx*, 4, 42.

11. Dobson, *Making of the National Poet*, 225–26.

12. Garber, *Shakespeare's Ghost Writers*, 12.

13. On Freud: Schoenbaum, *Shakespeare's Lives*, 367. Lacan, "Desire and the Interpretation of Desire in *Hamlet*," 50; Abraham, "Notes on the Phantom," 287; Plath, *Journals*, 244, 222.

14. Derrida, *Specters of Marx*, 10, 11.

15. Surette, *Birth of Modernism*, 11; Rabaté, *Ghosts of Modernity*, 4; Castle, "Phantasmagoria," 29.

16. Grady, *Modernist Shakespeare*, 94–100; Frank, "Spatial Form in Modern Literature."

17. Grady, *Modernist Shakespeare*, 87, 124.

18. Joyce, *Ulysses*, 463. The page numbers of all subsequent quotations are given in the text.

19. Castle, "Phantasmagoria"; Davidson, "Photographs of the Dead"; Miller, "Specters of Dickens's Study."

20. Garber, *Shakespeare's Ghost Writers*, 18, 13.

21. Blamires, *New Bloomsday Book*, 71.

22. As Joyce was apparently aware, spirit mediums since the mid–nineteenth century have frequently claimed Native Americans—Grace Cooke's White Eagle, Estelle Roberts's Red Cloud, Hannen Swaffer's Silver Birch, Helen Hughes's White Feather, and so forth—as their "spirit guides" or mediumistic "controls," ostensibly because such beings are more empathetic and spiritually powerful than are people of European extraction, having lived in a culture that revered the spirits of the dead and that understood death to be an extension of life. See Cooke, *Sun-Men of the Americas;* Barbanell, *Some Discern Spirits;* Silver Birch (Spirit), *Wisdom of Silver Birch;* Upton, *Mediumship of Helen Hughes*. All of these examples postdate *Ulysses*, but they document a phenomenon that was already well established by 1922.

23. Cheng, *Shakespeare and Joyce*, 88.

24. Schoenbaum, *Shakespeare's Lives*, 367, 381.

25. Brandes, *William Shakespeare;* Lee, *Life of William Shakespeare;* Harris, *The Man Shakespeare and His Tragic Life-Story;* Barton, *Links between Ireland and Shakespeare;* Vining, *Mystery of Hamlet;* Bleibtreu, *Lösung der Shakespeare-Frage;* Shaw, *Dark Lady of the Sonnets;* Wilde, *Portrait of Mr. W. H.*

26. Joyce, *Finnegans Wake*, 535.28–535.29. The page and line numbers of all subsequent quotations are given in the text.

27. Schoenbaum, *Shakespeare's Lives*, 359. Two of Dowden's most influential books were *Shakspere: A Critical Study of His Mind and Art* (London: King, 1875) and his school primer, *Shakespere* (New York: Appleton, 1878). According to Amazon.com's online database, Dowden's *Introduction to Shakespeare* (New York: Scribner, 1895) is due to be reissued in 2007.

28. Eglinton, *Irish Literary Portraits*, 67–68.

29. Schoenbaum, *Shakespeare's Lives*, 362.

30. Yeats, *Reveries over Childhood and Youth*, 101–2.

31. Yeats, *Letters of W. B. Yeats*, 602–3, 606.

32. Yeats, *Reveries over Childhood and Youth*, 105–6.

33. Yeats, *Essays and Introductions*, 519.

34. Yeats, *Letters of W. B. Yeats*, 349, 555.

35. Another real-life figure closely associated in Joyce's mind with the National Library was T. W. Lyster (1855–1922), who served as the library's director from 1895 to 1920. Although Lyster, the "Quaker librarian," comes off relatively lightly in *Ulysses*, he too was implicated in the web of literary connections binding together Joyce and Yeats with Edward Dowden. On 27 March 1926, Yeats spoke at the unveiling of a memorial to Lyster at the library: "He was, I think, something which we have not now in Dublin—a great scholar in literature. . . . He inherited that passion from a great friend of his youth, Edward Dowden, and from him also his interest in German and German literature. I myself would like to say that I am deeply indebted to Mr. Lyster. When I was a very young man, I read literature in the National Library . . . and it was Mr. Lyster who guided me." Yeats, *Reviews, Articles and Other Miscellaneous Prose*, 471.

36. Ellmann, *James Joyce*, 140, 411.

37. Skinner, "Two Joyce Letters concerning *Ulysses* and a Reply," 378.

38. Dowden, *Fragments of Old Letters*, 142.

39. Yeats, *Letters of W. B. Yeats*, 603.

40. Bentley, *Far Horizon*, 16, 26.

41. Wilde (Spirit), *Psychic Messages from Oscar Wilde*, 25. The page numbers of all subsequent quotations are given in the text.

42. Because Hester Travers Smith is listed on the title page as the book's editor (with Wilde as its author), it seems highly probable, despite the use of the third-person pronoun, that she wrote this editorial note herself.

43. Atherton, *Books at the Wake*, 47–48.

44. Joyce, *Letters of James Joyce*, 224.

45. Atherton, *Books at the Wake*, 48.

46. Eckley, introduction to *Steadfast Finnegans Wake*, n.p.; ibid., 261.

47. Travers Smith (née Dowden), *Voices from the Void*, 70; Stead (Spirit), *Life Eternal*.

48. Eckley, preface to *Steadfast Finnegans Wake*, n.p.; introduction ibid., n.p.; ibid., 38, 251, 132.

49. Schoenbaum, *Shakespeare's Lives*, 388. Both Schoenbaum and Garber offer lively, detailed, and often hilarious accounts of the Shakespearean authorship controversy. Schoenbaum notes that such respectable thinkers as Henry James, Mark Twain, and Sigmund Freud subscribed to alternate authorship theories (409–10, 441), while Garber observes that anti-Stratfordians have had "an uncanny propensity to appear a bit loony—literally" (as examples, she cites the surnames of the Oxfordian John Thomas Looney and the Baconian George M. Battey). On a more serious note, Garber goes on to observe that "the

Shakespeare authorship controversy presents itself [in history] at exactly the moment Michel Foucault describes as appropriate for appropriation: the moment when the 'author-function' becomes, in the late eighteenth and nineteenth centuries, an item of property, part of a 'system of ownership' in which strict copyright rules define the relation between author and text in a new way." Garber, *Shakespeare's Ghost Writers*, 4.

50. Cheng, *Shakespeare and Joyce*, 233–36.

51. Dodd, *Immortal Master*, 17, 33, 9–10.

52. Edward Dowden to C.M. Ingleby, 20 August 1883, an unpublished letter quoted in Schoenbaum, *Shakespeare's Lives*, 341.

53. Dodd, *Immortal Master*, 61.

54. Allen, *Talks with Elizabethans*, 32–33.

55. Ibid., 43, 97.

56. Abraham, "Notes on the Phantom," 287.

Chapter 4. Metaphorical Mediumship

1. Bürgin and Mayer, *Thomas Mann*, 61; Mann, "An Experience in the Occult," 219–20, 227, 256. The page numbers of all subsequent quotations for "Experience in the Occult" are given in the text. (The seance in question took place on 20 December 1922; Mann attended two subsequent sittings at Schrenck-Notzing's home on 6 and 24 January 1923.) As this chapter makes clear, popular spiritualism shared substantially the same characteristics—despite local differences in flavor and form—throughout the United States, Great Britain, and most of Europe.

2. Yeats, *A Vision* (1937), 24.

3. Letter to Edward Marsh, 10 May 19——, in Lawrence, *Letters of D. H. Lawrence*, 3:358; "Edgar Allan Poe," in Lawrence, *Studies in Classic American Literature*, 84.

4. Lawrence, *Complete Poems*, 739. The page numbers of all subsequent quotations from Lawrence's poetry are given in the text and refer to this edition.

5. Lawrence, "Glad Ghosts," 689, 667, 670, 689.

6. Yeats, *A Vision* (1937), 22.

7. Letter to Stephen Spender, 29 October 1934, in Woolf, *Letters of Virginia Woolf*, 5:341.

8. "The Supernatural in Fiction" (1918), in Woolf, *Collected Essays*, 1:294–95.

9. "Henry James's Ghost Stories," ibid., 3:324.

10. Johnson, "Haunted House," 247.

11. Royle, *Telepathy and Literature*, 119; Woolf, *Complete Shorter Fiction*, 92.

12. Woolf, *Mrs. Dalloway*, 135–36.

13. Johnson, "Haunted House," 249.

14. "Kew Gardens," in Woolf, *Complete Shorter Fiction*, 95.

15. Woolf, *Complete Shorter Fiction*, 123.

16. Robinson, "Unhaunted House," 172–73.

17. Entry for Sunday, 11 July, in Woolf, *Diary of Virginia Woolf*, 5:101.

18. "Il va sans dire qu'à aucun moment, du jour où nous avons consenti à nous prêter à ces expériences, nous n'avons adopté le point de vue spirite. En ce qui me concerne je me refuse formellement à admettre qu'une communication quelconque existe entre les vivants et les morts." Breton, "Entrée des médiums," 276.

19. Ibid., 274. Breton, *Conversations* (1952), as quoted in and translated by Polizzotti, *Revolution of the Mind*, 179.

20. "Lettre aux voyantes" (1925), reprinted as Breton, "Letter to the Seers," 199. For more on the many similarities (and differences) between spiritualism and surrealism, see Cottom, *Abyss of Reason*, especially the introduction.

21. Polizzotti, *Revolution of the Mind*, 581.

22. Rainey, "Taking Dictation," 125, 134, 136, 148.

23. See Thurn und Taxis-Hohenlohe, *Erinnerungen an Rainer Maria Rilke*, 72–76.

24. "Mich drängt's zur Unbekannten." Letter to Marie von Thurn und Taxis, 29 July 1913, in Rilke and Thurn und Taxis, *Briefwechsel*, 304.

25. "Les Esprits ne voulaient pas de moi évidemment." Letter to Marie von Thurn und Taxis, 21 October 1913, ibid., 322–23.

26. "Er dichtet manches, was ich nie gebilligt haben würde." Letter to Nanny Wunderly-Volkart, 30 November 1920, in Rilke, *Briefe an Nanny Wunderly-Volkart*, 349. For more on Rilke's encounters with spiritualism, see Morse, "Rainer Maria Rilke and the Occult."

27. "Ich bin . . . medial vollkommen unbrauchbar, aber ich zweifle keinen Augenblick, daß ich mich auf meine Weise den Einflüssen jener oft heimatlosen Kräfte eröffnet halte und daß ich nie aufhöre, ihren Umgang zu genießen oder zu erleiden." Letter to Nora Purtscher-Wydenbruck, 11 August 1924, in Rilke, *Gesammelte Briefe*, 295.

28. Sonnet 2:13, in Rilke, *Sämtliche Werke*, 1:759.

29. "Requiem: Für eine Freundin," ibid., 1:647–56.

30. Mann, *Magic Mountain*, 657. The page numbers of all subsequent quotations are given in the text.

31. Rainey, "Taking Dictation," 148.

32. Ackroyd, *T. S. Eliot*, 113; Surette, *Birth of Modernism;* Materer, *Modernist Alchemy.*

33. Eliot, *Complete Poems*, 135–36. The page numbers of all subsequent quotations are given in the text.

34. Eliot, *After Strange Gods*, 46.

35. Eliot, *Selected Essays;* idem, *Use of Poetry*, 144; idem, *Three Voices of Poetry*, 18.

36. Lawrence, *Complete Poems*, 849, 28.

37. Eliot, *The Waste Land: Facsimile and Transcript*, 125. The page numbers of all subsequent quotations from *The Waste Land* are given in the text and refer to this edition.

38. "Teeming city, city full of dreams, / where the specter accosts the passer-by in full daylight."

39. Virgil, *The Aeneid*, 6:113.

40. Cf. Ovid, *Metamorphoses*, 6:430–678.

41. Ibid., 3:316–38.

42. Smith, *T. S. Eliot's Poetry and Plays*, 76.

43. Eliot reviewed Huxley's *Crome Yellow* in the *Times Literary Supplement* of 10 November 1921 but could not have seen the published book until after he had drafted the Madame Sosostris passage. As Grover Smith notes, however, Eliot probably received an early presentation copy. In response to a query by Smith, Eliot replied that "he could remember reading Huxley's *Crome Yellow* on publication, but he was unaware that he had taken the name 'Sosostris' from it; he supposed he must have." Smith, *Waste Land*, 67, 113.

44. Koestenbaum, *Double Talk*, 120.

45. See, for instance, Miller, *T. S. Eliot's Personal Waste Land*, 85–86; Koestenbaum, *Double Talk*, 126.

46. Smith, *T. S. Eliot and the Use of Memory.* Yeats, among others, admired Moberly and Jourdain's book and desired to meet the authors (Yeats, *Yeats's Vision Papers*, 16). Their psychic adventure at the Petit Trianon continues to fascinate readers today. See, for instance,

Terry Castle's *The Apparitional Lesbian* (Castle argues that Moberly and Jourdain used "a supernatural third party to triangulate, and thereby legitimate, their lesbian relationship" [125]) and John Corigliano's 1991 *opera buffa, The Ghosts of Versailles.*

47. Kenner, *Pound Era*, 136; Smith, *T. S. Eliot's Poetry and Plays*, 286.

Chapter 5. Modernist Hauntology

1. See, for instance, Frederick Crews's review of Peter Washington's "comic masterpiece," *Madame Blavatsky's Baboon: A History of the Mystics, Mediums, and Misfits Who Brought Spiritualism to America.* Calling Yeats "perhaps the greatest of modern poets," Crews asks wonderingly, "How could otherwise discerning people have subscribed to such preposterous ideas?" ("Consolation of Philosophy," 26–27). For a brief but useful overview of recent criticism on Yeats and the occult, see also Howes, *Yeats's Nations*, 83.

2. See, for instance, Bachchan, *W. B. Yeats and Occultism;* Harper, *Yeats's Golden Dawn;* idem, *Yeats and the Occult;* Cullingford, *Gender and History in Yeats's Love Poetry.*

3. Yeats, *Reveries over Childhood and Youth*, 105; Murphy, "Psychic Daughter, Mystic Son, Sceptic Father," 26.

4. Yeats, *Reveries over Childhood and Youth*, 127–28.

5. Tynan, *Twenty-Five Years*, 209.

6. Blavatsky, *Isis Unveiled*, 588.

7. Cummins, *Unseen Adventures*, 87.

8. Ibid.

9. Yeats, "Swedenborg, Mediums, and the Desolate Places," 23.

10. See Goldman, "Yeats, Spiritualism, and Psychical Research," 109–13.

11. Unpublished letter, 29 December 1913, quoted in Harper and Kelly, "Preliminary Examination," 133. Brenda Maddox identifies the "personal matter" as the putative pregnancy (later revealed as a false alarm) of Yeats's mistress, Mabel Dickinson. Maddox, *Yeats's Ghosts*, 33–34.

12. Letter to John Butler Yeats, 5 August 1913. Yeats, *Letters of W. B. Yeats*, 584. Unpublished letter to Elizabeth Radcliffe, 28 July 1913, quoted in Harper and Kelly, "Preliminary Examination," 136.

13. Yeats, in Harper and Kelly, "Preliminary Examination," 141–42. The page numbers of all subsequent quotations are given in the text.

14. Yeats, *Essays and Introductions*, 28.

15. Yeats, *Collected Poems*, 177–78. The page numbers of all subsequent quotations of Yeats's poetry are given in the text and refer to this edition.

16. Yeats, "Swedenborg, Mediums, and the Desolate Places," 22. The page numbers of all subsequent quotations are given in the text.

17. Joanne A. Wood notes that British troops during the First World War suffered upward of 42,000 amputations; these numbers required the opening of at least one hospital devoted solely to the rehabilitation of "Limbless Sailors and Soldiers." Wood, "Lighthouse Bodies," 483.

18. Yeats, *Yeats's Vision Papers*, 6.

19. Yeats, "Leo Africanus," 38.

20. Yeats, *Mythologies*, 331.

21. Longenbach, *Stone Cottage*, 192.

22. Yeats, quoted ibid.

23. Yeats, *Critical Edition of a Vision* (1925), 229; Yeats, *A Vision* (1937), 238.

24. Longenbach, *Stone Cottage*, 190.

25. Yeats, *Yeats's Vision Papers*, 5.

26. Harper and Kelly, "Preliminary Examination," 141.

27. Yeats, *A Vision* (1937), 75.

28. Ellmann, *Yeats: The Man and the Masks*, xiv, xv.

29. Yeats, *A Vision* (1937), 8.

30. Harper, introduction in Yeats, *Yeats's Vision Papers*, 17.

31. Quoted in Yeats, *Yeats's Vision Papers*, 29.

32. Ibid., 21.

33. Goldman, "Yeats, Spiritualism, and Psychical Research," 127.

34. "I have a great sense of abundance—more than I have had for years. George's ghosts have educated me" (Yeats to Olivia Shakespear, 27 December 1930, in Yeats, *Letters of W. B. Yeats*, 781). Maddox, *Yeats's Ghosts*. For more on W. B. and Georgie Yeats's spiritualist collaboration, see also London, *Writing Double*, 179–209.

35. Marjorie Howes notes, however, that Yeats's occultism, like his spiritualism, was far from "escapist": "Yeats . . . turned to the occult in order to intervene more effectively in a potentially hostile public sphere, rather than to escape it." Howes, *Yeats's Nations*, 84.

36. Lane, who perished with the *Titanic*, left an unwitnessed codicil to his will in which he stipulated that his art collection should be housed in Dublin rather than London; the custodial dispute raged for decades until the two governments finally agreed to share the paintings.

37. Rosenheim, *Cryptographic Imagination*, 21.

38. H. D., *Collected Poems*, 292. The page numbers of all subsequent quotations are given in the text and, unless otherwise noted, refer to this edition.

39. On the Van Eck incident, see H. D., *Tribute to Freud*, 154–62, 182–87. See also H. D.'s unpublished manuscript, "Majic Ring," in the Yale Collection of American Literature, Beinecke Library. On the "writing on the wall" incident, see *Tribute to Freud*, 44–56; "Majic Ring," 72–73; and "H. D. by Delia Alton," 198–99. On the dance scenes, see "Majic Ring," 195–261, and *Tribute to Freud*, 172–73.

40. H. D., "Majic Ring," 145, as quoted in Sword, *Engendering Inspiration*, 157.

41. H. D., *Tribute to Freud*, 173.

42. Ibid., 93.

43. H. D., "Majic Ring," 118–19, as quoted in Sword, "H. D.'s *Majic Ring*," 354.

44. H. D., *The Gift*, 169. The page numbers of all subsequent quotations from *The Gift* are given in the text and refer to this edition.

45. For more on the relationship between the novel and H. D.'s seance experiments at the time, see Jane Augustine's excellent introduction to *The Gift*.

46. H. D., *Tribute to Freud*, 51. The page numbers of all subsequent quotations are given in the text.

47. Alec Marsh, unpublished paper presented at the Modernist Studies Association Conference, State College, Pennsylvania, October 1999.

48. Unpublished letter to Bryher, 27 March 1933 (Beinecke Library, Yale University).

49. Quoted in Friedman, *Psyche Reborn*, 19.

50. H. D., notes to "Majic Ring," as quoted in Sword, *Engendering Inspiration*, 168.

51. "Dark Room" is a chapter title in *The Gift*, 35–53. "Majic Ring," as mentioned earlier, is an unpublished manuscript (Beinecke Library, Yale University). "Writing on the Wall" is a section title in *Tribute to Freud*, 3–111. *Within the Walls* is a 1941–42 short story collection. "The Walls Do Not Fall" is a section title in *Trilogy* (*Collected Poems*, 509–43).

52. Derrida, *Specters of Marx*, xx.

53. "Before the Battle," in H. D., *Within the Walls*, 56.

54. For details about H. D.'s communications from the "R.A.F. boys," see Friedman, *Psyche Reborn*, 173–75; Guest, *Herself Defined*, 260–62.

55. In 1944–45, H. D. sent a series of letters speculating on the hidden meanings of her seances to former Air Chief Marshal Hugh Dowding, whose public lecture on spiritualism she had recently attended. For more on the circumstances surrounding her relationship to Dowding and her eventual turn from spiritualism, see Sword, "H. D.'s *Majic Ring.*"

56. H. D., "H. D. by Delia Alton," 200.

57. H. D., "The Sword Went Out to Sea," 211 (unpublished manuscript, Beinecke Library, Yale University).

58. H. D., *Helen in Egypt*, 303. The page numbers of all subsequent quotations are given in the text.

59. Poem 1222 in Dickinson, *Complete Poems*, 538.

Chapter 6. Ghostwriting Postmodernism

1. Yeats recounts his psychic experiences in prose, and elements of *A Vision*'s symbolic system can be traced in his verse, but apart from a brief four-line poem titled "Gratitude to the Unknown Instructors," he does not explicitly allude to his wife's mediumship in his poetry. H. D. describes her spiritualist involvement at length in such unpublished memoirs and romans-à-clef as "Majic Ring," "The Sword Went Out to Sea,*"* and the "Hirslanden Notebooks," but she mentions it only elliptically in her published works and not at all in her lyrical verse. Nor does Rilke address his 1912 planchette experiments anywhere in his poetry, although he frequently wrote about prophetic figures and visionary consciousness.

2. Many variations on this arrangement are possible: for instance, one can lay out scraps of paper representing the letters of the alphabet rather than inscribing them on a single sheet; one can write the letters in random sequence rather than in alphabetical order; and one can blindfold the sitters so that only the person who is transcribing the board's messages can see the words being spelled out.

3. Merrill, *Recitative*, 66.

4. Letter to the author from Evelyn M. Cuoco, Parker Brothers Consumer Relations, 23 April 1992. Parker Brothers reports having sold more than fifty million Ouija boards since it acquired the rights in 1966. The company claims that, historically, the Ouija board's popularity has tended to peak during wartime; in 1967, at the height of the Vietnam War, sales even topped those of Monopoly.

5. Hunt, *Ouija*, 6–7.

6. Merrill, *Recitative*, 66.

7. Vendler, "James Merrill," 83; Materer, *Modernist Alchemy*, 131.

8. Merrill, *Recitative*, 66; Jackson, "Lending a Hand," 301.

9. Merrill, *From the First Nine*, 66–67.

10. To be sure, the narrator of "Voices" never specifically indicates how many people assist him at the board. In fact, David Jackson recalls that his wife, Doris Sewell Jackson, was also present at that first seance in 1955. Jackson, "Lending a Hand," 301.

11. Merrill, *Changing Light at Sandover*, 278, 517. The page numbers of all subsequent quotations are given in the text.

12. See Spiegelman (whose interest in mirrors is surely "no accident"!), "Breaking the

Mirror," and Lehman, "Elemental Bravery," for further accounts of how images of rupture, shattered mirrors, and broken vessels figure in Merrill's visionary poetics.

13. Plath, *Collected Poems*, 77–78. The page numbers of all subsequent quotations of Plath's poetry are given in the text.

14. Hughes, notes in Plath, *Collected Poems*, 287.

15. Pollitt, "Note of Triumph," 96; Nims, "Poetry of Sylvia Plath," 60.

16. Plath, *Journals*, 112.

17. Materer, *Modernist Alchemy*, 130–31.

18. Ibid., 137.

19. "We keep telling Pan we want [to win] so we can have leisure to write and have lots of children," wrote Plath to her mother in 1957 (*Letters Home*, 294). Hughes notes that Pan, whose communications "were gloomy and macabre, though not without wit," could be maddening in his near-accuracy: "The first time he was guided through Littlewood's football coupon, he predicted all thirteen of the draws made on the following Saturday—but anticipated them, throughout, by just one match" (Plath, *Collected Poems*, 276). See also Hughes's poem "Ouija" in Hughes, *Birthday Letters*, 53–56.

20. Merrill, *Recitative*, 65.

21. Ibid., 53.

22. Ibid., 68.

23. Plath, *Letters Home*, 280, 276.

24. Plath, *Journals*, 245.

25. Ibid., 161, 173.

26. See H.D.'s unpublished memoir "Majic Ring," 238, 246 (in the Yale Collection of American Literature, Beinecke Library).

27. Merrill, *Recitative*, 71.

28. Plath, *Collected Poems*, 90–91.

29. Plath, *Journals*, 328.

30. Merrill, *Changing Light at Sandover*, 30; Plath, *Journals*, 245; Hughes, "Sylvia Plath and Her Journals," 155.

31. Plath, *Collected Poems*, 296.

32. Plath, *Letters Home*, 280, 480; Stevenson, *Bitter Fame*, 358.

33. Merrill, *Recitative*, 68.

34. Nabokov, *Pale Fire*, 52.

35. Ibid., 62–63.

36. See, for instance, Rowe, *Nabokov's Spectral Dimension*.

37. Boyd, "Shade and Shape in *Pale Fire*," 196. See Boyd's article for an excellent and thorough overview of critical approaches to *Pale Fire*.

38. Ibid., 196, 201, 210.

39. In Boyd's paraphrase, Hazel is supposed to "tell her father ('pada': pa, da, padre) not to go across the lane to old Goldsworth's, as an *atalanta* butterfly dances by, after he finished 'Pale Fire' ('tale feur'), at the invitation of someone from a foreign land who has told and even ranted his tall tale to him." Ibid., 202.

40. Byatt is an eminent scholar of Victorian literature who has carefully researched the spiritualist movement; see her review of Alex Owen's *The Darkened Room* (Byatt, "Chosen Vessels of a Fraud"). *Possession* is frequently designated a postmodern novel by literary critics; see, for just two of numerous examples, Buxton, " 'What's Love Got to Do with It?': Postmodernism and *Possession*," and Bronfen, "Romancing Difference, Courting Coherence: A. S. Byatt's *Possession* as Postmodern Moral Fiction."

41. See Porter, *Through a Glass Darkly.*

42. Byatt, *Possession,* 442.

43. For a detailed account of Hughes's occultism, especially in its literary manifestations, see Materer, *Modernist Alchemy,* 141–55.

44. Plath, *Collected Poems,* 77–78, 276–86; Hughes, *Birthday Letters,* 53–56. The page numbers of all subsequent quotations of *Birthday Letters* are given in the text.

45. Rose, *Haunting of Sylvia Plath,* 1.

46. Barthes, *Camera Lucida,* 14.

47. Hughes, "Myth and Education," 147.

48. For more on Hughes's administration of the Plath estate and his refusal to grant publication rights to critics with whose perspective on Plath he disagreed, see Rose, *Haunting of Sylvia Plath,* ix–xii; Alexander, *Rough Magic;* Malcolm, *Silent Woman.*

49. "L'Implosion du sens dans les média" in Baudrillard, *Simulacres et simulation,* 126. Quoted in Cottom, *Abyss of Reason,* 270 n. 17.

50. Http://www.math.unh.edu/black/cgi-bin/spirit.cgi (9 August 2000). The webmaster, Kelly Black, reports having been requested by Hasbro, Inc., which "owns the rights to the trademark to the word ouija," to delete *ouija* from the site's URL. It now contains the word *spirit* instead but can still be found with standard search engines by using the keyword *ouija.*

Epilogue. Ghostreading

1. On spiritualism in nineteenth-century Britain and America, see Logie Barrow, *Independent Spirits* (1986); Ruth Brandon, *The Spiritualists* (1983); Ann Braude, *Radical Spirits* (1989); Ann Douglas, *The Feminization of American Culture* (1977); R. Lawrence Moore, *In Search of White Crows* (1977); Geoffrey Nelson, *Spiritualism and Society* (1969); Janet Oppenheim, *The Other World* (1985); and Alex Owen, *The Darkened Room* (1990). On spiritualism in nineteenth-century literature, see Russell M. Goldfarb and Clare R. Goldfarb, *Spiritualism and Nineteenth-Century Letters* (1978); Kelvin I. Jones, *Conan Doyle and the Spirits* (1989); Howard Kerr, *Mediums, and Spirit Rappers, and Roaring Radicals: Spiritualism in American Literature, 1850–1900* (1972); and Katherine H. Porter, *Through a Glass Darkly: Spiritualism in the Browning Circle* (1958).

2. See Jacqueline Rose, *The Haunting of Sylvia Plath* (1991); Avery F. Gordon, *Ghostly Matters: Haunting and the Sociological Imagination* (1996); H. L. Hix, *Spirits Hovering over the Ashes: Legacies of Postmodern Theory* (1997).

3. See, for instance, Davidson, "Photographs of the Dead"; Johnson, "Haunted House"; Miller, "Specters of Dickens's Study"; Pencak, "Ghosts in Utopia"; Rainey, "Taking Dictation"; Tamen, "Phenomenology of the Ghost"; Viswanathan, "Ordinary Business of Occultism"; Weinstock, "Disappointed Bridge"; White, "Female Spectator, Lesbian Specter: *The Haunting.*"

4. Surette, *Birth of Modernism,* x.

5. Perdita Schaffner, letter to the author, 8 December 1988.

6. [Name withheld], letter to the author, 13 December 1988.

7. Braude, *Radical Spirits,* 28.

8. Culler, *On Deconstruction,* 97, 99, 102–5, 96.

9. Derrida, *Specters of Marx:* "deconstructive thinking of the trace," 75; ethics, xix; mourning, 9; the past, 4; the future, 39; inheritance, 21; religion, 144; translation, 18;

imagination, 100–101; phenomenology, 135; capitalism, 45; dialectical materialism, 63; political repression, 37; academic culture, 11; communication technologies, 54.

10. Basham, *Trial of Woman;* London, *Writing Double;* Brantlinger, *Rule of Darkness;* Howes, *Yeats's Nations;* Viswanathan, "Ordinary Business of Occultism"; Nunokawa, *Afterlife of Property;* Miller, "Specters of Dickens's Study"; Castle, *Apparitional Lesbian,* 6; Stevens, *Henry James and Sexuality;* White, "Female Spectator, Lesbian Specter: *The Haunting*"; Garber, *Shakespeare's Ghost Writers,* 14; Rose, *Haunting of Sylvia Plath;* Gordon, *Ghostly Matters;* Bergé, *Voix des esprits,* 44: Abraham and Torok, *Wolf Man's Magic Word: A Cryptonymy;* Rosenheim, *Cryptographic Imagination.*

11. Beer, "George Eliot: *Daniel Deronda* and the Idea of a Future Life" in *Darwin's Plots;* Davidson, "Photographs of the Dead"; Rainey, "Taking Dictation."

12. Derrida, *Specters of Marx,* 4.

13. "A historian is a bit like a spirit medium," acknowledges Ann Braude in *Radical Spirits;* "one's goal is to allow the dead to speak as clearly as possible" (xi). "I began with a desire to speak to the dead," confesses Stephen Greenblatt at the start of *Shakespearean Negotiations.* And in Byatt's novel *Possession,* the fictional poet R.H. Ash notes that "The Historian and the Man of Science alike may be said to traffic with the dead" (116).

14. McLuhan, *Gutenberg Galaxy.*

Bibliography

Abbott, David P. *Behind the Scenes with the Mediums.* Chicago: Open Court, 1907.

Abraham, Nicolas. "Notes on the Phantom: A Complement to Freud's Metapsychology." Translated by Nicholas Rand. *Critical Inquiry* 13 (winter 1987): 287–92.

Abraham, Nicolas, and Maria Torok. *The Wolf Man's Magic Word: A Cryptonymy.* Translated by Nicholas Rand. Minneapolis: University of Minnesota Press, 1986.

Ackroyd, Peter. *T. S. Eliot: A Life.* New York: Simon and Schuster, 1984.

Adorno, Theodor. "Theses against Occultism." Translated by E. F. N. Jophcott. In *Minima Moralia: Reflections from Damaged Life,* 238–44. London: Verso, 1978. Article first published in 1951.

Agnes, Dorothy. *The Voice of Marie Corelli: Fragments from "The Immortal Garden" through the Pen of Dorothy Agnes.* Manchester, England: Sherratt and Hughes, 1933.

Alexander, Paul. *Rough Magic: A Biography of Sylvia Plath.* New York: Viking, 1991.

Allen, Percy. *Talks with Elizabethans: Revealing the Mystery of "William Shakespeare."* London: Rider, 1947.

———. "Was It Hester Dowden?" *Light: A Journal of Spiritualism and Psychical Research* 69, no. 3350 (June 1949): 156–60.

Anglo-American Cataloging Rules. Ed. Michael Gorman and Paul W. Winkler. Chicago: American Library Association, 1978.

Asimov, Isaac. "The Immortal Bard." *Universe Science Fiction* 5 (May 1954).

Atherton, James. *The Books at the Wake: A Study of Literary Allusions in James Joyce's Finnegans Wake.* Mamaroneck, N.Y.: Appel, 1974.

Auden, W. H. "The Sea and the Mirror." In *Collected Poems,* 401–45. New York: Vintage, 1991. Poem written in 1942–44.

Bachchan, Harbans Rai. *W. B. Yeats and Occultism.* Delhi: Motilal Banarsidass, 1965.

Baer, Hans A. *The Black Spiritual Movement: A Religious Response to Racism.* Knoxville: University of Tennessee Press, 1984.

Baker, Michael. *Our Three Selves: The Life of Radclyffe Hall.* New York: William Morrow, 1985.

Barbanell, Sylvia. *Some Discern Spirits (The Mediumship of Estelle Roberts).* London: Psychic Press, 1945.

Barker, Elsa. *War Letters from the Living Dead Man.* London: Rider, 1915.

Barrett, Florence Elizabeth Perry, ed. *Personality Survives Death: Messages from Sir William Barrett.* London: Longmans, 1937.

Barrett Browning, Elizabeth. *The Letters of Elizabeth Barrett Browning.* Edited by Frederic G. Kenyon. 2 vols. London: Smith, Elder, 1897.

Barrow, Logie. *Independent Spirits: Spiritualism and English Plebeians, 1850–1910.* London: Routledge and Kegan Paul, 1986.

Barthes, Roland. *Camera Lucida: Reflections on Photography.* Translated by Richard Howard. New York: Hill and Wang, 1981.

Barton, Dunbar Plunket. *Links between Ireland and Shakespeare.* Dublin: Maunsel, 1919.

Basham, Diana. *The Trial of Woman: Feminism and the Occult Sciences in Victorian Literature and Society.* New York: New York University Press, 1992.

Baudrillard, Jean. *Simulacres et simulation.* Paris: Editions Gallilée, 1981.

Beecher, Charles. *Spiritual Manifestations.* Boston: Lee and Shepard, 1879.

Beer, Gillian. *Darwin's Plots: Evolutionary Narrative in Darwin, George Eliot, and Nineteenth-Century Fiction.* Boston: Routledge and Kegan Paul, 1983.

Benson, E. F. *All about Lucia: Four Novels.* New York: Sun Dial, 1940.

Bentley, Edmund. *Far Horizon: A Biography of Hester Dowden, Medium and Psychic Investigator.* London: Rider, 1951.

Bergé, Christine. *La voix des esprits: Ethnologie du spiritisme.* Paris: Editions Métailié, 1990.

Bergson, Henri. " 'Phantasms of the Living' and 'Psychical Research.' " In *Mind-Energy: Lectures and Essays,* translated by H. Wildon Carr, 75–103. London: MacMillan, 1920.

Blamires, Harry. *The New Bloomsday Book.* New York: Routledge, 1988.

Blavatsky, Helena Petrovna. *Isis Unveiled.* Vol. 2. 1877. Reprint, Los Angeles: Theosophy Company, 1975.

Bleibtreu, Karl. *Die Lösung der Shakespeare-Frage: Eine neue Theorie.* Leipzig: Thomas, 1907.

Bloom, Harold. *The Anxiety of Influence: A Theory of Poetry.* New York: Oxford University Press, 1973.

Bond, Frederick Bligh. *The Gospel of Philip the Deacon.* New York: Macoy, 1932.

Borges, Jorge Luis. "Everything and Nothing." In *A Personal Anthology,* edited and translated by Anthony Kerrigan, 116–17. New York: Grove, Weidenfeld, 1967.

Boucher, Gustave. *Une séance de spiritisme: Chez J.-K. Huysmans.* Niort, 1908.

Boyd, Brian. "Shade and Shape in *Pale Fire.*" *Nabokov Studies* 4 (1997): 173–224.

Boyd, Jane. *The Next World: Described by One Who Is There.* London: Longmans, 1942.

———. *What Are They Doing Now and How Can They Tell Us?* London: Longmans, Green, 1941.

Bradley, Dennis. *Towards the Stars.* London: T. Werner Laurie, 1924.

Brandes, Georg. *William Shakespeare: A Critical Study.* Translated by William Archer and Mary Morison. London: Heinemann, 1898.

Brandon, Ruth. *The Spiritualists: The Passion for the Occult in the Nineteenth and Twentieth Centuries.* New York: Knopf, 1983.

Brandon, Wilfred (Spirit). *Open the Door!* Transcribed by Edith Ellis. New York: Knopf, 1935.

Brantlinger, Patrick. *Rule of Darkness: British Literature and Imperialism, 1830–1914.* Ithaca: Cornell University Press, 1988.

Braude, Ann. *Radical Spirits: Spiritualism and Women's Rights in Nineteenth Century America.* Boston: Beacon, 1989.

Breton, André. "Entrée des médiums." In *Oeuvres complètes*, 273–79. Paris: Gallimard, 1988.

——. "Letter to the Seers." In *Manifestoes of Surrealism*, translated by Richard Seaver and Helen R. Lane, 197–203. Ann Arbor: University of Michigan Press, 1972. Essay first published in 1925.

Brogan, Kathleen. *Cultural Haunting: Ghosts and Ethnicity in Recent American Literature.* Charlottesville: University Press of Virginia, 1998.

Bronfen, Elisabeth. "Romancing Difference, Courting Coherence: A. S. Byatt's *Possession* as Postmodern Moral Fiction." In *Why Literature Matters: Theories and Functions of Literature*, edited by Rudiger Ahrens and Laurenz Vokmann, 117–34. Heidelberg: Universitätsverlag C. Winter, 1996.

Browning, Robert. "Mr. Sludge, 'The Medium.'" In *The Poetical Works of Robert Browning*, 397–412. Boston: Houghton Mifflin, 1974.

Bürgin, Hans, and Hans-Otto Mayer. *Thomas Mann: Eine Chronik seines Lebens.* Frankfurt a. M.: Fischer, 1965.

Burke, Carolyn. *Becoming Modern: The Life of Mina Loy.* New York: Farrar, Straus, and Giroux, 1996.

Burke, Jane Revere. *Let Us In: A Record of Communications Believed to Have Come from William James.* New York, 1931.

——. *The One Way.* New York: Dutton, 1922.

Buxton, Jackie. "'What's Love Got to Do with It?': Postmodernism and *Possession*." *English Studies in Canada* 22, no. 2 (June 1996): 199–219.

Byatt, A. S. "Chosen Vessels of a Fraud." *Times Literary Supplement*, 2 June 1989, 205.

——. *The Conjugial Angel.* In *Angels and Insects*, 187–337. New York: Random House, 1993.

——. *Possession: A Romance.* New York: Vintage, 1990.

Carroll, Lewis. *The Annotated Alice: Alice's Adventures in Wonderland and Through the Looking Glass.* Introduction and notes by Martin Gardner. New York: Meridian, 1960.

Castle, Terry. *The Apparitional Lesbian: Female Homosexuality and Modern Culture.* New York: Columbia University Press, 1993.

——. *The Female Thermometer: Eighteenth-Century Culture and the Invention of the Uncanny.* New York: Oxford University Press, 1995.

——. "Phantasmagoria: Spectral Technology and the Metaphorics of Modern Reverie." *Critical Inquiry* 15 (1988): 26–61.

Chamberlain, John. *The Enterprising Americans.* New York: Harper, 1963.

Charnes, Linda. *Notorious Identity: Materializing the Subject in Shakespeare.* Cambridge: Harvard University Press, 1993.

Cheng, Vincent John. *Shakespeare and Joyce: A Study of Finnegans Wake.* University Park, Pa.: Penn State University Press, 1984.

Coates, James, ed. *Has W. T. Stead Returned? A Symposium.* London: Fowler, 1913.

Coblentz, Flora. *For All Who Seek.* San Jose, Calif.: Redwood, 1973.

Collis, Maurice. *Somerville and Ross: A Biography.* London: Faber, 1968.

Conan Doyle, Arthur. "The Alleged Posthumous Writings of Great Authors." *Fortnightly Review,* 1 December 1927, 721–35.

——. *The New Revelation.* London: Hodder and Stoughton, 1918.

——. *Pheneas Speaks: Direct Communications in the Family Circle, Reported by Arthur Conan Doyle.* London: Psychic Press, 1927.

Conrad, Jessie. *Did Joseph Conrad Return as a Spirit?* Webster Groves, Mo.: International Mark Twain Society, 1932.

Cooke, Grace. *Sun-Men of the Americas.* Liss, Hampshire, England: White Eagle, 1985.

Cooke, Ivan. *"Thy Kingdom Come . . ." A Presentation of the Whence, Why, and Whither of Man. A Record of Messages Received from One of the White Brotherhood, Believed to Have Been Known on Earth as Arthur Conan Doyle.* London: Wright and Brown, 1933.

Corelli, Marie. *The Life Everlasting: A Reality of Romance.* London: Methuen, 1911.

——. *A Romance of Two Worlds.* London: Bentley, 1895.

Corigliano, John, composer. *The Ghosts of Versailles: A Grand Opera Buffa in Two Acts.* Libretto by William M. Hoffman. New York: Schirmer, 1991.

Cory, Winifred Graham. *My Letters from Heaven: Being Messages from the Unseen World Given in Automatic Writing to Winifred Graham by Her Father, Robert George Graham.* London: Hutchinson, 1923.

Cottom, Daniel. *Abyss of Reason: Cultural Movements, Revolutions, and Betrayals.* New York: Oxford University Press, 1991.

Coward, Noel. *Blithe Spirit: An Improbable Farce in Three Acts.* New York: French, 1941.

Crews, Frederick. "The Consolation of Philosophy." *New York Review of Books* 43, no. 14 (19 September 1996): 26–30, and 43, no. 15 (26 September 1996): 38–44.

Culler, Jonathan. *On Deconstruction: Theory and Criticism after Structuralism.* Ithaca: Cornell University Press, 1982.

Cullingford, Elizabeth. *Gender and History in Yeats's Love Poetry.* Cambridge: Cambridge University Press, 1993.

Cummins, Geraldine. *Beyond Human Personality: Being a Detailed Description of the Future Life Purporting to Be Communicated by the Late F. W. H. Myers. Containing an Account of the Gradual Development of Human Personality into Cosmic Personality.* London: Nicholson and Watson, 1935.

——. *Dr. E. Œ. Somerville: A Biography.* London: Dakers, 1952.

——. *Unseen Adventures: An Autobiography covering Thirty-four Years of Work in Psychical Research*. London: Rider, 1951.

Dallas, Helen Alex. *Mors Janua Vitae? A Discussion of Certain Communications Purporting to Come From F. W. H. Myers*. London: Rider, 1910.

Davenport, Reuben Briggs. *The Death-Blow to Spiritualism: Being the True Story of the Fox Sisters, as Revealed by the Authority of Margaret Fox Kane and Catherine Fox Jencken*. 1888. Reprint, New York: Arno, 1976.

Davidson, Cathy. "Photographs of the Dead: Sherman, Daguerre, Hawthorne." *South Atlantic Quarterly* 89, no. 4 (1990): 667–701.

Davies, F. T. A. *Six Million Men Killed in the Great War: Messages from the Dead to the Living*. London: Davies, 1921.

Dawson Scott, Catherine A. *From Four Who Are Dead: Messages to C. A. Dawson Scott*. Introduction by May Sinclair. London: Arrowsmith, 1926.

——. *Is This Wilson? Messages Accredited to Woodrow Wilson*. New York: Dutton, 1929.

DeLillo, Don. *White Noise*. New York: Penguin, 1985.

Delisle, Françoise. *The Return of Havelock Ellis: Or Limbo or the Dove?* London: Regency, 1968.

Derrida, Jacques. *Specters of Marx: The State of the Debt, the Work of Mourning, and the New International*. Translated by Peggy Kamuf. London: Routledge, 1994.

Dickens, Charles (Spirit). *Part Second of the Mystery of Edwin Drood: By the Spirit-Pen of Charles Dickens, Through a Medium*. Brattleboro, Vt.: T. B. James, 1873.

Dickinson, Emily. *The Complete Poems of Emily Dickinson*. Edited by Thomas H. Johnson. Boston: Little, Brown, 1960.

Dobson, Michael. *The Making of the National Poet: Shakespeare, Adaptation and Authorship, 1660–1769*. Oxford: Clarendon, 1992.

Dodd, Alfred. *The Immortal Master*. London: Rider, 1943.

Doten, Lizzie. *Poems from the Inner Life*. Boston: William White, 1867.

Doucé, P. M. *Incredible Alliance: Transmissions from T. S. Eliot through the Mediumship of P. M. Doucé*. Philadelphia: Dorrance, 1975.

Douglas, Ann. *The Feminization of American Culture*. New York: Knopf, 1977.

Dowden, Edward. *Fragments of Old Letters: E. D. to E. D. W., 1869–1892*. London: Dent, 1914.

Dowden, Hester. See Travers Smith, Hester.

Dowding, Hugh. *Lychgate*. London: Rider, 1945.

——. *Many Mansions*. London: Rider, 1943.

Dowding, Muriel. *Beauty—Not the Beast: An Autobiography*. Jersey, England: Spearman, 1980.

Drouét, Bessie Clark. *Station Astral*. London: G. P. Putnam's Sons, 1932.

Ebon, Martin. *They Knew the Unknown*. New York: World, 1971.

Eckley, Grace. *The Steadfast "Finnegans Wake": A Textbook*. New York: University Presses of America, 1994.

Eddy, Mary Baker. *Science and Health: With Keys to the Scriptures*. 1875. Reprint, Boston: Trustees of Mary Baker Eddy, 1934.

Eglinton, John. *Irish Literary Portraits*. London: Macmillan, 1935.

Eliot, George. *The George Eliot Letters*. Edited by Gordon S. Haight. 9 vols. London: Oxford University Press, 1954–78.

Eliot, T. S. *After Strange Gods: A Primer of Modern Heresy*. London: Faber and Faber, 1934.

——. *The Complete Poems and Plays, 1909–1950*. New York: Harcourt Brace Jovanovich, 1971.

——. *Selected Essays, 1917–1932*. New York: Harcourt Brace Jovanovich, 1964.

——. *The Three Voices of Poetry*. London: National Book League, 1953.

——. *The Use of Poetry, and the Use of Criticism: Studies in the Relation of Criticism and Poetry in England*. London: Faber and Faber, 1933.

——. *The Waste Land: A Facsimile and Transcript of the Original Drafts Including the Annotations of Ezra Pound*. Edited by Valerie Eliot. New York: Harcourt Brace Jovanovich, 1971.

Ellmann, Richard. *James Joyce*. Oxford: Oxford University Press, 1982.

——. *Yeats: The Man and the Masks*. New York: Penguin, 1979.

Emery, Linda. *Houdini Unmasked: Code Message Received by Beatrice Houdini*. Lily Dale, N.Y.: Dale News, 1947.

Evans, Colin. "Spiritualism and Language." *Psychic Review* 5, no. 5 (April 1943).

Flammarion, Camille. *Spirit Communications*. London: Putnam, 1925.

Foucault, Michel. "What Is an Author?" In *Textual Strategies: Perspectives in Post-Structuralist Criticism*, edited by J. V. Harari, 141–60. Ithaca: Cornell University Press, 1979.

Frank, Joseph. "Spatial Form in Modern Literature." *Sewanee Review* 53 (1945): 221–40, 433–56, 643–53.

Freud, Sigmund. *The Future of an Illusion*. Translated by W. D. Robson-Scott. Edinburgh: Horace Liveright and the Institute of Psycho-Analysis, 1928.

——. "Thoughts for the Times on War and Death." In *The Standard Edition of the Complete Psychological Works of Sigmund Freud*, translated by James Strachey, 14:273–300. London: Hogarth, 1957. Lecture first presented in 1915.

——. "The 'Uncanny.'" In *The Standard Edition of the Complete Psychological Works of Sigmund Freud*, translated by James Strachey, 17:219–52. London: Hogarth, 1955. Essay first published in 1919.

Friedman, Allan Warren. *Fictional Death and the Modernist Enterprise*. New York: Cambridge University Press, 1995.

Friedman, Susan Stanford. *Psyche Reborn: The Emergence of H. D.* Bloomington: Indiana University Press, 1981.

Fripp, Peter. *The Book of Johannes*. London: Rider, 1945.

Fuller, John G. *The Airmen Who Would Not Die*. London: Corgi, 1981.

Garber, Marjorie. *Shakespeare's Ghost Writers: Literature as Uncanny Causality*. New York: Methuen, 1987.

Garrett, Eileen. *Many Voices: The Autobiography of a Medium*. New York: G. P. Putnam's Sons, 1968.

Gaudon, Jean, ed. *Ce que disent les tables parlantes: Victor Hugo à Jersey*. Paris: Jean-Jacques Prevert, 1963.

Gauld, Alan. *The Founders of Psychical Research.* London: Routledge and Kegan Paul, 1968.

Gibson, William. *Mona Lisa Overdrive.* New York: Bantam, 1988.

Gilbert, Sandra M., and Susan Gubar. *The Madwoman in the Attic: The Woman Writer and the Nineteenth-Century Literary Imagination.* New Haven: Yale University Press, 1979.

——. *No Man's Land.* 3 vols. New Haven: Yale University Press, 1988–94.

Gillespie, Edward Acheson (Spirit). *Knowledge of Thy Truth: By an Anglican Priest (Edward Acheson Gillespie) Speaking from Beyond Death through His Wife in Collaboration with Mrs. Hester Dowden.* London: Daniel, 1939.

Gillson, the Rev. E., M.A., Curate of Lyncombe and Widcombe, Bath. *Table-Talking; Disclosures of Satanic Wonders and Prophetic Signs. A Word for the Wise.* Bath: Binns and Goodwin, [1853]. Pusey House Pamphlet Collection, Oxford, catalog no. 3326.

Goldfarb, Clare R. "From Hydesville to Yasnaya Polyana: Leo Tolstoy and Modern Spiritualism." *Centennial Review* 33 (1989): 228–42.

Goldfarb, Russell M., and Clare R. Goldfarb. *Spiritualism and Nineteenth-Century Letters.* London: Associated University Press, 1978.

Goldman, Arnold. "Yeats, Spiritualism, and Psychical Research." In *Yeats and the Occult,* edited by George Mills Harper, 108–29. Toronto: Macmillan, 1975.

Gordon, Avery F. *Ghostly Matters: Haunting and the Sociological Imagination.* Minneapolis: University of Minnesota Press, 1996.

Grady, Hugh. *The Modernist Shakespeare: Critical Texts in a Material World.* Oxford: Clarendon, 1991.

Greenblatt, Stephen. *Shakespearean Negotiations: The Circulation of Social Energy in Renaissance England.* Berkeley: University of California Press, 1988.

Grove, Harriet McCrory, and Mattie Mitchell Hunt, eds. *Gone West: By a Soldier Doctor.* New York: Knopf, 1919.

Guest, Barbara. *Herself Defined: The Poet H.D. and Her World.* New York: Doubleday, 1985.

Hardy, Thomas. *The Complete Poems.* New York: Macmillan, 1976.

Harper, George Mills. *The Making of Yeats's "A Vision": A Study of the Automatic Script.* Carbondale: Southern Illinois University Press, 1987.

——. *Yeats's Golden Dawn.* London: Macmillan, 1974.

——, ed. *Yeats and the Occult.* Toronto: Macmillan, 1975.

Harper, George Mills, and John S. Kelly. "Preliminary Examination of the Script of E[lizabeth] R[adcliffe]." In *Yeats and the Occult,* edited by George Mills Harper, 130–71. Toronto: Macmillan, 1975.

Harris, Frank. *The Man Shakespeare and His Tragic Life-Story.* London: Frank Palmer, 1909.

Harris, Sara. *Talks with Spirit Friends, Bench and Bar: Being Descriptions of the Next World and Its Activities by Well-Known Persons Who Live There, Given through the Trance Mediumship of the Late Miss Sara Harris to a Retired Public Servant and Recorded by Him.* London: Watkins, 1931.

Harrison, Eva. *Wireless Messages from Other Worlds*. London: Fowler, 1915.

Hawley, Elizabeth, and Columbia Rossi. *Bertie: The Life after Death of H. G. Wells*. London: New English Library, 1973.

Hawthorne, Nathaniel. *The Blithedale Romance*. Boston: Ticknor and Fields, 1859.

H. D. *By Avon River*. New York: Macmillan, 1949.

——. *Collected Poems, 1912–1944*. Edited by Louis L. Martz. New York: New Directions, 1983.

——. *The Gift*. Edited by Jane Augustine. Gainesville: University Press of Florida, 1998.

——. "H. D. by Delia Alton." *Iowa Review* 16, no. 2 (1986): 174–221. First written in 1949 and titled "Notes on Recent Writing."

——. *Helen in Egypt*. New York: New Directions, 1974.

——. *Tribute to Freud*. New York: New Directions, 1974.

——. *Within the Walls*. Iowa City: University of Iowa Press, 1993.

Heaney, Seamus. "Station Island." In *Selected Poems, 1966–1987*, 181–212. New York: Farrar, Straus, and Giroux, 1990. The poem was first published in 1984.

Hix, H. L. *Spirits Hovering over the Ashes: Legacies of Postmodern Theory*. New York: State University of New York Press, 1997.

Horn, Henry J. *Strange Visitors: A Series of Original Papers, Embracing Philosophy, Science, Government, Religion, Poetry, Art, Fiction, Satire, Humor, Narrative, and Prophecy. By the Spirits of Irving, Willis, Thackeray, Bronte, Richter, Byron, Humboldt, Hawthorne, Wesley, Browning, and Others Now Dwelling in the Spirit World*. New York: Carleton, 1869.

Horn, Susan G. *The Next World: Fifty-six Communications from Eminent Historians, Authors, Legislators, Etc. Now in Spirit-Life*. London: James Burns, 1890.

Horwood, Harold. *Mary Baker Eddy: Her Communications from beyond the Grave*. London: Max Parrish, 1964.

Howells, William Dean. *The Undiscovered Country*. Boston: Houghton Mifflin, 1880.

Howes, Marjorie. *Yeats's Nations: Gender, Class, and Irishness*. Cambridge: Cambridge University Press, 1996.

Hughes, Ted. *Birthday Letters*. New York: Farrar, Straus, and Giroux, 1998.

——. "Myth and Education." In *Winter Pollen: Occasional Prose*, edited by William Scammell, 136–53. London: Faber and Faber, 1994. Essay originally published in 1976.

——. "Sylvia Plath and Her Journals." In *Ariel Ascending: Writings about Sylvia Plath*, edited by Paul Alexander, 152–64. New York: Harper, 1985.

Hunt, Stoker. *Ouija: The Most Dangerous Game*. New York: Harper and Row, 1976.

Huxley, Aldous. *Brave New World*. London: Chatto and Windus, 1932.

——. *Crome Yellow*. London: Chatto and Windus, 1921.

Huxley, Leonard. *Life and Letters of Thomas Henry Huxley*. 2 vols. New York: Appleton, 1900.

Jackson, David. "Lending a Hand." In *James Merrill: Essays in Criticism*, edited by David Lehman and Charles Berger, 298–305. Ithaca: Cornell University Press, 1983.

Jackson, Shirley. *The Haunting of Hill House.* New York: Viking, 1959.

James, Henry. *The Bostonians: A Novel.* New York: Macmillan, 1886.

Johnson, George M. "A Haunted House: Ghostly Presences in Woolf's Essays and Early Fiction." In *Virginia Woolf and the Essay,* edited by Beth Rosenberg and Jeanne Dubino, 235–54. New York: St. Martin's Press, 1998.

Jones, Kelvin I. *Conan Doyle and the Spirits: The Spiritualist Career of Sir Arthur Conan Doyle.* Wellingborough, England: Aquarian, 1989.

Joyce, James. *Finnegans Wake.* 1939. Reprint, New York: Viking, 1971.

———. *The Letters of James Joyce.* Edited by Stuart Gilbert. New York: Viking, 1957.

———. *Ulysses: The Corrected Text.* Edited by Hans Walter Gabler. New York: Random House, 1986.

Jung, C. G. "On the Psychology and Pathology of So-Called Occult Phenomena." Translated by M. D. Eder. In *Collected Papers on Analytical Psychology,* edited by Dr. Constance E. Long, 1–93. New York: Moffat Yard, 1917.

———. "The Psychological Foundations of Belief in Spirits." *Proceedings of the Society for Psychical Research* 31, no. 79 (May [1920]): 75–93.

Keen, Linda. *John Lennon in Heaven: Crossing the Borderlines of Being.* Ashland, Ore.: Pan, 1994.

Kenner, Hugh. *The Pound Era.* Berkeley: University of California Press, 1971.

Kerr, Howard. *Mediums, and Spirit Rappers, and Roaring Radicals: Spiritualism in American Literature, 1850–1900.* Urbana: University of Illinois Press, 1972.

Kingsmill, Hugh. *The Return of William Shakespeare.* In *The Dawn's Delay.* London: Eyre and Spottiswood, 1948. Novella originally published in 1929.

Kipling, Rudyard. "Wireless." In *Mrs. Bathurst and Other Stories,* 23–41. Oxford: Oxford University Press, 1991. Story originally published in 1902.

Koestenbaum, Wayne. *Double Talk: The Erotics of Male Literary Collaboration.* New York: Routledge, 1989.

Koestler, Arthur. *The Ghost in the Machine.* New York: Macmillan, 1968.

Kubis, Patricia, and Mark Macy. *Conversations beyond the Light: Communication with Departed Friends and Colleagues by Electronic Means.* Boulder, Colo.: Griffin, 1995.

Lacan, Jacques. "Desire and the Interpretation of Desire in *Hamlet.*" *Yale French Studies* 55/56 (1977): 11–52.

Lawrence, D. H. *The Complete Poems.* Edited by Vivian de Sola Pinto and Warren Roberts. 1960. Reprint, New York: Penguin, 1980.

———. "Glad Ghosts." In *Complete Short Stories of D. H. Lawrence,* 3:661–700. London: Heinemann, 1955. Story originally published in 1926.

———. *The Letters of D. H. Lawrence.* 7 vols. Cambridge: Cambridge University Press, 1979–93.

———. *Studies in Classic American Literature.* New York: Doubleday, 1953.

Lay, Wilfred. *Man's Unconscious Spirit: The Psychoanalysis of Spiritism.* London: Kegan Paul, 1921.

Leary, Penn. *The Cryptographic Shakespeare: A Monograph Wherein the Poems and Plays Attributed to William Shakespeare Are Proven to Contain the Enciphered Name of the Concealed Author, Francis Bacon.* Omaha, Neb.: Westchester House, 1987.

Lee, Sidney. *A Life of William Shakespeare.* London: Macmillan, 1898.

Lehman, David. "Elemental Bravery: The Unity of James Merrill's Poetry." In *James Merrill,* edited by Harold Bloom, 149–61. New York: Chelsea House, 1985.

Lehmann, Rosamond. *The Swan of the Evening: Fragments of an Inner Life.* London: Collins, 1967.

Leichtman, Robert R. *Eileen Garrett Returns.* Columbus, Ohio: Ariel, 1980.

Levertov, Denise. "Relearning the Alphabet." In *Relearning the Alphabet,* 110–21. New York: New Directions, 1970.

Lodge, Sir Oliver J. *Raymond; Or, Life and Death, with Examples of the Evidence of Survival of Memory and Affection after Death.* London: Methuen, 1916.

London, Bette. *Writing Double: Women's Literary Partnerships.* Ithaca: Cornell University Press, 1999.

Longenbach, James. *Stone Cottage: Pound, Yeats, and Modernism.* Oxford: Oxford University Press, 1988.

Lowell, James Russell. "The Unhappy Lot of Mr. Knott." In *The Poetical Works of James Russell Lowell,* 283–309. Boston: Houghton Mifflin, 1858. Poem originally published in 1851.

Maddox, Brenda. *Yeats's Ghosts: The Secret Life of W. B. Yeats.* New York: Harper-Collins, 1999.

Maeterlinck, Maurice. *Our Eternity.* Translated by Alexander Teixera de Mattos. New York: Dodd, Mead, 1913.

———. *The Unknown Guest.* Translated by Alexander Teixera de Mattos. New York: Dodd, Mead, 1914.

Malcolm, Janet. *The Silent Woman: Sylvia Plath and Ted Hughes.* New York: Knopf, 1994.

Mallarmé, Stéphane. "The Book: A Spiritual Instrument." Translated by Bradford Cook. In *Critical Theory since Plato,* edited by Hazard Adams, 690–92. New York: Harcourt, Brace, Jovanovich, 1971. Essay originally published in French in 1896.

Mann, Thomas. "An Experience in the Occult." In *Three Essays,* translated by H. T. Lowe-Porter, 219–61. New York: Knopf, 1929. Essay originally published in German in 1923.

———. *The Magic Mountain.* Translated by H. T. Lowe-Porter. New York: Knopf, 1927. Volume originally published in German in 1924.

Materer, Timothy. *Modernist Alchemy: Poetry and the Occult.* Ithaca: Cornell University Press, 1995.

Maynard, Nettie Colburn. *Was Abraham Lincoln a Spiritualist? Or, Curious Revelations from the Life of a Trance Medium.* Philadelphia: Hartrauft, 1891.

McLuhan, Marshall. *The Gutenberg Galaxy: The Making of Typographic Man.* Toronto: University of Toronto Press, 1962.

Melville, Herman. "The Apple-Tree Table." *Putnam's* 7 (May 1856): 465–75.

Menotti, Gian Carlo. *The Medium: A Tragedy in Two Acts.* New York: Schirmer, 1947.

Merrill, James. *The Changing Light at Sandover.* New York: Atheneum, 1982.

———. *From the First Nine: Poems 1946–1976.* New York: Atheneum, 1982.

——. *Recitative: Prose by James Merrill.* Edited by J. D. McClatchy. San Francisco: North Point, 1986.

——. *The Seraglio.* New York: Knopf, 1957.

Miller, Andrew H. "The Specters of Dickens's Study." *Narrative* 5, no. 3 (1997): 322–41.

Miller, J. Hillis. "The Limits of Pluralism, III: The Critic as Host." *Critical Inquiry* 3 (spring 1977): 439–47.

Miller, James E., Jr. *T. S. Eliot's Personal Waste Land.* University Park, Pa.: Penn State University Press, 1977.

Moberly, Charlotte Anne, and Eleanor Jourdain. *An Adventure.* London: Macmillan, 1911.

Moore, E. M. *Spirit-Messages: Conveyed by Automatic Writing through the Hand of E. M. Moore.* London: Stockwell, 1928.

Moore, R. Lawrence. *In Search of White Crows: Spiritualism, Parapsychology, and American Culture.* New York: Oxford, 1977.

Morse, B. J. "Rainer Maria Rilke and the Occult." *Journal of Experimental Metaphysics* (1945–46).

Murphy, William M. "Psychic Daughter, Mystic Son, Sceptic Father." In *Yeats and the Occult,* edited by George Mills Harper, 11–26. Toronto: Macmillan, 1975.

Nabokov, Vladimir. *Pale Fire.* 1962. Reprint, New York: Vintage, 1989.

Nelson, Geoffrey. *Spiritualism and Society.* London: Routledge and Kegan Paul, 1969.

Nims, John Frederick. "The Poetry of Sylvia Plath: A Technical Analysis." In *Ariel Ascending: Writings about Sylvia Plath,* edited by Paul Alexander, 46–60. New York: Harper, 1985.

Nunokawa, Jeff. *The Afterlife of Property: Domestic Security and the Victorian Novel.* Princeton: Princeton University Press, 1994.

Oates, Joyce Carol. *A Bloodsmoor Romance.* New York: Dutton, 1982.

Oliphant, Margaret Oliphant W. *Memoir of the Life of Laurence Oliphant and of Alice Oliphant, His Wife.* 2 vols. New York: Harper, 1891.

Oliphant, Rosamond Dale. *The Mediators.* Worthing, Sussex, England: E. G. Stead, 1939.

One Step Higher: Communications from Beyond. Collected by A. B. London: C. W. Daniel, 1937.

Oppenheim, Janet. *The Other World: Spiritualism and Psychical Research in England, 1850–1914.* Cambridge: Cambridge University Press, 1985.

Ortzen, Tony. *When Dead Kings Speak: Psychic Stories Featuring Royalty, Popes, Politicians, and Statesmen . . . Dead and Alive!* London: Regency, 1985.

Osborne Leonard, Gladys. *My Life in Two Worlds.* 1931. Reprint, London: Cassell, 1992.

Ovid. *Metamorphoses.* Translated by Rolfe Humphries. Bloomington: Indiana University Press, 1983.

Owen, Alex. *The Darkened Room: Women, Power, and Spiritualism in Victorian England.* Philadelphia: University of Pennsylvania Press, 1990.

Owen, G. Vale. *The Life beyond the Veil: Spirit Messages Received and Written Down by the Rev. G. Vale Owen.* London: Butterworth, 1920.

Owen, G. Vale, and H. A. Dallas, eds. *The Nurseries of Heaven: A Series of Essays by Various Writers concerning the Future Life of Children, with Experiences of Their Manifestation after Death.* London: Kegan Paul, Tranch, Trubner, 1920.

Payne, Edward Biron. *The Soul of Jack London.* London: Rider, 1926.

Pencak, William. "Ghosts in Utopia: Semiotics of the Post-Historical World." In *Worldmaking,* edited by William Pencak, 335–54. New York: Peter Lang, 1996.

Plath, Sylvia. *The Collected Poems.* New York: Harper, 1981.

———. *The Journals of Sylvia Plath.* New York: Dial, 1982.

———. *Letters Home.* New York: Harper, 1975.

Pole, Wellesley Tudor. *Private Dowding: A Plain Record of the After-Death Experiences of a Soldier Killed in Battle, and Some Questions on World Issues Answered by the Messenger Who Taught Him Wider Truths.* London: Watkins, 1918.

Polizzotti, Mark. *Revolution of the Mind: The Life of André Breton.* New York: Farrar, Straus, and Giroux, 1995.

Pollitt, Katha. "A Note of Triumph: On the Collected Poems." In *Ariel Ascending: Writings about Sylvia Plath,* edited by Paul Alexander, 94–99. New York: Harper, 1985.

Porter, Katherine H. *Through a Glass Darkly: Spiritualism in the Browning Circle.* Lawrence: University of Kansas Press, 1958.

Pound, Ezra. *The Cantos of Ezra Pound.* New York: New Directions, 1948.

Pullman, Philip. *The Subtle Knife.* New York: Knopf, 1997.

Rabaté, Jean-Michel. *The Ghosts of Modernity.* Gainesville: University Press of Florida, 1996.

Rainey, Lawrence. "Taking Dictation: Collage Poetics, Pathology, and Politics." *Modernism/Modernity* 5, no. 2 (April 1998): 123–53.

Rilke, Rainer Maria. *Briefe an Nanny Wunderly-Volkart.* Frankfurt a. M.: Insel, 1977.

———. *Gesammelte Briefe.* 6 vols. Frankfurt a. M.: Insel, 1936–39.

———. *Sämtliche Werke.* 6 vols. Frankfurt a. M.: Insel, 1987.

Rilke, Rainer Maria, and Marie von Thurn und Taxis. *Briefwechsel.* Zurich: Niehans, 1951.

Roberts, Daisy Oke. *How Do We Live? By Some Who Know: Letters from Writers in the Spirit World.* London: Roberts, 1950.

Roberts, Daisy Oke, and Collin E. Woolcock. *Elizabethan Episode: Incorporating Shakespeare and Co., Unlimited.* London: 1961.

Robertson, Mary Nixon. *"The Other Side God's Door": Messages from Lord Kitchener, Mary Baker Eddy, and Others.* London: Kegan Paul, Trench, Trubner, 1920.

Robinson, Lennox. "The Unhaunted House." In *Curtain Up: An Autobiography,* 169–76. London: Michael Joseph, 1942.

Ronell, Avital. *Dictations: On Haunted Writing.* Bloomington: Indiana University Press, 1986.

———. *The Telephone Book: Technology, Schizophrenia, Electric Speech.* Lincoln: University of Nebraska Press, 1989.

Rose, Jacqueline. *The Haunting of Sylvia Plath.* Cambridge: Harvard University Press, 1991.

Rosenheim, Shawn. *The Cryptographic Imagination: Secret Writing from Edgar Poe to the Internet.* Baltimore: Johns Hopkins University Press, 1997.

Rouse, C. H. *Through Séance to Satan: Or, the Lure of Spiritism.* London: Robert Scott, 1921.

Rowe, William. *Nabokov's Spectral Dimension.* Ann Arbor, Mich.: Ardis, 1981.

Royle, Nicholas. *Telepathy and Literature: Essays on the Reading Mind.* Oxford: Blackwell, 1991.

Sagan, Carl. *Contact: A Novel.* New York: Simon and Schuster, 1985.

Saunders, R. H. *The First Successful Attempt to Broadcast Spirit Voices.* London: Sanders, 1924.

Sayers, Dorothy. *Strong Poison.* New York: Harper, 1958.

Schoenbaum, S. *Shakespeare's Lives.* Oxford: Clarendon, 1991.

Shakespeare, William (Spirit). *My Proof of Immortality: By Shakespeare's Spirit, Through the Medium of His Pen Sarah Taylor Shatford.* New York: Torch, 1924.

———. *Shakespeare's Revelations: By Shakespeare's Spirit, Through the Medium of His Pen Sarah Taylor Shatford.* New York: Torch, 1919.

Shaw, George Bernard. *The Dark Lady of the Sonnets.* London: Constable, 1910.

Shelley, Percy Bysshe (Spirit). *The Fortune of Eternity. Taken through the Clairaudience of Shirley Carson Jenney, Psychic.* Ilfracombe, Devon, England: Stockwell, 1950.

Sherard, Robert. *The Real Oscar Wilde: To Be Used as a Supplement to, and in Illustration of "The Life of Oscar Wilde."* London: T. Werner Laurie, 1915.

Sherwood, Jane. *The Country Beyond: A Study of Survival and Rebirth.* London: Rider, 1945.

———. *Post-Mortem Journal: Communications from T. E. Lawrence.* London: Neville Spearman, 1964.

Silver Birch (Spirit). *Wisdom of Silver Birch.* London: Psychic Book Club, 1944.

Simon, Gustave. *Chez Victor Hugo: Les table tournantes de Jersey.* Paris: Louis Conard, 1923.

Sinclair, Upton. *Mental Radio.* Pasadena, Calif.: Sinclair, 1930.

Singer, Isaac Bashevis. "The Séance." In *The Séance and Other Stories*, 3–15. New York: Farrar, Straus, and Giroux, 1968.

Sinnett, A. P. *Tennyson an Occultist as His Writings Prove.* London: Theosophical Publishing House, 1920.

Skinner, Charles. "Two Joyce Letters concerning *Ulysses* and a Reply." *James Joyce Quarterly* 15, no. 4 (1978): 376–78.

Smith, Grover. *T. S. Eliot and the Use of Memory.* Lewisburg, Pa.: Bucknell University Press, 1996.

———. *T. S. Eliot's Poetry and Plays: A Study in Sources and Meaning.* Chicago: University of Chicago Press, 1956.

———. *The Waste Land.* London: Allen and Unwin, 1983.

Smith, Stevie. "Mrs Simpkins." In *Collected Poems*, 22. London: Allen Lane, 1975.

Spiegelman, Willard. "Breaking the Mirror: Interruption in Merrill's Trilogy." In

James Merrill: Essays in Criticism, edited by David Lehman and Charles Berger, 186–210. Ithaca: Cornell University Press, 1985.

Staff, Vera. "Communication with Robert Browning." *Psychic Science: Quarterly Transactions of the British College of Psychic Science* 12, no. 3 (1943): 96–103.

Stead, Estelle Wilson. *Faces of the Living Dead: Remembrance Day Messages and Photographs.* Manchester, England: Two Worlds, 1925.

——. *Spirit Return of W. T. Stead.* London: Spiritualist Press, 1947.

——, ed. *Communication with the Next World: The Right and Wrong Methods. A Text-Book Given by W. T. Stead from "Beyond the Veil" through Madame Hyver.* London: Stead, 1921.

Stead, W. T. *After Death: A Personal Narrative.* New and enlarged edition of *Letters from Julia* (1898). New York: George Doran, 1914.

Stead, W. T. (Spirit). *The Blue Island: Experiences of a New Arrival beyond the Veil.* London: Rider, 1922.

——. *Life Eternal.* London: Wright and Brown, 1933.

——. *Message from William T. Stead.* Chicago: W. T. Stead Memorial Center, 1917.

Stearn, Jess. *The Search for a Soul: Taylor Caldwell's Psychic Lives.* Garden City, N.Y.: Doubleday, 1973.

Steiner, Rudolf. *The Dead Are with Us: Lecture Given in Nuremberg, 10th Feb. 1918.* London: Rudolf Steiner Press, 1973.

——. *The Presence of the Dead on the Spiritual Path: Seven Lectures Held in Various Cities between April 17 and May 26, 1914.* Translated by Christian von Arnim. Hudson, N.Y.: Anthroposophic Press, 1990.

Stephenson, Neal. *Snow Crash.* New York: Bantam, 1993.

Stevens, Hugh. *Henry James and Sexuality.* Cambridge: Cambridge University Press, 1998.

Stevenson, Anne. *Bitter Fame: A Life of Sylvia Plath.* Boston: Houghton Mifflin, 1989.

Surette, Leon. *The Birth of Modernism: Ezra Pound, T. S. Eliot, W. B. Yeats, and the Occult.* Montreal: McGill-Queens University Press, 1993.

Swaffer, Hannen. *Adventures with Inspiration.* London: Morley and Mitchell, 1929.

——. *My Talks with the Dead.* London: Spiritualist Press, 1962.

——. *Northcliffe's Return.* London: Hutchinson, 1925.

Sword, Helen. *Engendering Inspiration: Visionary Strategies in Rilke, Lawrence, and H. D.* Ann Arbor: University of Michigan Press, 1995.

——. "H. D.'s *Majic Ring.*" *Tulsa Studies in Women's Literature* 14, no. 2 (1995): 347–62.

Tait, James A. *Authors and Titles: An Analytical Study of the Author Concept in Codes of Cataloging Rules in the English Language, from That of the British Museum in 1841 to the Anglo-American Cataloguing Rules in 1967.* Hamden, Conn.: Archon Books and Clive Bingley, 1969.

Tamen, Miguel. "Phenomenology of the Ghost: Revision in Literary History." *New Literary History* 29, no. 2 (1998): 295–304.

Tennyson, Alfred. *In Memoriam A. H. H.* London: Edward Moxon, 1850.

Thompson, Elizabeth M. *Life in the Hereafter*. London: Regency, 1969.

Thurn und Taxis-Hohenlohe, Marie von. *Erinnerungen an Rainer Maria Rilke*. Frankfurt a. M.: Insel, 1966.

Tisdall, E. E. P. *Queen Victoria's Private Life*. London: Jarrolds, 1961.

Todorov, Tzvetan. *The Fantastic: A Structuralist Approach to a Literary Genre*. Translated by Richard Howard. Cleveland, Ohio: Press of Case Western Reserve University, 1973.

Tolstoy, Leo. *Anna Karenina*. New York: Crowell, 1886.

Travers Smith [née Dowden], Hester. *Voices from the Void: Six Years' Experience in Automatic Communications*. New York: Dutton, 1919.

Tryphonopoulos, Demetres P. *The Celestial Tradition: A Study of Ezra Pound's "The Cantos."* Waterloo, Ontario, Canada: Wilfrid Laurier University Press, 1992.

Turgenev, I. S. (Spirit). *Beyond Earth's Fears: Dictated by I. S. Turgeniev to Ida M. Everett Keeble*. Ipswich, England: W. E. Harrison, 1936.

Twain, Mark. "Schoolhouse Hill." In *Mark Twain's Mysterious Stranger Manuscripts*, edited by William B. Gibson, 175–220. Berkeley: University of California Press, 1969.

Twain, Mark (Spirit). *Jap Herron: A Novel Written from the Ouija Board*. New York: Michael Kennerley, 1917.

Tweedale, Charles L. *News from the Next World: Being an Account of the Survival of Antonius Stradiuarius, Frederick Chopin, Sir Arthur Conan Doyle, the Brontës, and of Many of the Author's Relatives and Friends*. London: T. Werner Laurie, 1940.

Tynan, Katharine. *Twenty-Five Years: Reminiscences*. New York: Devin Adair, 1913.

Tyndall, John. "Science and the 'Spirits.'" In *Fragments of Science: A Series of Detached Essays, Addresses and Reviews*, 467–75. London, 1899.

The Uncanny. Special issue of *Paradoxa: Studies in World Literary Genres* 3, nos. 3–4 (1997).

Upton, Bernard. *The Mediumship of Helen Hughes*. London: Spiritualist, 1946.

Vendler, Helen. "James Merrill." In *James Merrill*, edited by Harold Bloom, 69–93. New York: Chelsea House, 1973.

Vining, Edward P. *The Mystery of Hamlet: An Attempt to Solve an Old Problem*. Philadelphia: Lippincott, 1881.

Virgil. *The Aeneid of Virgil*. Translated by Allen Mandelbaum. New York: Bantam, 1971.

The Visitation, or, an Interview between the Ghost of Shakespear and D-V-D G-RR—K, Esq. London: Privately printed, 1755.

Viswanathan, Gauri. "The Ordinary Business of Occultism." *Critical Inquiry* 27 (autumn 2000): 1–20.

Vivian, Joyce M. (Spirit). *Christmas Dinner, and Other Stories: By "Heather."* Folkestone, England: Warde, 1950.

——. *The Curtain Drawn: By "Heather," Written from Another World*. London: Psychic Press, [1949].

Ward, J. S. M. *Gone West: Being the Experiences of Our Soldiers and Others after Death as Seen and Told by the Author*. London: Rider, 1917.

Washington, Peter. *Madame Blavatsky's Baboon: A History of the Mystics, Mediums, and Misfits Who Brought Spiritualism to America*. New York: Schocken, 1995.

Weinstock, Jeffrey A. "The Disappointed Bridge: Textual Hauntings in Joyce's *Ulysses*." *Journal of the Fantastic in the Arts* 8, no. 3 (1997): 347–69.

White, Patricia. "Female Spectator, Lesbian Specter: *The Haunting*." In *Inside/Out: Lesbian Theories, Gay Theories*, edited by Diana Fuss, 142–72. New York: Routledge, 1991.

Wilcox, Ella Wheeler. *The Worlds and I*. 1918. Reprint, New York: Arno, 1980.

Wild, Cyril A. *No Matter: Guided by Lalasal and Marie Corelli*. London: Regency, 1969.

Wilde, Oscar. *The Portrait of Mr W. H.* 1889. Reprint, London: Methuen, 1958.

Wilde, Oscar (Spirit). *Psychic Messages from Oscar Wilde*. Edited by Hester Travers Smith [née Dowden]. London: T. Werner Laurie, 1924.

Winter, Alison. *Mesmerized: Powers of Mind in Victorian Britain*. Chicago: University of Chicago Press, 1998.

Wood, Joanne A. "Lighthouse Bodies: The Neutral Monism of Virginia Woolf and Bertrand Russell." *Journal of the History of Ideas* 55, no. 3 (July 1994): 483–502.

Woodward, George. *Familiar Verses, from the Ghost of Willy Shakspeare to Sammy Ireland*. London: Richard White, 1796.

Woolf, Virginia. *Collected Essays*. 4 vols. London: Hogarth, 1966–68.

——. *The Complete Shorter Fiction of Virginia Woolf*. London: Hogarth, 1989.

——. *The Diary of Virginia Woolf*. 5 vols. Edited by Anne Olivier Bell and Andrew McNeillie. New York: Harcourt Brace Jovanovich, 1984.

——. "How Should One Read a Book?" In *The Second Common Reader*. New York: Harcourt, Brace and World, 1960.

——. *Jacob's Room*. 1922. Reprint, Harmondsworth, England: Penguin, 1968.

——. *The Letters of Virginia Woolf*. 5 vols. Edited by Nigel Nicolson and Joanne Trautmann. New York: Harcourt Brace Jovanovich, 1975–80.

——. *Mrs. Dalloway*. 1925. Reprint, London: Granada, 1983.

——. *Night and Day*. 1919. Reprint, Harmondsworth, England: Penguin, 1969.

Yeats, William Butler. *The Autobiography of William Butler Yeats*. New York: Macmillan, 1965.

——. *The Collected Poems of W. B. Yeats*. New York: Macmillan, 1956.

——. *A Critical Edition of Yeats's "A Vision" (1925)*. Edited by George Mills Harper. London: Macmillan, 1978.

——. *Essays and Introductions*. London: Macmillan, 1961.

——. *The Letters of W. B. Yeats*. Edited by Allan Wade. London: Rupert Hart-Davis, 1954.

——. "The Manuscript of 'Leo Africanus.'" Edited by Steve L. Adams and George Mills Harper. *Yeats Annual* 1 (1982): 3–47.

——. *Mythologies*. 1959. Reprint, New York: Touchstone, 1998.

——. "Preliminary Examination of the Script of ER." See Harper and Kelly.

——. *Reveries over Childhood and Youth*. New York: Macmillan, 1916.

——. *Reviews, Articles and Other Miscellaneous Prose*. Vol. 2 of *Uncollected Prose by*

W. B. Yeats, general editors John P. Frayne and Colton Johnson. London: Macmillan, 1975.

——. "Swedenborg, Mediums, and the Desolate Places." In *If I Were Four-and-Twenty,* 21–68. Dublin: Cuala, 1940.

——. *A Vision.* New York: Macmillan, 1937.

——. *The Words upon the Window Pane: A Play in One Act, with Notes upon the Play and Its Subject.* Dublin: Cuala, 1934.

——. *Yeats's Vision Papers.* 3 vols. Edited by George Mills Harper. Iowa City: University of Iowa Press, 1992.

Yellen, Sherman. "Sir Arthur Conan Doyle: Sherlock Holmes in Spiritland." *International Journal of Parapsychology* 7 (1965): 33–56.

Index

Abbott, David, 2
Abraham, Nicolas, 46, 55, 74, 164
Ackroyd, Peter, 93, 167 n. 2
Adorno, Theodor, 12
Agnes, Dorothy, 169 n. 4, 174 n. 26
Alexander II, 168n. 6
Alexander, Paul, 184 n. 48
Allen, Percy, 42, 73, 74, 170 n. 16, 173 n. 52
American Library Association, 27–29
Apophrades, 32–33, 40, 45
Ashbery, John, 32
Asimov, Isaac, 52–53
Atherton, James, 68
Auden, W. H., 50, 103, 132; spirit of, 45, 140, 142, 144
Augustine, Jane, 181 n. 45
Austen, Jane, spirit of, 145
Automatic writing, ix, x, 2, 8; and Eliot, 94; and Futurism, 85; and Joyce, 71; and Mann, 90; and Merrill and Plath, 132–33, 147–48; and modernist-era mediums, 14, 17, 26–27, 42, 52, 58; and Rilke, 86; and surrealism, 85; and Yeats, 103–15. *See also* Ghostwriting; Ouija board

Bachchan, Harbans Rai, 180 n. 2
Bacon, Delia, 71
Bacon, Francis, 60, 71–74; spirit of, 14, 30, 71–74
Baer, Hans, 3, 168 n. 4
Baker, Michael, 171 n. 36
Balfour, Arthur, 53, 168 n. 6, 173 n. 12
Balfour, Eleanor Mildred, 168 n. 6
Barbanell, Sylvia, 171 n. 40, 174 n. 22, 176 n. 22
Barker, Elsa, 14, 175 n. 38
Barrett, Florence, 171 n. 25

Barrett, William, 168 n. 6; spirit of, 171 n. 25, 174 n. 22
Barrett Browning, Elizabeth, 7, 34; spirit of, 42
Barrow, Logie, 3, 168 n. 4, 184 n. 1
Barthes, Roland, 155
Barton, D. P., 61
Basham, Diana, 3, 8, 160, 163, 168 n. 4, 171 n. 22, 173 n. 8
Battey, George M., 177 n. 49
Baudelaire, Charles, 96, 101–2
Baudrillard, Jean, 157
Beach, Sylvia, 58
Beecher, Charles, 19, 169 n. 9, 174 n. 26, 175 n. 31
Beer, Gillian, 164
Bell, Alexander Graham, 168 n. 6
Bennett, Arnold, 53, 66
Benson, E. F., 6
Bentley, Edmund, 170 n. 11, 174 n. 20, 176 n. 5, 177 n. 40
Bergé, Christine, 164
Bergson, Henri, x, 168 n. 6
Berman, Marshall, 76
Bhaduri, Arthur, 123, 126–29
Blake, William, 11
Blamires, Harry, 176 n. 21
Blavatsky, Helena Petrovna, 98, 105, 168 n. 6
Bleibtreu, Karl, 61, 64
Bloom, Harold, 32–33, 40, 45, 165
Bond, Frederick Bligh, 25, 172 n. 52
Borges, Jorge Luis, 49–50
Bornhauser, Fred, 140
Boucher, Gustave, 169 n. 9
Boyd, Brian, 150
Boyd, Jane, 169 n. 2, 170 n. 9, 173 n. 53
Bradbrook, W. R., 22

205